❧ *Antoinette Brown Blackwell* ❧

Antoinette Brown Blackwell, ca. 1890

ANTOINETTE BROWN BLACKWELL,

A Biography

ELIZABETH CAZDEN,

The Feminist Press
Old Westbury, New York

LIBRARY OF CONGRESS CATALOGING IN PUBLICATION DATA
Cazden, Elizabeth, 1950-
    Antoinette Brown Blackwell, a biography.

    Bibliography: p.
    Includes index.
    1. Blackwell, Antoinette Louisa Brown, 1825-
1921. 2. Unitarian churches—Clergy—Biography.
3. Clergy—United States—Biography. 4. Feminists
—United States—Biography. I. Title.
BX9869.B6C38   288'.33'0924   [B]   82-4986
ISBN O-935312-00-5   AACR2
ISBN O-935312-04-8 (pbk.)

The text of this book was typeset in Baskerville and the display heads were set
in Garamond by Duarte Phototypesetting Co. The book was manufactured
by R. R. Donnelley, Crawfordsville, Indiana.

Text design by Lea Smith.

PHOTOGRAPH AND ILLUSTRATION ACKNOWLEDGMENTS
Cover and frontispiece: courtesy of Schlesinger Library, Radcliffe College
    (Women's Rights Collection).
Chapter 1: courtesy of Henrietta Town Historian, Henrietta, New York.
Chapters 2, 3, 4, 6, 7, 8, 12, 13, 14, 15: courtesy of Schlesinger Library, Radcliffe
    College (Blackwell Collection).
Chapter 5: courtesy of Oberlin College Archives. Susan Hayes Ward, *History
    of the Broadway Tabernacle Congregational Church*, (New York:
    private, 1901).
Chapter 9: courtesy of Schlesinger Library, Radcliffe College. Antoinette
    Brown Blackwell, *The Island Neighbors*, (New York: Harper Bros.,
    1871), p. 85.
Chapter 10: courtesy of Schlesinger Library, Radcliffe College (Alma Lutz
    Collection).
Chapter 11: courtesy of Schlesinger Library, Radcliffe College (A-33, vol. 2,
    collection by Julia Ward Howe, 1893, portraits of women ministers).

❧ *Dedication* ❧

To the women writers in my family: my grandmother, Courtney Borden (Courtney Letts d'Espil); my great-aunt, Joyce Borden Baloković; my aunt, Miriam Plotkin Levine; my mother, Courtney Borden Cazden; and my sister, Joanna Cazden.

CONTENTS

LIST OF ILLUSTRATIONS

ACKNOWLEDGMENTS

This book contains threads of contributions from numerous individuals and printed sources, threads that I can, in many cases, no longer trace.

Some people deserve special thanks. Roberta Barstad Miller, then a lecturer in history at Oberlin College, first encouraged me to delve into the research for this volume during a course she taught on the History of Women in America in the spring of 1971. The Oberlin College Library staff kindly located manuscript materials in the attic of the old Carnegie Library, as well as in the stacks. William Bigglestone and Gertrude Jacobs of the Oberlin College Archives and Philip J. Tear, editor of the Oberlin Alumni Magazine, have also provided assistance concerning Oberlin materials and photographs.

E. Gale Huntington, head of the Duke's County Historical Society (and a grand-nephew, by adoption, of my subject), escorted me around Martha's Vineyard in October 1974, showing me all the Blackwell houses and the arboretum Antoinette planted in her later years, and regaling me with anecdotes that did not appear in any printed materials. Mrs. Ethel (Jones) Whidden, Antoinette's granddaughter, welcomed me into her home and filled in some of the family history.

Catherine and Elmer Frangenberg, the current owners of the stone house that Joseph Brown built in 1830, greeted me graciously when I arrived at their doorstep with no advance warning and shared their enthusiasm for Antoinette, her family, and their home. Vivian Heffernan, town historian of Henrietta, New York, provided photographs from the town's collection.

Florence Howe at The Feminist Press first suggested that Antoinette Brown Blackwell was worthy of a full-length biography and insisted that my Oberlin term paper be expanded into a book. Sue Davidson acted as editor during the book's formative years, and her questions and criticism helped shape the material presented here. Barbara M. Solomon, Ellen Dubois, Karen Blair, Paul Lauter, and John Blackwell read the

manuscript at various stages and offered comments and suggestions. Any errors of fact and opinions on issues expressed in this
volume are, however, my own responsibility.

Manuscript materials used here are printed with the kind
permission of the following: The New York Public Library,
Astor, Lenox and Tilden Foundations, Rare Books and Manuscripts Division (Horace Greeley Papers); The George Arents
Research Library, Syracuse University (Gerrit Smith Collection); the Mabel Smith Douglass Library, Rutgers University,
(Theodore Stanton Collection); Oberlin College. The volumi-
nous Blackwell papers, consisting of manuscripts, correspondence, newspaper clippings, photographs, and the like, are
divided between the Library of Congress Manuscript Division
and Schlesinger Library, Radcliffe College. The Blackwell
Collection at the Library of Congress is labeled as being in
public domain. The remaining Blackwell materials are used
with the permission of Schlesinger Library, Radcliffe College,
and of George, John, and Lane Blackwell on behalf of the
wider Blackwell family.

Finally, I owe much to the typists who turned my cut-up,
pasted, written-over fragments into neat pages ready for a fresh
round of editing and rewriting.

Elizabeth Cazden
Manchester, New Hampshire
October, 1982

Antoinette Brown Blackwell

Brown farmhouse, Henrietta, New York

Monroe Academy, Henrietta, New York

WHY SHOULD I NOT PRAY?

The Brown family gathered that Sunday for evening prayers in their stone farmhouse. They were a large group: the gentle grandmother who read Bible stories to the children; father, rather short and stout; mother, tall, thin, energetic; Aunt Eliza; and ten children ranging from grown-up Rebecca and William to baby Ellen. It had been a long day: the regular morning service at the Congregational Church down in the village, a picnic lunch, a Bible study class, and a shorter afternoon service. Eight-year-old Antoinette enjoyed Sundays; they were a change from the weekday routine of home and school and a time when she could give full attention to the inner stirrings and wondering that connected her to God.

The family prayer gathering was a memorable one that evening. At the end of the meeting, much to everyone's astonishment, Antoinette Brown spontaneously spoke a sweet and simple prayer. As the gathering broke, her brother William took her on his knee and asked, "Why did you pray, Nettie?" She answered confidently, "Because I think I am a Christian, and why should I not pray?"[1] As far as she was concerned, it was that simple, and neither William nor the rest of her family expressed any disagreement. Within her own family, the child Antoinette felt strong in her beliefs and free to express them.

Later that year, just before her ninth birthday, Antoinette decided that it was time for her to join the church. During the regular Sunday service, the minister invited anyone who wanted to unite with the church to come forward to the front seats. Without hesitation, Antoinette stood up and walked alone to the designated place. The minister, not used to examining a young child, asked her one or two simple questions. She responded with her own statement of why she considered herself a Christian and wanted to be connected with the Lord's people.[2] Despite some misgivings about her age, the church voted unanimously to receive her into membership. In later years, Antoinette Brown remarked that "I was as deeply and truly religious at that time, though but nine years of age, as I have ever been at any age."[3]

She entered into the life of the church with an enthusiasm that some people considered precocious. Soon she began speaking and praying at informal prayer meetings at the church and among her school friends, as well as within her family. On one of these occasions, an elder of the church intoned piously, "Out of the mouths of babes and sucklings, the Lord has perfected praise." Antoinette was indignant; she later commented, "It seemed somehow to refer to me and yet I was neither a babe nor a suckling—nine or ten years old feels itself pretty well grown."[4]

Upstate New York in the 1830s was an ideal environment for nurturing Antoinette's independence, assertiveness, and religious commitment. Like most of their neighbors, her parents were transplanted Yankees, descended from six generations of New England farmers. Abigail Morse Brown was born in southern Massachusetts in 1793. She probably attended a "dame school"; even girls were expected to be able to read the Bible and keep household accounts. Before she was twelve her parents died, leaving her to care for a younger brother and sister. At seventeen she married Joseph Brown, eight years older than she, and moved to his home in Connecticut to work side by side with him on the farm and help him care for his invalid father. Joseph Brown was a farmer by necessity rather than choice. Always fonder of reading than of manual labor, he had studied theology for a time, until his father's illness called him home. Their first child, Rebecca, was born in 1812, and a son, Joseph Addison, two years later. When Joseph Brown went away to fight in the War of 1812, Abby Brown ran the farm alone.

After his father died, Joseph Brown grew restless and dissatisfied with the rock-covered farm. He convinced his wife, his mother, and his unmarried younger sister Eliza that they should move toward the frontier. In 1819 they packed their belongings and children—two boys and two girls—into an ox-drawn wagon and joined the steady flow of Yankees to the fertile lands of western New York, following the ancient pathway along the Mohawk River. Joseph followed his brother, a physician, to the area around Rochester, and bought 100 acres of land with a two-room log cabin on it near the village of Henrietta.

It was new country, settled by English-speaking farmers only since 1800, but by 1820 its farms were fruitful and prosperous. Traders along the Hudson and Mohawk Rivers brought manufactured goods and foreign products such as molasses from New York City, and took back wheat, cheeses, and fruit from the upstate farms. In 1825, the year Antoinette Brown was born, the Erie Canal opened from the Hudson River to the Great Lakes, extending trade routes to the frontier states of Ohio, Indiana, Illinois, and Michigan. With this added stimulus, as well as the protective tariffs on imported goods imposed by the government in Washington, a few water-powered factories opened in western New York. Over the next century, the new system of factories, wage labor, and mass-produced store-bought goods would profoundly alter both the technological details of daily life and the patterns of community interaction and family structure that were based on relatively stable farm homesteads.[5] In the 1820s the dislocations caused by the shifting economy showed up in a nationwide economic depression, with occasional outbursts of violence; an apparent increase in alcoholism, prostitution, and crime; and a vague moral discontent, as the trust and cooperation of village life were replaced by distant corporations with little conscience or accountability. But in western New York, relatively shielded from the worst impact of the financial crises, the new system was perceived as progress.

Joseph and Abby Brown prospered in their new home. Their family continued to grow; like many women of her time, Abby bore a child about every two years, getting pregnant as soon as she weaned the previous baby. By May 1825, when Antoinette Louisa was born, there were six older children, three boys and three girls, ranging in age from two to thirteen.

Antoinette's earliest memories were of the large kitchen, the main living area of the house, where her cradle was placed. In one corner was a large spinning wheel; in another, the wooden loom on which her mother wove all of the family's clothing. In the center of one wall was a large fireplace with an iron bar, from which pots were suspended, and a brick oven for baking bread, pies, and cakes. In this room the women of the family spent most of the day, cooking, washing, weaving, sewing, preserving food. In an adjoining room was the big bed where Antoinette's parents slept, with her trundle bed underneath; the older children slept in the loft. Outside, Joseph Brown, his three sons, and a hired man took care of the livestock and crops. The family grew or gathered most of its food, wood to heat and cook with, and flax for linen clothing. Surplus food was sold so that the family could purchase tools, wool, and cotton, as well as such luxuries as white sugar.

When Antoinette was two and a half, she lost her position as the baby in the family. She later recalled:

> I can clearly remember my first visit, taken with my oldest sister, where I spent the night, sat on a little chair on the grass, played with a little dog and ate cake. When we returned home we found a new baby sister.[6]

With a new baby to care for, Abby Brown was glad to let Antoinette join the older children at play.

The next spring, when she was not quite three, Antoinette went with her next oldest brother and sister to the local district school half a mile from home. Antoinette learned to read easily, probably from the rhymed pages of the *New England Primer*. She later remembered sitting on her teacher's lap to recite her lessons. Like her brothers and sisters, Antoinette "ran as naturally to books as young ducks to water."[7]

When Antoinette was five, her family moved from their cramped cabin to a new larger stone house down the road.[8] It stood sedately on top of a rise, overlooking broad fields. Antoinette and several of the other children slept in the large open attic.

At home, the children's play often merged with work. Antoinette described the farm as "a place of perpetual variety ... like a far off fairyland."[9] Even the youngest child could help gather apples, peaches, plums, cherries, currants, and nuts from the forest. They tagged after the adults as they tapped maple trees and boiled the sap down into delicious syrup. At harvest time the children sat in gaps in the fence to keep animals out of the fields. Antoinette taught a new calf to drink milk from a pail, letting the calf suck her small fingers dipped in warm skimmed milk.

Until Antoinette's seventh year, her family had little formal religious life. Although her father had once wanted to become a minister, he accepted the prevailing view that any internal conversion experience would take place in a time and manner determined wholly by God, without any initiative on his part. He waited patiently for that change of heart to occur.

The only person in the household who considered herself a committed Christian was Antoinette's grandmother. Antoinette and the other small children spent much time in the elderly woman's room, listening to her read from *Pilgrim's Progress* or the large family Bible, and talking with her about what had been read. Antoinette later commented that "to this dear grandmother must be attributed much of the thoughtfulness which we children seem to have early acquired."[10] Antoinette's first religious teacher, then, was a woman, someone who shared her daily life in a manner quite distinct from a clergyman.

Religion was a lively topic of conversation for most of the adults in upstate New York. It was in the air, like democracy, or the price of hogs. The Yankees who settled western New York had brought more than axes, plows, and featherbeds to their new homes; they also carried the moral and religious intensity of New England churches. Among the settlers were hundreds of Congregational and Presbyterian ministers; by 1824 half the Presbyterian clergy for the entire nation lived in New York state.

Religion and the churches, in the turbulent decades when Antoinette was growing up, were the source of opposing forces for stability and change. On the one hand, the "aristocrats of wealth," both the old landed gentry and the newer business entrepreneurs, saw religious institutions as a critical bulwark against the wave of anticlerical atheist mob violence that they feared would spread from Republican France to the young United States. Many ordinary people turned to religious groups and their preaching of rock-solid faith as a source of personal reassurance, comfort, and community ties, in a time when geographic mobility and changes in economic structure fostered disruption and instability.

For some clergy and laypeople, on the other hand, Christianity in its true form was a force for radical personal and social change. It inspired and strengthened organized drives for social reforms ranging from attacks on alcohol and prostitution to political campaigns for the abolition of slavery and equal rights for women. With an optimism nurtured in the War of Independence, they believed that America, unlike corrupt Europe, could become indeed a heaven on earth. Religious fervor also spawned a variety of unusual sects, small but influential, which chose to withdraw from the "progress" of the world: the Shakers, in their well-ordered celibate communities; the Mormons, with new scriptures and polygamous marriage; the followers of William Miller, who believed that Christ would return to earth for the Last Judgment within a few years.[11]

Out of this amalgam the people of western New York developed a unique religious style, which combined a firm belief in a future millennium ushering in the Kingdom of Heaven with moral crusades aimed at improving life here and now. This religious and moral fervor was a wellspring for most of the social reform movements of pre-Civil War America, and its influence would continue to the end of the century.

During the early decades of the nineteenth century, waves of intense religious excitement swept through western New York. Traveling evangelical preachers called their listeners to renewed Christian faith and to moral perfection in this world. A whole community might vibrate for months with the excitement of new spiritual discoveries.

One of the most popular preachers was Charles Grandison Finney, a self-taught lawyer-turned-preacher, whose mission was to bring the Gospel to bear directly on the lives of individuals and on society. By all accounts, Finney had an unusual ability to appeal to each person individually, in a way that changed that person's view of God and of his or her place in the world.[12] Finney stressed that each person had a duty to work actively for a personal conversion. For Finney, this meant not just a single flash of salvation, but the beginning of a life of commitment to God and to working toward a more perfect society. It was this dual commitment that deeply shaped Antoinette Brown's religious beliefs.

Finney's influence peaked in a series of revival meetings in Rochester during the winter of 1831, when Antoinette was six years old. People flocked to hear him—rich people and poor, bankers, day laborers, farmers, schoolgirls. The meetings went on every day, long into the evening, for nearly a week. Essential chores somehow got done, but everything else was put aside while souls were examined. Antoinette's oldest sister Rebecca, sobered by a fall from a carriage while coming home from a dancing party, first attended Finney's meetings, and persuaded her parents to accompany her. Joseph Brown, like many of his neighbors, was deeply moved by Finney's dramatic preaching, and experienced at last the internal conversion he had long awaited. The next morning he paused before serving breakfast, and in great anguish, tears streaming down his cheeks, reaffirmed the commitment of the prophet Joshua: "As for me and my house, we will serve the Lord."[13] William Brown wrote that Finney's preaching "changed ... the whole current of our family life. It was the commencement of our religious history."[14]

The small Henrietta church, which the Browns attended, was part of the "liberal" branch of the Congregational Church. "Orthodox" preachers stressed that human beings were sinful, depraved, and utterly helpless before a distant and powerful God, who condemned them to eternal punishment if they disobeyed. Liberal Congregationalists, on the other hand, stressed God's mercy and forgiveness, as well as human initiative and goodness. Neither Antoinette's church nor her family sought to impress upon the Brown children the terrors of future punishment. Instead, Antoinette, like her sisters and brothers, learned to envision God as a friendly presence. For her, God was as accessible as the nearby forest; she was delighted "to steal away alone and lie on the grass or leaves looking up at the blue sky, or in the evening at the moon or the stars as they came out one after another. It seemed as though I had found a new heaven and a new earth."[15]

Even the death of her beloved grandmother, when Antoinette was nine, seemed to confirm her faith in a kindly God. William later reported that their grandmother, just before she died, said to him, "I have been talking with the angels and they are all around me now." He felt that "she passed the portal seemingly under their guidance and as peacefully and joyfully as if she had been a child going to visit dear friends."[16]

The middle years of Antoinette's childhood were shaped by the routines of church, school, play, and farm chores. From a very early age—probably at about the same time that she started school—she was expected to help with housekeeping. Before she could go out and play, she had to sit and knit the prescribed number of rows on her own socks and mittens. She later confessed that "sewing was always my detestation, although the two older sisters enjoyed it."[17] From an early age, Antoinette decided that "the routine of cooking and dishwashing is in itself distasteful." Her attitude toward housework came in part from her mother, who, as Antoinette later remarked, "never seemed very fond of ordinary housework."[18]

Antoinette much preferred outdoor work to indoor. One year the threshing crew was shorthanded, and she was allowed to fill the empty place, putting hay into the mows or building up the straw stacks. She commented matter-of-factly, "My youngest brother was five years my senior. It was convenient to have a little boy about the farm, and I was that little boy."[19] Her father insisted on paying her for her work, indicating that he considered it not only acceptable, but actually valuable. Antoinette felt that "it was delightful to earn this first money, and equally so to spend it on my own dresses, with a feeling of personal independence."[20] Growing up, she could see that society's stereotypes of women's and men's work did not match her own choice of activities. Her parents, stuck in their roles by circumstances more than choice, encouraged Antoinette to reach beyond those stereotypes.

The rhythm of farm work and school was interrupted occasionally by visits from relatives and neighbors. Uncle William was a favorite guest, often bringing his blind daughter Susan, who was just Antoinette's age. Joseph Brown was also a justice of the peace, and people who came to him with disputes to settle sometimes brought their children to play while the informal court was in session. Now and then women from a neighboring farm would drop in for an impromptu afternoon visit. Antoinette's mother and older sisters, no doubt glad for the companionship, would then put aside their everyday chores and take up their sewing or knitting while they chatted. At tea time a quick fire was built, a fresh baking of cream biscuits prepared, the table set with the "company" dishes, and an array of homemade relishes brought out.[21] Antoinette grew up accustomed to this easy warm style of hospitality and social interaction among women.

Her memories were of a loving, happy family. She later described a typical evening from her childhood:

> The large family was gathered about the table with its several tallow candles, the older children studying their lessons, the women of the family sewing or reading, one brother with an iron candlestick with a hook at the top hung over a chair, slate in hand ciphering, my father with two kitchen chairs turned on their faces and an old scythe suspended between them, he seated at one end of it with a large basket of corn at his side, shelling it upon the edge of the scythe. The cobs were thrown to one side and eagerly seized upon by the smaller girls for cob houses. Soon a tall brother left his books and made us a mimic church with a long cob for the steeple, the whole so tightly pressed together that we could lift our little meeting-house by its steeple, and when it finally fell apart the scattering of the cobs was another source of merriment.[22]

Although Antoinette's immediate experience was limited to friends and relatives in the small village of Henrietta, she was not isolated from the broader world. Her father subscribed to a number of liberal newspapers: the *Rochester Democrat*, the abolitionist *National Era* (which later published *Uncle Tom's Cabin*), and the *Moral Reform Journal*.

Her education was fairly ordinary for the time. The district school terms ran four months each, in summer and winter, leaving children free for farm chores at planting and harvest times. The teachers generally had at best a high school education; one year Antoinette's teacher was her twenty-year-old brother William, with fifteen-year-old Samuel hearing the youngest children's lessons. Antoinette's young mind was probably as acute as that of the young Margaret Fuller, the nineteenth-century intellectual and author. Unlike Fuller, Antoinette could not study Latin or Shakespeare, nor have access to the other resources of a classical education. Her mind was honed on—and to some extent limited by—the primitive resources of a small, semifrontier town.

Within that limited context, she excelled. Antoinette's writing ability appeared early in her childhood. She began writing short verses and compositions as easily as she had learned to read. At first the other children in the small district schoolroom teased Antoinette by quoting bits of her "literary productions" back at her. She resorted to hiding her writings in a secret compartment in a bureau drawer. Soon, however, her compositions "became the family pride."[23] Her family's only complaint, as she later reported, was "that letter paper disappeared much too rapidly, sometimes rather unaccountably."[24] The support she received for these early efforts at self-expression must have strengthened her sense of the value of her work and encouraged her to pursue writing seriously.

Antoinette's favorite teacher and companion was her brother Samuel, who was five years older than she. Sam, who showed great promise as an inventor while still in his teens, introduced her to the world of nature and science. Scientific theory had not yet fragmented into physics, engineering, optics, chemistry, and a host of other disciplines. In the 1830s, science was still a unified study of "natural philosophy," supported by experiments in backyards and other home laboratories. Antoinette and Samuel, far removed from any university, got their inspiration from books such as Dick's *Popular Guide to the Observations of Nature*, which they borrowed from the

newly established public library. These books, she later said,
"gave me a new and better appreciation of nature and had a
considerable effect on my subsequent life."[25]

Not content with reading, Samuel—with his younger sister's assistance—devised his own experiments. Antoinette later
described one of their attempts to design a perpetual motion
system of siphons:

> Never shall I forget the beautiful illumination of [his]
> young face when he thought we were at last successful;
> then came the sudden blank of disappointment [as] the
> water in one vessel was largely drawn out while another
> was almost filled.[26]

In 1838, when Antoinette was thirteen, she graduated from
the district school and joined Samuel and another sister at
Monroe County Academy. The academy, the first secondary
school in the county, drew students from all over western New
York. It was housed in a three-story brick building on a large
slope near the Congregational Church, about two miles from
the Browns' home. In the summer Antoinette and her brother
and sister could walk back and forth each day, taking a short-
cut through the fields. In the winter, however, other arrangements were required. One winter they rode in a horse-drawn
sleigh. Another year Antoinette boarded with a family in the
village, coming home only on Sundays. One particularly cold
winter, Antoinette and Samuel stayed at home teaching the
three younger girls and hearing each others' lessons as well.

The academy students were considered responsible and
independent. Many of them lived too far away from the school
to stay at home with their families. One winter, students from
several families kept house together near the academy, with
little adult supervision. Each Monday they brought food from
home, ready to be warmed over during the week. The young
people were trusted to take care of themselves and each other,
and apparently did so with few problems. Antoinette later
explained that no one seemed concerned about boys and girls
living in the same house: "It was not thought anything peculiar or not adapted to the times. A different state of morality
certainly existed in our country neighborhoods at that time."[27]
Had Antoinette lived in a city, she might have experienced
more constraints on the "proper" behavior of a young lady.

Antoinette was fortunate in having access to a secondary school. The academy offered her a much better education than she could have found at one of the "female seminaries" scattered across New England and New York. Those institutions focused on polishing the social skills that would make young women more attractive wives, mothers, and hostesses. Monroe Academy, on the other hand, provided serious academic work, within the constraints of a semifrontier community. As in many such academies, boys and girls studied together. The curriculum included mathematics, composition and rhetoric, .and French; by the time she graduated, Antoinette "could read easy French fairly well, but the pronunciation must have been worse than the patois of any known tongue."[28]

Antoinette Brown finished Monroe Academy in 1840, when she was fifteen. The next spring she was asked to teach the youngest children in a small district school in a nearby town. An old farmer came to pick her up on the first day in a farm wagon; in honor of "Miss Brown," the usual rough plank seat was replaced by two fine cane-seated chairs. Antoinette was to board with one of her pupils' families until Saturday, when one of her sisters would come on horseback to take her home for the weekend. Though barely sixteen, she does not seem to have been nervous about the transition from being a daughter and pupil to being a "school marm" living away from home. On the contrary, with her usual vitality, she welcomed the experience: "[I went with] great glee, for I was in high spirits.... In the neighborhood were a number of girls my own age, who helped me from being homesick."[29] The next summer she taught farther away, near the Genesee River. She was paid $1.50 a week, plus board. She gave most of the money to her parents, but kept one precious dollar to buy writing paper for her compositions.

Antoinette knew that teaching school could well become her permanent work. It was one of the few jobs readily available to unmarried women; other occupations, such as nursing and secretarial work, barely existed until after the Civil War. At least one of Antoinette's sisters taught school all her life. A few outstanding women—Emma Willard, Mary Lyon, Catherine Beecher—went beyond teaching basic skills to a vision of education as a means of improving the position of women. Antoinette probably knew of their efforts through reports in reform newspapers and adopted some of their ideas. When she thought about a career in education, she saw herself founding and running a school:

> One favorite early dream of mine was the building of an institution where girls could be educated along social, moral, and religious lines as well as those of the intellect. I had even selected the spot where I should like to erect such an institution, a broad and handsome field almost in front of my father's farmhouse.[30]

But she did not find teaching itself particularly satisfying.

Antoinette Brown could more readily imagine herself becoming a published writer. "An author," she wrote, "always seemed to me a most enviable and revered personage."[31] On a short trip when she was sixteen, she eavesdropped on a young woman talking with a friend about her own literary work. The woman, only two years older than Antoinette, was Grace Greenwood (Lippincott), who had already published some poems in Rochester newspapers and was working on a book of stories. Antoinette "listened with intense eagerness, feeling how charming it would be to make her acquaintance."[32]

Antoinette Brown assumed that she could have a future outside of her small home town. She apparently did not envision herself in her mother's role, as mistress of a large farm. She later commented that her mother's life "was never an easy one, although she superintended her family even when in feeble health."[33] Antoinette sympathized with her mother's confinement to chores she neither chose nor enjoyed. Many people throughout the nineteenth century feared that education "would beget distaste for the pleasures of domestic life and would unfit women for family and social duties."[34] In Antoinette's case, it is more likely that her dislike of domestic chores was one factor in her decision to seek further education and nondomestic work. Rather early, too, she set sights on her own accomplishments—writing, teaching, preaching. Her visions of the life stretching before her varied: now she was a famous author, now headmistress of a school, now a religious leader. She felt that the progress around her was exciting and promising and that its promise included her.

At some point during her teens, Antoinette formulated the ambition that would thrust her into historical prominence: she wanted to become a minister. It was not unusual for young women to show a strong interest in religious work during the

1840s. The world around them was changing rapidly—cities growing, the western frontier opening up, machines taking over manual chores. Antoinette could see the changes in her own household: first, the spinning wheel in the corner of the main room was replaced by a mechanical spinning jenny; before long, homespun cloth was replaced altogether by store-bought goods manufactured in the textile mills of New England. Many people felt confused about what part they should play in the new order. This identity crisis particularly affected young single women, and frequently made them open to greater involvement in religious activities.[35] Despite other changes in their lives, they could still play an important part in society through the church and the various social reform organizations. In fact, both women and the church would increasingly be called upon to preserve and represent values of cooperation, sharing, and nurturing that were cast aside by the prophets of economic progress.

Women were not, however, expected to become public leaders of the religious community. No woman anywhere had ever been ordained as a priest or minister. One Methodist woman had tried to preach in New York some twenty years earlier, but stopped because of public pressure. Within unorthodox groups like the Society of Friends, who believed that all members were ministers, women sometimes spoke in worship services. When Quaker abolitionists Sarah and Angelina Grimké traveled around New England giving public speeches, however, the Massachusetts Council of Congregationalist Ministers responded with a Pastoral Letter condemning such public work as un-Christian and unladylike.[36]

Antoinette Brown's interest in religion was quite normal for a young woman in her place and time. Early in her youth, however, she showed an unusual capacity for spiritual leadership. Her brother William reported that on one occasion she gathered the girls in her class in the cloakroom and told them how pleasant it was to love and serve the Lord, offering a "tender and touching prayer" that left the girls in tears.[37]

In her teens she participated actively in the Henrietta church, speaking often in informal prayer meetings, where any member was free to speak. She seems to have felt comfortable in that role, taking for granted that God's call was not limited by gender. Many people in her community, noting her religious interest, assumed she would marry a minister and labor by his side. They appreciated women like Antoinette's grandmother, who taught, counseled, and prayed within their own homes. The minister of her church warmly encouraged her to become a missionary overseas, another acceptable role for religious women. Even her mother "suggested that it would be much easier to become a foreign missionary than to meet the prejudices of a so-called Christian community in that day if I engaged in public religious work and certainly if I tried to become a minister."[38] Nevertheless, Antoinette decided that was what she wanted to do, and set about working toward it with remarkable persistence.

She knew she would need more education than could be gleaned from Monroe Academy and the books in the Henrietta public library. Many of the young men in her class had gone on to Dartmouth College; but neither Dartmouth nor most other colleges accepted women students. Women's colleges such as Vassar and Radcliffe were twenty-five years away. The few postsecondary schools for women primarily offered religious and moral self-improvement, as well as social adornments. Sometimes their course included training for teaching. But Antoinette Brown had little use for a course of study designed to help women be better wives and mothers. She shared the views of one of her contemporaries, who wrote:

> I have felt unwilling to go to most of our Seminaries, where the great object is to make mere butterflies of females. I wish to go where not only the intellect, but the moral principle will be cultivated, disciplined and trained for active service in the vineyard of the Lord.[39]

Antoinette Brown set her sights on Oberlin Collegiate Institute, far away in the swampy woods of Ohio. By the 1840s Oberlin was well-known as a hotbed of antislavery sentiments. Charles Grandison Finney, who had been the Brown family's spiritual leader, was the college's president. Antoinette's older brother William went to study theology at Oberlin and wrote back enthusiastic letters about his work and the young woman he wanted to marry. Best of all, Oberlin admitted women to study with men at the college level. Its first catalog announced that one of its purposes was "the elevation of female character by bringing within the reach of the misjudged and neglected sex all the instructive privileges which hitherto have unreasonably distinguished the leading sex from theirs."[40] Antoinette had high hopes that she, like her brother, would be able to study theology. In short, Oberlin College was clearly the logical next step for her.

Her family had mixed feelings about her plans. The idea of a girl going to college did not shock them. In fact, Antoinette's oldest sister, Rebecca, and a friend had planned to go Oberlin; but when the friend accepted a sudden marriage proposal, Rebecca was too shy to go alone on such a long journey. But Antoinette's father felt that she was needed at home to help her mother. He also was not sure they could afford Oberlin's nominal tuition. So Antoinette continued to teach school for three more years, saving her earnings, dreaming, and hoping.

The winter of 1843, when Antoinette was seventeen, was a strange one throughout upstate New York. William Miller, a well-meaning fanatic, thought he had determined the exact time and place of Christ's return to earth. On the appointed day, thousands of sincere religious people dressed in white and waited in groups on top of hills and barns to be gathered up by the Lord. The event made a vivid impression on Antoinette:

> One night I was awakened from sleep by the sound of heavy teams rolling one after another past our house on the frozen ground. The almost empty rooms echoed with the sound, and I trembled with the belief that the end of the world had really come. Too frightened to cry out, I lay terror stricken until the startling roar passed by.[41]

In the morning, it was of course quickly discovered that the end of the world had not come.

In another sense, however, the world of Antoinette's childhood was coming to an end. That winter her mother was sick, worn out by hard work and repeated childbearing. Antoinette's oldest brother, William, was troubled by what he termed an "incessant and irrepressible" cough. And her favorite brother, Sam—kind, clever, gifted Sam—was gravely ill with tuberculosis, then called "lung fever."[42] At that time no one knew that the disease was infectious, and until the discovery of antibiotics decades later there was no effective treatment. It was a difficult and challenging time for Antoinette; one can imagine her caring for Sam, reading the Bible with him, listening to him cough night after night, watching him grow weak and emaciated. He died on May 25, a few days after Antoinette's eighteenth birthday. Her closest sister, fifteen-year-old Ophelia, died of the same disease the following October; two older sisters died within the next two years. By the time she was twenty, Antoinette was left alone between two sisters much younger than herself and three siblings much older.

In retrospect, Antoinette Brown said of these illnesses and deaths only that they "were the shadows of that early home life."[43] But, almost certainly, the experience planted in her deep questions about the nature of God and human life. Antoinette's only previous encounter with a death in her family was that of her grandmother ten years earlier—an elderly person slipping away quietly after a full life. Her brother William wrote that their siblings "all died in the Christian hope," that is, fully believing in a life in Christ after death.[44] At the time, Antoinette seems to have shared their belief; in fact, given her own religious strength, she may well have helped her sisters and brother prepare spiritually for their deaths. Nevertheless, the untimely deaths of her closest brother and sisters were more difficult to reconcile with her childhood faith that "God was always just as well as merciful and that no wrong could or would be done."[45]

The loss of a significant set of family members also influenced Antoinette's close relations with people.[46] These events may have encourged her to look for emotional support and intimacy outside of her biological family. The profound changes in family architecture may well have been an additional factor in encouraging her to leave home, as she was now soon to do.

Antoinette Brown, ca. 1846-1850

OBERLIN, STAR OF HOPE

In the spring of 1846, close to her twenty-first birthday, Antoinette Brown set out in great excitement for Oberlin. It took several days to make the 300-mile trip. She took a mule-drawn barge down the Erie Canal to Buffalo, then a new steamer, the "Niagara," across Lake Erie to Cleveland. To save money, Brown slept on a hard wooden bench on the open deck, instead of bunking in a stuffy cabin with most of the other women. From Cleveland, a crowded stagecoach took her the last twenty-five miles, over rough, muddy roads, to Oberlin. It was on this final stage of the journey that Brown first heard the name of Lucy Stone. A family friend who happened to be on the stagecoach warned her that she should not become too friendly with Stone, whom he described as "a very bright girl, but eccentric, a Garrisonian, and much too talkative on the subject of woman's rights." Brown said nothing; but she "resolved then and there to know more of Lucy Stone."[1]

Oberlin's appearance must have been disappointing to someone accustomed to the beautiful hills and well-kept farms of western New York. The area was utterly flat, swampy, and wild. The town of Oberlin was still almost a pioneer settlement; the first brush had been cleared only thirteen years earlier. The town's four streets, ankle-deep rivers of sticky mud, formed a square that served as both village green and farm. It was named after New York reformers Arthur and Lewis Tappan, who had lent both moral and financial support to the new community. In the early spring, when Antoinette Brown arrived, Tappan Square would have been marked out into small tracts for individual gardens. There were probably buds on the community's peach and mulberry trees, the latter the remnants of an ill-fated experiment in silkworm culture. Despite some attempts at fence building, hens, hogs, and cattle ran at large. Sanitation was primitive, and Brown would learn all too well that such illnesses as cholera, pneumonia, and tuberculosis were a chronic problem.[2]

She took her belongings to one of the sparsely furnished rooms in the Ladies Boarding Hall, where she would live for the next two years. That evening she joined the other students

for supper in the house's large dining room. Meals were the
center of Oberlin's social life. Men and women sat side by side
at long tables, and friendships and romances flourished. The
food was wholesome but simple, usually bread or johnnycake
and milk. Meat was served infrequently, reflecting the community's limited funds as well as its sympathy with the dietary
philosophy of reformer Sylvester Graham. Brown saw Lucy
Stone at the next table, engaged in an active discussion with a
professor and two male students. Stone, small, plump, and
neatly dressed, looked about eighteen. Antoinette Brown's first
impression was that "she was too pert and forward for so young
a girl in discussion with an almost middle-aged clergyman."[3]
She regretfully decided that she would not like Stone.

Brown had a few days before classes started to explore her
new surroundings. Her room was on the second floor of the
Ladies Boarding Hall, overlooking Tappan Square. In the
center of the square stood Tappan Hall, a large brick building
containing classrooms on the ground floor and the men's dor-
mitory above. Beyond it, across the street, Brown could see the
brand-new brick Congregational Church. To the west, along
Professor Street, were the homes of some of the college faculty;
to the east, across Main Street, was the town's one hotel and its
small business district. Like any small and growing town,
Oberlin attracted an assortment of grocers, blacksmiths, tai-
lors, and carpenters. It also boasted a bookstore. Next to the
Ladies Hall, on College Street, sat Colonial Hall, one of the
earliest classroom buildings.

Oberlin had been carved out of the wilderness in 1833 by a
group of ministers and their families from New England and
western New York. Like the founders of Brook Farm, Oneida,
New Harmony, and a host of other experimental communities
in the Northeast, these sincere men and women sought to create
a new community that would embody their ideals and serve as a
model for the larger society. Attempts to save the world by
establishing a "pilot plant," a "City on a Hill," were a venerable
part of the American tradition, from the English Separatists
who had sailed to Massachusetts two centuries before, to the
dozens of utopian communities that dotted the frontiers of New
York, Ohio, and Indiana before the Civil War.[4] Oberlin soon
developed its own peculiar ideology, a mixture of liberal religion, practical training, and reform politics.

The Congregational Church was the town's first institution. In the fall of 1834, a Collegiate Institute was established to

train ministers, missionaries, and teachers to spread the Gospel at home and abroad. A report issued in November 1834 announced:

> Its grand object is the diffusion of useful science, sound morality, and pure religion among the growing multitudes of the Mississippi Valley. It aims also at bearing an important part in extending these blessings to the destitute millions which overspread the earth.[5]

Students flocked to Oberlin, mostly from Ohio, New England, and New York, drawn to a school where education and piety were closely linked.

In 1835 Charles Grandison Finney, fresh from evangelical revivals in New York state, came to Oberlin to be professor of theology, pastor of the church, and spiritual leader of the entire community. The man who had had such a profound influence on Antoinette Brown's parents thus became her mentor. Finney's eloquent sermons and teaching reflected his conviction that intellectual talent and training should be devoted to the dual work of saving individual souls and transforming society. His preaching infused Oberlin with a contagious sense of moral urgency. Antoinette Brown would react to his sermons with "a certain zest of enjoyment," finding them "fearfully vivid, artistic, and realistic to an intense degree."[6] Her classmate Sallie Holley said that she "had never heard enough praying in all her life until she came to Oberlin."[7]

A month after its founding, Oberlin was strengthened and radicalized by an influx of white and Negro students and teachers known as the "Lane rebels," who had left Lane Seminary near Cincinnati after a bitter dispute over the abolition of slavery. By the time Brown arrived in Oberlin, more than ten percent of the town's people were black or mulatto, some of them escaped slaves who had come from North Carolina and Virginia on the underground railroad, some of them free Negroes.[8] Oberlin soon became a storm center of antislavery debates between "voting abolitionists," who believed in working within the political framework, and the "come-outers," followers of William Lloyd Garrison who favored more radical tactics.

In keeping with its egalitarian philosophy and a vision of economic self-sufficiency, Oberlin expected all students to share in the manual labor necessary for the community's survival. In the first few years, when the town was new and poor, four hours of work each day were required. As in any well-ordered family of the day, the work was largely divided along gender lines. Men students spread manure, gathered hay, cleared brush, erected and repaired buildings, and cut wood for the stoves that heated every room. Women had most of the responsibility for the ironing, washing, mending, and cooking.[9] Although wages were low—three to ten cents an hour—many students were able to work off most of their fees. By the late 1840s manual labor, no longer essential to the physical survival of the community, remained a firm part of Oberlin's philosophy, in the hopes that it would keep body and soul healthy and discourage less virtuous pastimes. *Learning and Labor* became Oberlin's official motto.

Antoinette Brown's first job was washing dishes in the boarding hall. Such chores provided an opportunity for informal fellowship. Brown found Lucy Stone sweeping the parlor floor, while Kenyon Cox, later an army general, in an apron and paper cap and sleeves rolled up, baked whole-wheat crackers for Sunday morning breakfast.[10] Before long, Brown was promoted from domestic chores to teaching drawing, an employment that was more to her liking as well as better paid.

The students' lives were well regulated. They were expected to live by normal standards of etiquette and Christian morality; most disciplining was for petty violations such as swearing, smoking, blasphemy, unauthorized trips out of town, or gambling on the Sabbath. The earliest and most important social rule, believed crucial to the success of Oberlin's experiment in coeducation, prohibited any visitors of the opposite sex in students' rooms—a rule that survived virtually intact until the late 1960s.[11] By the late 1840s additional rules prohibited men and women students taking walks together, even on the open paths between the college buildings. A committee of faculty and faculty wives concluded in 1845 that such rules were necessary, because otherwise young men and women had "a tendency to spend too much time & to be too much engrossed in each others society," at the expense of their studies.[12] In addition to these rules, all women students were expected to join the Female Moral Reform Society, an antiprostitution organization whose goal was "to protect and purify the home and reclaim the fallen," and to keep an eye out for unchaste behavior.[13] These restrictions must have come as an unwelcome surprise to

Antoinette Brown; it was the first time her activities had
been curbed in the name of ladyhood.[14]

Once classes began, the rigorous routine left Brown little
time for loneliness. She was awakened at five each morning,
and after dressing and cleaning her room spent a half-hour in
private meditation. Next came breakfast and family-style prayers. Following this, all students attended classes and studied
from seven to five o'clock, with an hour break for midday
dinner and recreation. On Tuesday and Thursday afternoons
everyone was expected to attend a religious lecture or sermon.
At five each evening there were prayers in the chapel, followed
by supper. Evenings were reserved for studying; unless there
was a special prayer meeting or other activity, women had to be
in their rooms by eight o'clock with candles blown out by ten.
On Sunday, everyone went to church services in both the morning and the afternoon.

The curriculum at Oberlin was rigorous, modeled after
the prestigious eastern colleges, but with fewer pagan classics
and more Christian theology. The classical course, leading to a
bachelor's degree, included Greek, Latin, and Hebrew; mathematics, astronomy, and "natural philosophy"; chemistry, geology and biology; logic and rhetoric; and weekly lectures on the
Bible. The literary course omitted the more rigorous subjects—
classical languages, rhetoric, and advanced mathematics—and
substituted for them English poetry, American history, and art.
The literary course was designed for women students, and lead
only to a diploma, not a degree.

From the beginning, however, some women at Oberlin
asked to take the classical course. Reluctantly Oberlin agreed.
In 1837 four brave women entered the classical course; the three
who graduated in 1841 were the first women at any American
college to receive bachelor's degrees. By the mid 1840s, a third of
the women chose the classical course. Antoinette Brown did
not. She felt rusty in languages and mathematics. Because of
the preparation she received at Monroe Academy, she could
skip portions of the less demanding literary curriculum and
finish that course in two years instead of the usual four. The
difference between the two programs would not, she believed,
affect her plans to study theology.[15]

She soon found new friends among the other women students. There was Sarah Pellet, an interesting young woman
from western Massachusetts, who, like Lucy Stone, was one day
to become a well-known public speaker. There was Sallie

Holley, a devout Unitarian, later an abolitionist crusader, who introduced Brown to the liberal thought of Ralph Waldo Emerson. There was Lettice Smith from Ann Arbor, an apt scholar who shared Brown's interest in theology.

Brown also began to get acquainted with Lucy Stone. She learned that Stone, who had come to Oberlin from western Massachusetts, was already twenty-seven, much older than most of her classmates. Because her authoritarian father opposed any higher education for women and refused to help her in any way, Stone had to earn all of her expenses. Stone's neat appearance hid strong opinions and a fiery temper; she was a radical abolitionist, a follower of Garrison. Stone had come to Oberlin specifically to learn skills in public speaking as preparation for work in the abolition and woman's rights movements. She was halfway through the classical course when Antoinette Brown arrived. Brown came to regard Stone with "the intense admiration of a younger girl for one much more experienced and influential."[16] Away from her family for the first time, and still feeling the loss of her older brothers and sisters, Brown looked to Lucy Stone for her primary emotional support for the next few years.

Like Antoinette, these young women had come to Oberlin to obtain a thorough college education in preparation for public work. They had high expectations; Lucy Stone later wrote, "In our despair, Oberlin, away in the West, became our star of hope, our Mecca."[17] The women quickly discovered that Oberlin had no intention of training them as public speakers. Throughout the college, in classes and in extracurricular activities, women were prohibited from speaking in mixed groups. Although women shared classes with men, they were "excused" from participation in discussions, debates, or rhetorical exhibitions. They learned to write; men learned to write and to speak. Officially the rule rested on the famous words of Paul: "Let a woman learn in silence with all submissiveness."[18] Public speaking was considered unseemly for proper young ladies.

But more than simple propriety was involved. Training in rhetoric was an essential part of the preparation of Oberlin men, most of whom expected to become lawyers, ministers, or teachers.[19] Such training was considered unnecessary for female students, who were not expected to enter the professions for which it was needed.

Despite Oberlin's radical reputation and its interest in social reform, the college shared common prejudices about women's roles. Female education, according to this traditional view, should be geared toward moral and religious self-improvement, which would contribute to women's preordained roles as wives, mothers, and moral teachers. Although the founders of Oberlin yielded to the insistence of Father John Shipherd, one of their leaders, that women be admitted as students, few of them held any new or unusual views of women's roles. Oberlin's first Annual Report stated quite clearly that women students "will be permitted to enjoy the privilege" of partaking of such intellectual work "as shall best suit their sex, and prospective employment."[20]

The primary defender of coeducation, James H. Fairchild, an Oberlin graduate himself and professor of mathematics and natural philosophy, believed firmly that woman's place was in the home. "The woman is the natural housekeeper," he told the assembled student body in 1849. "There may be other objects of interest and effort to her, but these are incidental and must hold a second place. The claims of the household are paramount, all others are secondary."[21] Fairchild fully expected that Oberlin's education of women would be consistent with that fact; he "could not cheerfully bear a part in a system of female education which is false to nature and blots out God's handwriting."[22]

Even Charles Grandison Finney, who had encouraged the young Antoinette Brown to participate in informal prayer meetings, did not believe that women needed training in public speaking. Finney believed that the evangelical work of teaching the Gospel on the frontier and overseas demanded the best efforts of everyone, men and women. In particular, he felt that a man going into a rugged and potentially hostile environment needed a companion who could share his convictions and support his work. And what better way to provide a pool of suitable wives than to educate them side by side with their future husbands? In addition, the presence of women students would improve the atmosphere for the male students, aiding the process of transforming coarse farm boys into mature well-mannered Christian gentlemen.[23] Of all the professors at Oberlin in the late 1840s, only President Asa Mahan fully supported proposals to allow women to participate in discussions and debates, and he was consistently outvoted by the faculty.[24]

Lucy Stone, Antoinette Brown, Sallie Holley, and several other women were bitterly disappointed by this policy. Stone wrote home, "I hoped when I came to Oberlin that the course of study would permit such practice, but I was never in a place where women are so rigidly taught that they must not speak in public."[25] Stone, older and more self-confident than some of the others, quickly set out to challenge the rule. Despite severe censure from the college community, she spoke at a public celebration of the tenth anniversary of the West Indian emancipation of slaves. For this daring act she was soundly reprimanded by the Ladies Board, an official group of faculty wives who watched over both the academic progress and the personal development of the female students. Brown described these women as "lovely educated women, much more conservative than their husbands."[26] They were steeped in Christian virtue and middle-class morality, and held traditional views of what "ladies" ought and ought not to do with their lives. The Ladies Board had a particular dislike for "advanced" women, those who challenged accepted norms and defined their lives in ways other than as prospectuve wives for their classmates.[27]

Lucy Stone's example encouraged her classmates to take similar direct action. In June 1846 Stone, Antoinette Brown, Lettice Smith, and several of their classmates reactivated the dormant Young Ladies Association of Oberlin Collegiate Institute for the Promotion of Literature and Religion, commonly known as the Ladies Literary Society, as a framework for training themselves in speaking.[28] The group met as often as it could, at the home of a black woman—one of Lucy Stone's pupils—on the outskirts of town. They slipped out quietly to keep the meetings from arousing the interest of the Ladies Board. Some women who were not interested in learning to speak came to listen and lend their support to the venture. The topics selected for essays and debates ranged from "Egotism" and "The Qualifications of a Minister's Wife," to a report on the Seneca Falls women's rights convention in 1848.[29] In the early 1850s, after Stone and Brown had both left, the Society resolved "that ladies have the right to debate and declaim in public"—a view that official Oberlin would reluctantly accept only in 1874.

During the autumn that followed their revival of the literary society, Brown and Stone convinced James Thome, their rhetoric professor, to allow them to stage a debate in class. Thome was one of the "Lane Rebels" and a firm believer in coeducation; he offered them valuable coaching, criticism, and encouragement. Due to their experience in their own debating society and their enthusiasm for breaking the gag on women's speaking, they did a brilliant job. The incident provoked such a vehement reaction from both the faculty and the Ladies Board that the debate experiment was not repeated.

In the winter of 1846-47, during Oberlin's three-month vacation, Antoinette Brown left Oberlin to teach at a large private academy in Rochester, Michigan. It was customary, during the vacation, for Oberlin students to scatter to small towns throughout the country to teach in district schools, gaining valuable experience and earning up to twenty dollars toward tuition. Brown still felt that "God never made me for a school teacher,"[30] but she had no other means of earning money.

On the train from Cleveland to Michigan, she had a long conversation with Rev. Henry Fairchild, brother of the Oberlin professor, about the proper role for women. Like his brother, Rev. Fairchild believed "not only in St. Paul but also that the woman's place, the one befitting her modesty and real interest, was home, social-life and life in the pews as a lay member of the church." His final words to her were, "Whatever you may think ought to be, the place and position of woman will never be greatly different from what it is now."[31] Brown wrote to Lucy Stone as soon as she reached Rochester:

> He was very kind and good-natured about it, but it put me into such an agony as I never wish to feel again, and for once I did wish God had not made me a woman (I do not wish so now).[32]

At the Rochester Academy, Brown took over the girls' department, while the headmaster, Peter Moyers, taught the older boys. After a few weeks he began to switch classes with her without any warning, forcing her to teach extemporaneously. She also started a literary society for the older girls. She reported to Stone:

> There are some young ladies here of superior talent, all take a deep interest in the exercises and I must say I have never before improved so rapidly in my life in the use of the tongue....We are all getting to be Woman's Rights Advocates.[33]

Peter Moyers also encouraged Brown to give her first public speech, in the village church. With great excitement she accepted his invitation. When it was all over she could report with satisfaction that "It was fairly well received by the students and the community."[34] It was altogether a profitable and enjoyable winter.

That winter was a turning point in Brown's relationship with Lucy Stone. Alone and perhaps homesick, she missed Stone's companionship. At the end of February, when Brown returned to Oberlin, she focused her emotional attention on Stone. Their friendship deepened, unrestricted by the rules of etiquette that governed relationships between men and women. Brown later recalled:

> 1847—that was the time when I used to slip over and sleep with Lucy and talk almost all night, of everything, present, future, and more or less of the past. Of our studies, and of how we could get money to carry out our plans; and also of the comfort of being cuddled up together.[35]

They may have become lovers, bound together by sexual intimacy as well as by emotional ties.[36] The emotional intensity of the relation was reflected in letters written while they were apart. Brown wrote:

> We believed no more things in common than any other of my classmates, perhaps *not as many*, & yet I loved you more than all the rest together . . . .[37]

She was afraid that Lucy Stone did not feel the same way, a fear that would continue to haunt her:

> You tell me you do not wish to become acquainted with a very good and amiable young lady because you are afraid you will learn to love her and then she will go away and leave you. Pardon me dear Lucy, but you do need a severe rebuke. Why are you becoming so misanthropic? . . . Have I caused you more sad than happy hours, and do you regret having known me?[38]

Stone's answer, for the moment, was a clear no:

> I do not feel more of "pain, than pleasure, on account of our previous intimacy." The short memories that cluster around it, and the knowledge that in the wide world *one* heart understands me, can *feel* what I feel, and sympathize with me is an infinity of good to me.[39]

Antoinette Brown shared these sentiments; two years later she recalled, "I loved you Lucy as I seldom loved any human being & as I much fear I shall never love another."[40]

Their friendship was peppered with frequent disagreements. Brown, like her father, was a "voting abolitionist," while Stone was an ardent Garrisonian. Brown was firmly committed to the ideology and institutions of organized Christianity; Stone had withdrawn angrily from the Congregational Church because it sanctioned slavery and opposed women speaking in public. Stone, who dressed in Quakerlike simplicity, criticized the artificial flowers on Brown's bonnet, feeling that such decoration was frivolous for someone who wanted to be a public speaker. Worst of all, Brown discovered that Stone scorned her own aspirations:

> We were one evening facing a beautiful sunset when we both stopped and stood looking at this evening glory. I told her of my intention to become a minister. Her protest was most emphatic. She said, "You will never be allowed to do this. You will never be allowed to stand in a pulpit, nor to preach in a church, and certainly you can never be ordained." It was a long talk but we were no nearer to an agreement at the end than at the beginning. My final answer could only be, "I am going to do it."[41]

Brown was deeply disappointed that Stone did not support her. Her friend's opposition did not, however, mar their underlying friendship, nor alter Brown's determination to study theology.

In the summer of 1847, both Antoinette Brown and Lucy Stone finished their college work. Brown went home to Henrietta for a few weeks to see her family before commencement. Once more she wrote long letters to Stone about her ideas, her aspirations, and her feelings:

> I go out into the barn and make the walls echo with my voice occasionally but the church stands on the green in such a way that I have too many auditors when I attempt to practice there. The barn is a good large one however and the sounds ring out merrily or did before Father filled it so full of hay.

She added, "I have wished you were here a dozen times a *dozen* times.... Oh Lucy I wish I could see you only one hour."[42]

At Oberlin's commencement, as in its classes and debating societies, male students prepared orations. Their female classmates were "excused" from that exercise, as they had been throughout their formal education. Women in the classical course were permitted to write essays to be read by a professor. For Lucy Stone, the offer of such a restricted role conflicted with her deepest convictions concerning women's abilities and roles, and she refused to participate. Antoinette Brown, on the other hand, was to receive only a literary diploma. Because the literary commencement was officially a ladies' event, the women students were invited to read their essays aloud even to a mixed audience, and Brown accepted. She returned to Oberlin early in August to prepare her essay. Its subject, "Mind Adapted to Originality of Thought or Investigation," reflected her interest in philosophy and psychology.

As soon as they had graduated, Stone left Oberlin to begin her work as a public speaker by lecturing on abolition throughout New England. Brown remained at Oberlin—there was no vacation before fall term—to commence the study of theology.

Lucy Stone, ca. 1855

ঌ Chapter 3 ঌ

NO CROSS, NO CROWN

As Oberlin's new term began in September 1847, Antoinette Brown began her serious study of theology. With clarity and conviction, she felt that she was called to study theology with the intention of being ordained as a parish minister. She accepted fully the exhortations of Charles Grandison Finney and others that young men and women use their full talents in the Lord's service. In her culture and her experience, a minister was "an oracle and a political and social arbiter,"[1] as well as a trained scholar, a nurturer of human relationships, and a sign of God's presence within the community. It was a vocation that would draw on her own religious experience, her probing and broad-reaching intellect, her gifts as a speaker, and her concern for social reform. Perhaps—if a parish accepted her—it would also enable her to earn her living through work more satisfying to her than teaching school. If she needed Biblical confirmation of her choice, she found it in the words of the prophet Joel: "And it shall come to pass in the last days, saith God, I will pour out my spirit upon all flesh; and your sons and your daughters shall prophesy."[2]

Brown knew that it would be difficult for her to be accepted as a future minister. She nevertheless applied for formal admission to the Theological Department. The Oberlin faculty may not have discussed her application at all.[3] Its position in that period, however, was firm: Oberlin allowed women a general education, but had no intention of training women for active roles in professions other than teaching. In a speech to the student body in 1848, Professor James Fairchild expressed the prevailing attitude toward women lawyers or ministers:

> Can woman occupy these stations to an equal extent
> with man? The answer must be, No, for two general
> reasons: it is improper and impossible .... It is a thing
> positively disagreeable to both sexes to see a woman a
> public character. The reason why we are so made as to
> dislike to see a woman a public character, is found in the
> fact that in general it is impossible that she should be.[4]

Fairchild advised women who wanted a more active and public role:

> Remember then that woman's lot is on you, lest, if you forget it now, you may one day learn it and regret the error with bitterness of heart. . . . If the lot seems too hard and the burden greater than you can bear, then learn self-denial of the Captain of your salvation, and as you deliver up your trust to Him you shall receive the highest praise which mortal ever received from Him—"She hath done what she could."[5]

Brown found the women of the Ladies Board equally discouraging:

> Mrs. Finney, having heard that I intended to study theology, appealed to me not to do so, at least not to become a public speaker or a minister. When she had brought many stereotyped arguments her last appeal was, "You will never feel yourself wise enough to go directly against the opinions of all the great men of the past." As that was exactly what her husband had done and was doing, it was necessary for me to reply, "That is exactly what Professor Finney is doing, and we all feel that he is making a great advance of thought."[6]

The informal pressure of a small, family-like community must have been as hard on Brown as a formal no. She felt that "The tremendous weight of public opinion seemed to be inexorably bearing me down."[7] Officially, she and Oberlin reached an uneasy compromise. For the next three years Brown was listed in the catalog under the heading of the Young Ladies Department, as a "resident graduate pursuing the theological course," a status that acknowledged her studies but left unanswered the question of her professional future.[8]

This official ambiguity did not deter her from the goal she had been seeking for seven years. In fact, at first she rather enjoyed her unique position. She told Lucy Stone:

> I have a grand chance to bring the subject up almost every time I meet an old friend or a stranger for generally the first question after finding out what I am studying is, "Are you going to preach, be a minister, a public lecturer, etc.," or else such remarks as "You can write sermons for your brother or for your husband" or something else of the sort

and so the subject comes in without dragging. Sometimes they ... believe I am joking, sometimes stare at me with amazement and sometimes seem to start back with a kind of horror. Men and women are about equal and seem to have their mouths opened and their tongues loosed to about the same extent.[9]

In the Theological Department, as in the rest of the community, women had their accepted place. They were most welcome to reap the benefits of its teaching by sitting in on classes, as long as their only goal was self-improvement. Oberlin's first Annual Report stated plainly, "The Female Department's higher classes will be permitted to enjoy the privilege of such professorships in the Teacher's, Collegiate, and Theological Departments as shall best suit their sex, and prospective employment.[10] Many women did just that, especially young women waiting for their fiancés to graduate.

One of Brown's classmates, Lettice Smith, was a more serious student of theology than the other women who attended classes. She shared Brown's semiofficial status in the department. But Smith's presence never aroused the opposition that Brown's did. Everyone knew that Smith would soon marry her classmate Thomas Holmes; her prospective role as a minister's wife made her studies much more acceptable than Brown's. Nor did Smith challenge the accepted view of woman's place at Oberlin. Brown complained to Lucy Stone, "How I do wish Lettice would take part in these exercises. She does well in her studies but she has no confidence in herself & she never talks at all in the class."[11] Lettice Smith did not provide Brown with an ally, nor with the solidarity that had enabled Brown and Lucy Stone to challenge the "no speaking" custom in their undergraduate classes.

The short fall term of 1847 was a difficult one for Brown. She was lonely, sick, and under emotional strain. She had no money even to pay for her room and board. To reduce her expenses and free herself from institutional supervision, she moved from the Ladies Boarding Hall and kept house for herself in a room rented from Deacon Beecher, who had relatives in Henrietta. She had expected to earn her way by teaching younger girls in the Preparatory Department, but the Ladies Board passed a resolution, apparently aimed specifically at Brown, prohibiting female Oberlin graduates from teaching in the Preparatory Department. In desperation, she wrote to Peter Moyers, principal of the Rochester Academy, where she had taught the previous winter; he readily offered to send her the money she needed. When he died suddenly before he could send the money, she "shed nearly all the tears of my entire life."[12] By November she was more than ten dollars in debt, a considerable sum at a time when most wages at Oberlin averaged less than ten cents an hour. She wrote to Lucy Stone:

> After you left here you know how the ladies board thought of me & of my being prevented from teaching in the institution. Those were dark weeks. I felt that I ought to study but had not a penny of money nor any means of obtaining any except by working at 3 cents an hour or going away to teach. To add to my trials I took a severe cold which lasted many weeks attended with a hard cough. ... Sarah attributed it to my not wearing wrappers &c but all the wrappers in the world could not have prevented me from taking cold while I was constantly exposing myself to the damp air in such a state of mind.[13]

Finally Mary Atkins, the assistant principal of the Ladies Department, arranged for Brown to teach perspective drawing on an independent basis, outside of the college. The classes became popular; even Professor James Fairchild and some of the theological students began to attend them. Brown reported to Lucy Stone:

> Last fall I was ready to teach at 18 pence an hour & there was a prospect of a small class at that, but this spring [1848] I raised the price to a dollar for 40 lessons & went on perfectly independent of the institution. The class was full & I earned 20 dollars in 8 weeks, 50 cts. an hour. Another class has now been continued for a week & this is filled to overflowing so that we have had to bring additional seats into the assembly room & I shall have earned enough by commencement to carry me through the whole winter for I intend to remain here & study. Whatever you may think of this I certainly regard it as a favor directly from the hand of God & I have no fear now either of being unable to sustain myself during my studies or of not being able to talk or do anything else that seems [my] duty when I am through my studies.[14]

Having resolved her financial crisis, Brown encountered other difficulties in the Theological Department. Oberlin's general prohibition against women's oral recitation at first prevented her from participating fully in her classes. She knew she was academically qualified to participate; she had shared instruction with these same male students for the past two years. In addition to her other work, she had studied Hebrew and Greek on her own. Moreover, with her experience in the Ladies Literary Society and at Rochester Academy, she was confident of her abilities as a speaker. The restriction on speaking was an especially damaging one in the Theological Department, where classroom recitation was practice for preaching. Since Antoinette Brown planned to preach, she was determined to have the same opportunity as her classmates to speak, to be heard and criticized.

The conflict surfaced early in the fall of 1847, at a religious meeting during which each of the twelve new theological students was asked to tell why he wanted to become a minister. Brown described the meeting to Lucy Stone:

> When he [Finney] called for those who already had not [spoken], [James] Tefft mentioned Lettice & I. Once he looked as though he did not know what to say & the next time said, "Oh, we don't call upon the ladies." They had all told me we should have to speak & I felt so badly at what he said that I just began to cry & was obliged to leave the room. It was the first & last time that I have cried about anything connected with this matter this spring, but it came so unexpectedly. After I went out they talked over the matter & it seems Prof. Finney did not know we were members of the department in any other sense than the other ladies are who go in to hear the lectures. He said he was willing any lady should speak if she wished to.... I went over to see him & he certainly seemed to forget that he was talking with a woman. We conversed more than an hour sometimes upon gravest subjects of Philosophy & Theology & he expressed himself freely upon the true position of women. Said he did not care how much she was educated that her education had been fundamentally wrong—that though he did not think she was generally called upon to preach or speak in public because of the circumstances did not demand it, still that there was nothing right or wrong in the thing itself & that sometimes she was specially called to speak.[15]

Finney encouraged her to speak in all of his classes, but told her that each of the other professors would have to make his own decision. "From that time on," Brown felt, "no one could have been more helpful or more considerate in making my position both easy and satisfactory than Professor Finney."[16]

Finney's theology class, one of the most popular in the department, was an exciting and challenging experience for her:

> In Professor Finney's teaching of theology the names of all the class were written on slips of paper. He gathered them up in his hand and while he turned his face the other way we saw him throw them into his hat and then draw out a name at random. The person selected was required to stand and give his opinion of the point or doctrine under discussion.... The teacher and any pupil who chose were expected to ask questions or make objections to which the student holding the floor was expected to reply if possible, holding the floor as long as anything remained to be stated or illustrated. It was an exercise which required every faculty to be alert and resourceful. For one, I came in time to thoroughly enjoy it and it certainly was the most helpful class that any of us ever attended.[17]

Brown had more difficulty gaining access to the Theological Literary Society, an extracurricular club largely run by the students. At least two members—James Tefft and Thomas Holmes—fully supported Brown's desire to participate, but the faculty advisor, Professor John Morgan, definitely did not. The committee of students who made the list of assignments for presenting essays put Brown's name on it. When Morgan saw the list, he dismissed the class early and asked the committee why they had included a woman. The committee members reminded him that their constitution required every member to participate in the exercises. Morgan took the issue to a special faculty meeting. Brown reported to Lucy Stone:

> They talked & talked about preventing me but at last let it go. Professor Morgan said if he was the teacher he would not let me sustain any other relation to the department than the ladies do to the college classes ie he would have no discussion or declamation from ladies but as it was a society the members had a right to say what I might do & they were too evenly divided to prevent me from speaking.[18]

Morgan felt constrained by the words of the Oberlin charter, which permitted women to participate in all departments of the institution. With full participation in the Theological Literary Society and in Professor Finney's classes, Brown now felt that she had the same advantages as the official students.

There were, however, additional hurdles to overcome. In one of their classes, Antoinette Brown and Lettice Smith were assigned to write essays on the Biblical passages that forbade women to preach:

> Let your women keep silence in the churches, for it is not permitted unto them to speak.... Let the women learn in silence with all subjection. I suffer not a woman to teach, nor to usurp authority over the man, but to be in silence.[19]

Brown realized that this was not just a routine assignment; it was a direct challenge to use all her intellectual skills to justify her position. When she went home to Henrietta during the winter vacation of 1847-48, she devoted herself to studying the passages. She wrote to Lucy Stone:

> I have been examining the bible position of women a good deal this winter—reading various commentaries—comparing them with each other & with the bible, & hunting up every passage in the scriptures that have any bearing on the subject either near or remote. My mind grows stronger & firmer on the subject & the light comes beaming in, full of promise. Lately I have been writing out my thoughts to see if they will all hang together but have not finished yet. It is a hard subject & takes a long time to see through it doesn't it. But "no cross no crown."[20]

Over the next few months she finished her exegesis, including her own translations from the Greek text. Professor Asa Mahan considered her paper good enough for publication in the *Oberlin Quarterly Review*; it appeared in the same issue that contained Professor Fairchild's conservative speech on "Women's Rights and Duties."

In her essay, Brown suggested that Paul's words had been twisted by later generations to serve a purpose the apostle did not intend. She took the position that Paul meant only to warn against "excesses, irregularities, and unwarrantable liberties" in public worship:

> This exegesis makes the passage have nothing whatever to do with the question of public teaching. The females were

not forbidden to take part in the work of instructing the church, of speaking "either by revelation, or by knowledge, or by prophesying, or by doctrine," or of doing anything else which they had the wisdom and ability to do, ... and moreover, ... being taught by the Spirit of the mighty God, they did actually take part in these exercises.... In what portion of the inspired volume do we find any commandment forbidding woman to act as a public teacher, *provided* she has a message worth communicating, and will deliver it in a manner worthy of her high vocation? Surely nowhere....This was too sacred a subject to be coldly decided by the voice of law, and they left it, where it must ever remain, at the portal of the individual conscience of every moral agent.[21]

Unlike her dear friend Lucy Stone, Antoinette Brown made a concerted effort to integrate orthodox Christianity with reform politics and especially with woman's rights. She believed that her rational explanations would change people's opinions. The process was slow, however. She found ministers, whom she looked to as models, the least receptive to her views— and the least interested in discussing the idea of a woman being ordained. She complained to Stone:

I can hardly find anyone to talk with. Some of them can't talk, and some of them won't talk on this question. Associated as I have been this winter frequently with ministers, I have not found one who has been both ready and willing to talk over the matter candidly.... Some of them around here at least begin to feel a little uneasy at their old position and are not quite ready to advocate that nor quite ready to get a new standing point.[22]

Regardless of the reception given her ideas, when Brown returned to Oberlin in the spring of 1848, she was inspired with a renewed sense of her goal and her religious faith. She tried to explain this to Lucy Stone:

You know I decided to stay here and as I told you "trust Providence" for assistance & Lucy Providence has assisted me. I learned then to cast myself on the Lord as I had never done before & I learned to pray to him as I had never prayed before. Perhaps you will think me superstitious but I have learned to talk with God as I would with a friend & I feel that to have his sympathy is all I need. You know we used

to wish sometimes that we could live on & feel no need of
the sympathy of any one & I have learned to feel so. I do not
mean that I do not wish for sympathy but I can feel
perfectly happy without it, & when any thing troubles me I
can tell it all to God & he certainly does comfort me even in
the most trifling griefs.... I have never been happier in the
world for the last few months but it is a new kind of
happiness.[23]

She felt more confident about her work, too; at the end of
the long summer term she wrote to Stone:

I have grown very happy lately & do not feel half so sad for
the good cause is prospering though we have hard struggles & if they think Public Opinion will prevent us from
studying Theology very long, they don't know us yet.[24]

But although she claimed that she did not need sympathy
or support from other people, Brown's letters to Lucy Stone
reflect a deep loneliness. Lettice Smith apparently never
became a very close friend, despite their somewhat common
position. Sarah Pellet to some extent replaced Stone as Brown's
day-to-day companion, but Brown told Stone that "I never
made [Sarah] a confidant. It could not be so for we are not
alike."[25] Nor could she depend upon her family for support.
The matter was, in fact, reversed: of necessity, she had taken on
responsibility for her younger sister Augusta, who had joined
her at Oberlin. It soon became apparent that Augusta was
afflicted with the tuberculosis that had killed the other Brown
siblings. Brown wrote to Stone from Henrietta:

My sister grew rapidly worse & I dared not let her remain at
Oberlin any longer. She could not travel alone & there was
no one I knew of going East so I have come home with
her.... When we rushed home we found *Mother* sick with
a kind of intermitting fever. She is very weak but sits up
part of the time.... O Lucy it is hard to have our friends
afflicted. My heart feels sad to day.... I have just been into
the garden & sat down under a cherry tree and cried. How I
should like to see you now.[26]

Her relationship with Lucy Stone seemed all the more
precious to her now. Her ties with her family were no longer the
primary bonds in her life; she was lonely even in Henrietta. In

long letters to Stone, she tried to assuage her loneliness—as well as some doubts of her friend's continuing devotion:

> Lucy Dearest,
> Perhaps you will almost wonder at this [long letter] when you think of the short & far between little notes that you have condescended to send me lately. Do you not stand self convicted on this point Lucy, & do you not think my forebodings of last fall may possibly be realized that you may yet cease to write from your heart   But no Lucy dearest dear Lucy I do not believe this. I know if you were here now you would talk with me just as you used to & that you will write so too the next letter if you are not too busy. But somehow that last letter did seem to me to be just such a one as I often write to an *acquaintance* with whom *concience* & *custom* compells me to correspond   It had no soul in it. . . . But Lucy I don't know why I am writing in this way. . . . My heart has just been called back to the time when we used to sit with our arms around each other at the sunset hour & talk & talk of our friends & our homes & of ten thousand subjects of mutual interest till both our hearts felt warmer & lighter for the pure communion of spirit.[27]

Stone's response should have put to rest her friend's fears:

> O Nette how I do wish we could meet and talk, all that our hearts want to so much. . . . Sure there are few, *very* few who can understand, and enter into the soul's holy of holies, but the few, or that human one, *is needed*, and any one is *better* who *shares* his soul's holiest emotions, aye, and *stronger* too. I never had a friend like you Nette, to whom I wished to *trust everything*, and who could understand me. I had friends who came into the "outer Court." But into the *sanctum*, none but you ever went. . . . Is not our *soul* sympathy an eternal bond? And is there not then a life-long bond, or tie, between us?[28]

Despite these expressions of mutual affection, circumstances did not permit them to see one another. Antoinette lamented:

> O how glad I should be to have your arm around me & my arm around you & to walk with you again. . . . Dear dear Lucy when shall I see you again & when shall we walk together & talk together as we used to. Will it be ever again—ever in this world or in the next?[29]

Stone's lecture schedule kept her in New England, while Brown shuttled between Oberlin and Henrietta.

Brown was also hurt by Stone's lack of support for her theological studies. Stone repeatedly warned her about "that *wall* of bible, brimstone, church and corruption, which has hitherto buried *women* into *nothingness*." For a woman to gain a place in a hierarchical and oppressive institution seemed, to Stone, of dubious value. Her letter continued:

> I wonder if you have any idea how dreadfully I feel, about your studying that old musty theology, which already had its grave clothes on, and is about to be buried in so deep a grave that no resurrection trumpet can call it into being, and no Prophet voice clothe its dry bones with *living* life? ... The great *soul* of the *Present*, hungering & thirsting for the bread and water of Life, falters by the wayside, finding no green pastures or living foundations that are not all polluted with the horrid stench which goes up from the decaying corpse of such a theology, with which Humanity, and God himself are weary. Yet *my own dear Nette* is spending *three* precious years of her life's young prime, wading through that deep slough, from the stain of which she can never wash herself and by which, I *fear*, her vision will be so clouded that she can only see *men* through creeds.... It creeps over me again, like the cold sense of "coming ill," that you will be *only* a *sectarian*, and never dare to throw yourself out like "incense to the breeze," careful only that the healing fragrance shall be spread abroad—but you will have to be politic so as not to injure your *sect*.[30]

Brown wrote back with equal vehemence:

> And you are afraid I am getting bigoted exclusive and narrow minded No no I am not I *am not* at any rate I think so. One thing is certain I am not afraid to act as my conscience dictates no matter what the world may think and Dearest Lucy I am not timeserving I am not "Politic" in the bad sense of that term. But what use is there in saying what one is when actions speak louder than words and at present I cant act in such a way at least as to vindicate myself. But dont think too hardly of me my dear sister "wait a bit" and see.[31]

She was not able to explain to Stone the basis of her conviction, or the ways in which she felt that her direct relationship with

God, rather than binding her, freed her to act independently of
social pressure—as she had now been doing for some years.

Yet that winter, for the first time, her confidence in the
course she had chosen seemed to falter. Because of Augusta's
illness, she decided not to remain at Oberlin during the winter
vacation of 1849-50. She went home to Henrietta and once
again, reluctantly, agreed to teach as a way of earning badly
needed money. At Monroe Academy, which she had attended
ten years earlier, she taught philosophy, algebra, geometry, and
physiology. She did not enjoy it; she wrote to Stone: "How I do
wish I was doing something besides teaching this winter but
the time has not come yet for me to do much as a public
teacher."[32]

She debated whether or not to return to Oberlin that spring
for her final term of theological study. She wrote to Stone:

> Do you know any thing about my thinking of applying to
> some other Theological Seminary for admition. I had
> concluded to do so if the way seemed prepared for this but
> although my friends would not oppose me in this and even
> favor it to some extent yet they see but little reason for my
> leaving O[berlin] and are anxious to have me get through
> my studies So they will not think it best to assist me to
> means and as I am anxious to get through studying also
> and am so very nervous already have about concluded not
> to spend any more time and strength for the sake of what
> might be gained by going to some other Institution.
> Besides it is so uncertain whether I could be admitted
> elsewhere.[33]

In addition to—or perhaps because of—her ambivalence,
she felt physically sick all winter:

> If I could feel strong and well I have no doubt I should be
> able to do a considerable [amount] towards discharging
> my debts or assisting myself in [the] future. But Lucy I am
> almost sick this winter and as nervous as I can be
> almost.... I say as little about it as possible for it makes
> my friends so anxious but I shall get to be as figety as can
> be if I am not careful so I have given up all hard thinking
> for the present and have very little to do with the subject of
> Womans Rights or any other exciting question. All I need
> is rest and no excitement and yet I never was so anxious to
> do something as now.[34]

While some of Brown's health problems may have been the result of the inadequate sanitation in the community and a poor diet, her own words suggest that the main cause was her "state of mind," induced by the unorthodox role she had chosen.

In this uncertain period, she also caught fleeting glimpses of other visions of herself, images and possibilities pushed aside in the concentration on her goals at Oberlin. In a letter to Stone, she outlined a future that connected with her teenage dreams. She proposed to find a large building, probably in Cincinnati, hire a housekeeper, and adopt seven "little ragged starving outcasts" into her household. In her home she could have a good reference library, and a haven to which she could retreat. She told Stone:

> I do not think with my temperament health &c &c I can do as much good by giving up my time exclusively to lectur-ing or preaching as I could by doing various other things in connection with these. Besides much is to be accom-plished in reforming the world by writing; more persons are accessible by this means than by any other and it seems to me that almost any one can accomplish more by both methods than by being confined to either . . . . Then again I cant go wandering up and down the earth without any home. Not cant because it would require too much self denial, but because I should get too excited and too down-hearted from reaction to accomplish anything . . . I need a pleasant happy home to rest in and some pleasant happy children there to keep me from becoming a misanthrope.[35]

Brown's feelings arose more from her own experience of, and yearning for, the warmth and support of a family home than from Professor Fairchild's stern lectures on woman's place.

Whatever the attractions of her alternate dreams of the future, Brown was at this time not ready to pursue them. Oberlin offered her the opportunity to continue the theological study that was the keystone of her intellectual and moral life. For Antoinette Brown, theology, broadly conceived, embraced the world—"the whole range of human thought open for investigation, and all human relations ready for the applica-tion of perceived principles."[36] Theology was not only prepa-ration for the specific career of parish minister; it was also a window to a far-reaching exploration of the nature of the universe and of the human psyche.

And so she returned to Oberlin at the beginning of the spring term in 1850—with the same ambiguous status as before. She resigned herself to her situation, and tried once again to explain her decision to Stone:

> It is a fine pleasant afternoon, just such an one as makes me think of you....
>
> "Don't go to Oberlin Nette" those words are ringing in my ears. Thank you L. for your kind advice. I would have heeded it but suspected you did not know all the circumstances.... Providence did not open the way for me to go elsewhere. I had neither money nor health for this year, and was anxious to get through studying that I might commence acting. There are but few months longer and I shall be greatly profited by them every way. Our studies have never been more interesting.[37]

Stone was appalled. She was convinced that by remaining at Oberlin without official recognition, Brown was tacitly accepting Oberlin's view that women should listen, but not preach:

> Nette I am so sorry you are at Oberlin, on terms which to me seem *dishonorable*. They trampled your womanhood and you did not spurn it. I do believe that even *they* would have thought better of you if you have stayed away. O Nette, I am sorry you returned, but for all this, you *know* I *love you dearly*, and will say no more about it....
>
> I don't like the idea of your "settling"—I am afraid you will settle into just what other ministers do. No not *just* what they are, for you will always be *more*, but I am afraid you will settle into something *less* than *you* ought to be.[38]

Brown tried once more to explain her decision:

> You think I have come back to Oberlin upon dishonorable terms? Then you dont know me. I never did a dishonorable public act that could make me blush to look any body in the face, never!
>
> I came back here just upon no terms at all. They refused to recieve me into the Institution. I came back to study Theology and get knowledge. I do get it, they dont interfere. I am not responsable for their conduct or decisions. I have nothing to do with these but I am bound to

put myself into the most favorable position for improvement possible while the day for improvement lasts; and
when I go out to work I shall work in the field where I
think I can do most good and what if they, or any body else
think I act unwisely, or dishonorably, or foolishly what
can that be to me. I respect their advice but I do not abide
by their decisions. Why should I? I never spite myself for
their errors and I would scorn myself for resenting injus-
tice done me for there is no time to spare for such
things .... I believe I acted wisely and if they respect me
any the less it is because they dont understand me else it
were the more shame for them ...

I am no more conservative, creed-loving, time-serving
or bigoted than I was three years since. I am no less of a free
thinker or independent actor; but I *have* more settled and
consistent views and more self reliance or rather more
implicit reliance upon an arm that will never fail me and
will hold me up in opposition to a mistaken world if need
be. In short I have a great deal more individuality so please
dear Lucy dont lecture me any more about the folly or
danger of my course or rather do lecture me for it can do no
harm and may do much good. I like to have you speak
what you think. If you did not do it with our great difference of views I should think we had ceased to be true
friends.[39]

The paradox of Brown's position is a classic one for those
seeking to break through social barriers. If she accepted—that
is, by studying theology on "their" terms, without formal
recognition—she appeared to be countenancing "their" policy
that women should not become ministers. But if she had taken
the position Stone advocated, staying away until she could
study on the same terms as men, she could not have gotten the
training she needed to enter a male profession. Brown chose to
accept education on Oberlin's terms. She felt that she would
not regret the time spent at Oberlin even if she should ultimately abandon the ministry as a vocation:

Lucy, if I believed I should one day throw away the
bible—should one day come to believe that prayer to God
was impious, that the sabbath was an ordinance of man,
that the church was the great resovoir of iniquity and that
the present system of Theology was composed of blas-
phemous dogmas, still I firmly believe that I should continue to be thankful that I had spent three years in the

> Theological investigations at Oberlin merely for the sake
> of the mental discipline I have acquired and which I
> believed could be obtained no other way.[40]

That spring Antoinette Brown first raised, in an overt way,
the issue of her official right to preach and to perform the
sacraments—something no woman had ever done. Responsibility for ordaining Oberlin graduates lay with the Lorain
County Congregational Association, an independent group
made up almost exclusively of Oberlin faculty. The association
customarily gave preaching licenses to students in the final
year of their studies, which authorized them to give sermons in
nearby churches, but not to perform any of the sacraments. The
college rules stated that it was "out of order" for any student to
lecture or preach outside of Oberlin without such a license.[41]
Wanting to be treated on an equal footing with other students,
Brown applied for a preaching license along with her classmates in the spring of 1850. After much deliberation, the association sidestepped the controversial issue of recognizing a
woman as a preacher. Brown later wrote, "They were willing to
have me preach, but not to themselves endorse this as a principle . . . . They decided, after much discussion, that I must preach
if I chose to do so on my own responsibility."[42] It was both a
denial of the offical recognition she wanted, and a grudging
acknowledgment that she was beyond their control. Brown
chose to lecture on the popular topic of temperance and to
preach whenever she could in the small-town churches in
Oberlin's vicinity. Her classmate James Tefft often helped her
arrange these lectures, and went along for moral support.

In the spring of 1850 Antoinette Brown reached the final
decision facing her at Oberlin: whether to ask to be ordained.
Normally Congregational ministers were ordained by the individual churches that called them. Some Oberlin students, however, feared that the liberal theological and political views
associated with Oberlin would be a stumbling-block to ordination in the more orthodox parishes;[43] others expected to go
forth into frontier communities or foreign countries where no
established churches existed. As a result, each year several Oberlin graduates chose to be ordained by the Lorain County Congregational Association.

James Tefft was to be ordained at Oberlin immediately
after commencement in August, before leaving for missionary

work in Liberia. He suggested that Brown be ordained at the same time, and set about finding ministers willing to participate in the unprecedented ceremony. It was rumored around Oberlin that Tefft wanted Brown to marry him and accompany him to Africa. But she assured Lucy Stone, "Do not fear my getting married. I have neither opportunity nor inclination at present to take such an irredeemable step."[44] Perhaps it was unusual for young women to have close male friends who were not suitors. Or perhaps people could not believe that an attractive woman like Antoinette Brown would choose to remain single.

Despite Tefft's urgings, Brown decided not to press for ordination at Oberlin. She felt that it would be "a delicate thing" to ask for the use of Oberlin's First Church and the participation of Oberlin professors, given the diversity of views on women ministers in the community. She also preferred to follow the traditional pattern of ordination by a local parish that wanted her as its pastor; she had "an instinctive desire to be ordained in my own church, and a belief that I could one day in the future be ordained by my own denomination which was then the Orthodox Congregational."[45]

As the end of the summer term approached, Brown had to face the choices and conflicts of finding a niche in a world that was barely prepared to accept her skills and talents. She turned to Stone for advice:

> What shall I do Lucy when my studies are finished I dont like the idea of teaching at all and am some in debt for my education. Please suggest something if you can.... Work for the Lord and he'll board you is Prof Finneys motto and I believe it but I must work better than I have done or I shall have to get in debt for a part of it.[46]

She thought of going to visit her older brother, William, a minister in Andover, Massachusetts, perhaps to study at Andover Seminary. But she confessed to Stone that "I do not want to spend any more time at present in the study of Theology." She was hungry for "actual contact with the world"; she wrote, "now come the sterner conflicts of real live and God helping me I am ready for them."[47]

She was not without apprehension as she faced a complete unknown:

Now you will ask what I am intending to do. I don't know except that I am going to follow the leadings of Providence. The probability is I shall go to Cincinnati and do whatever I find to do there and in that great city there'll be enough. As for a support I have not the least idea where it is coming from except it will doubtless come from the Lord. Am I following a chimera and depending on a bauble? I think not but there is not a friend in the wide world as far as I know that can feel that I am acting wisely and at the call of God. O dear! Well I must stand alone....

Everything is pleasant and my heart is so full it is almost running over with happiness and yet I sometimes feel a vague sensation of dread or apprehension when I think of the dim unknown future.[48]

The final days at Oberlin must have been a swirl of emotions, as she said goodbye to the friends who had shared the last five years of her life. James Tefft, newly ordained, would be leaving soon for Africa. Sarah Pellet and Sallie Holley would remain at Oberlin for one more year to finish the literary degree. Lettice Smith and Thomas Holmes were married, headed for a parish in New Hampshire.

Neither Smith nor Brown had any part in the commencement exercises; Brown later commented:

We were not supposed to graduate, as at that time to have regularly graduated women from a theological school would have been an endorsement of their probable future careers.[49]

Their names did not appear in official listings of the theological class of 1850 until 1908.

Antoinette Brown left Oberlin at the end of the summer term in 1850. She was twenty-five years old and had gotten the education she wanted from Oberlin, despite its opposition. Although she did not know what she would do from that point on, she was nevertheless able to tell Stone, "I am happy and hopeful and all the world looks bright."[50]

Antoinette Brown, sketch, ca. 1850-1860

ᔍ Chapter 4 ᔋ

STRANGER IN A STRANGE LAND

At home in Henrietta, preparing to begin her public religious work, Antoinette Brown for the first time faced active opposition from her family:

> It was not until I reached home after graduation in 1850 that my family began to feel the imminent need of discouraging me in my plan to become a public speaker. They brought up all the objections that appealed to them, urging the certainty of failure and the hard strain and suffering it must be for me to combat public opinion in this unusual way. Reverend Mr. Freeman, my teacher in the Academy, a dear elderly clergyman, tried to mold me after his own heart, joining with my mother in appealing to me to graduate at Mount Holyoke into a chronic teacher or to become a missionary in some foreign land rather than a hopelessly handicapped woman minister in a civilized community.[1]

Brown knew that she did not want to become a "chronic teacher." But she did not see clearly how to begin the work she envisioned for herself as a minister.

Lucy Stone, excited by the newly organized woman's rights movement, wrote to invite Brown to the first National Woman's Rights Convention, to be held in Worcester, Massachusetts, in October 1850. Stone begged her friend to give a speech, because "we need all the women who are accustomed to speak in public."[2] Brown replied with mixed feelings:

> You urge me to go East to the Convention in October. I should like nothing better than to be there but there are great obstacles in the way and I fear they may not be removed.... If I should go East it would take it all [my money] even suppose the Convention should pay my expenses as you propose....
>
> Then why should your Convention pay any portion of my expenses. I might go there and speak against them in many things for I do not believe exactly with your party even on the subject of woman's rights and I would not be

bought to silence.... I should still like to attend the convention but do not know that it will be best. I should be a
stranger in a strange land and it would be hard for people
to understand me.[3]

The reference to "your party" apparently referred to the Garrisonian branch of the antislavery movement, which lent organizational support to the new woman's rights movement. Brown
assumed, with some basis, that the leaders of the convention
would share Stone's commitment to the radical methods of the
Garrisonians. The split in the antislavery movement—the
most important political reform group—thus colored both the
beginning of feminist organization and Brown's attitude
toward the women who could be allies in her own search for
recognition in an all-male profession.

In the meantime, Brown found that "the way opened for
me as it always did so long as my strength was given almost
entirely to public work." The path led not to Cincinnati, as she
had anticipated, but to New York City:

My friend Mrs. Barnes, ... who used to bring her knitting
to our Oberlin class exercises, spent much of her time in
New York and was interested in many of its benevolences.
She now made this proposition to me—if I would go to
work in charities and in the slums, speaking as I could find
opportunity in public and private, she would guarantee
me a very fair salary and would find me a boarding-place
with Zeruiah Porter Weed of the Class of 1838 Oberlin
Literary....

I accepted, making a stipulation for freedom to do any
kind of public preaching or lecturing which would not
interfere with my New York duties.[4]

She went first to Henrietta, where her sisters—more skilled at
needlework than she was—helped prepare a suitable wardrobe
for her new role.

As soon as her traveling outfit was finished, Brown made
her "first venture in really public life" by attending an antislavery convention in Oswego, New York. She went eagerly, hoping to take part in the proceedings. It was a convention of
"voting abolitionists" who, like Brown and her family,
believed in working for change through existing government
channels. That branch of the antislavery movement did not,
however, permit women an active role. To Brown's disappoint-

ment, even the more liberal men present did not invite her to speak, even though some of them knew of her experience as a public speaker. Instead of crusading within the organization for her right to speak, she chose to express her opinions in writing:

> The opposition of my family together with the certainty (after my return from the convention) that I should not be welcome on the antislavery platform with which my father had always been allied and in whose methods I believed, led me to begin almost at once to write brief articles in a disguised hand with a heavy pen for Frederick Douglass' *North Star*.[5]

Frederick Douglass, a former slave, was principally allied with William Lloyd Garrison and was a warm supporter of the woman's rights movement in its early years. By using a pseudonym, Brown hoped to avoid the stigma of being clearly allied with the Garrisonian faction.

Soon afterward, despite her misgivings, Brown decided to make the trip to Worcester for the National Woman's Rights Convention. The convention, the first feminist gathering to call itself a "national" meeting, attracted almost all of the women who had been pressing for change in some aspect of public life. Here Brown met the leaders of the new movement—women whose names she knew from newspaper accounts—including Elizabeth Cady Stanton and Lucretia Mott, organizers of the now-famous Seneca Falls Convention of 1848. The convention was primarily concerned with sharing ideas on a wide range of issues; specific planning for united action would come later. Women like Antoinette Brown, who had been thinking about some aspects of women's lives and work, had an opportunity to share their insights. As Stone had hoped, Brown reworked her Oberlin paper into a speech refuting the Biblical argument that women should not speak in public. Despite her own ambivalence, her listeners received her speech with enthusiasm, recognizing Brown's struggle for recognition as a minister as part of their common cause.

With this introduction, Brown was drawn into the loose-knit network of women and men throughout the Northeast who were working actively for a variety of social reforms. Lettice Smith Holmes, her former classmate, wrote from New Hampshire, "Let me congratulate you on your introduction into society. That Worcester convention was a fine thing for you. You could not have discovered any better way of becoming known if you had searched a long time."[6]

After she spoke at the Worcester Woman's Rights Convention, Brown found that despite her own ambivalence toward organized feminism, she was viewed as one of the radicals. She noticed "a decided change in the atmosphere" among the New York women she expected to work with, and she "began to feel that there might be strained relations caused by our unlike methods of thought and action." She decided that instead of staying in New York City under the protective wing of Mrs. Barnes, as she had planned, she would "make my own way as best I could in the public field as a speaker and teacher."[7] She confessed to Stone:

> For my part I am glad to be again free from any connection with any one in laboring, for I believe with nobody, & I could not work perfectly well with any one. I will for the present at least be employed by no society not only, but by no individual either, & will make no engagements for any length of time. Then I shall be free to believe what I please, & to act as I please responsible to my own conscience & to God. Then I can go & come when & where I please, can lecture write or rest as the spirit moves me; and above all can feel free—as free at least as it is possible in a world where we must more or less involve others in our trials, cares & rewards, our honors or disgraces.[8]

This experience confirmed what Brown had feared before she left Oberlin: that her unique beliefs and her choice of methods would make it difficult for her to work with organized groups, either of feminists or of more conservative women.

She decided to try to earn her living as Lucy Stone did, as a public speaker. During the mid-nineteenth centry the lyceum, or lecture series, was an important source of ideas and entertainment for people throughout the Northeast.[9] In an age before television, radio, or feature magazines, people looked to the lyceum for entertainment, discussion of controversial ideas, and an opportunity to broaden their intellectual horizons. Their staid Puritan ancestors had frowned on fashionable balls and parties, so New Englanders spent their "evenings out" listening to lectures or debates on theology, botany, abolition, and even on woman's rights. The lyceum circuit drew speakers ranging from medical quacks and spiritualists to some of the finest thinkers of the era, including Ralph Waldo Emerson, Henry Thoreau, Harriot Hunt, Lucy Stone, Louis Agassiz, and Antoinette Brown.

For the speakers, a lecture series meant hard work. Essays had to be prepared—two or three would serve for one tour—and appointments set up in a dozen or more cities and small towns. Often a manager helped set up speaking engagements. Since both the speaker and the manager were trying to earn money on the tours, they crammed in as many engagements as possible.

The lyceum circuit, somewhat comparable to present-day college speaking tours, was a vital source of income for an entire generation of social reformers and intellectuals. A good speaker, especially a man, could earn $100 a night or even more, though in small towns the fee would often be closer to $25.

At first, Brown was apprehensive about relying solely on lecturing for her livelihood. Of the reformers she knew, only Lucy Stone had no other source of income:

> It seemed reckless to begin my work financially a pauper and (if public speaking should fail) almost worse than a pauper in hoping for any other means of support from a public which would be prejudiced against me as a "Come Outer" and a worker for woman's rights. Mrs. Barnes with her strong sympathy with me realized the difficulties of my situation and cheerfully lent me enough money to inaugurate my independent venture.[10]

As in other occupations, women were generally paid less than men. Brown found it necessary in making arrangements for one lecture to specify that "my terms, from principle, are never less than the best prices received by the gentlemen of the particular association where I speak."[11]

Many of the people she met at the Worcester Convention helped Brown break into the lecture circuit; she later noted, "About that time I began to be invited to speak in lecture-courses and my good friends also obtained for me opportunity to speak with the usual compensation."[12] Most often it was male reformers who were in positions to help her, especially when she wanted to preach as well as lecture. Liberal ministers such as Samuel J. May and William Henry Channing, converted to feminism by Margaret Fuller some ten years before, invited Brown to preach from their pulpits and encouraged their colleagues to do the same.[13] Even her oldest brother, William, who had originally opposed her desire to preach, opened his Andover church to her.

With a tight schedule to meet, a speaker could pay little attention to her own health and comfort. An extended tour involved many days and nights of traveling in sooty railroad cars or in stagecoaches over rough and muddy roads, stopping at irregular intervals for often unpalatable meals at country inns. She often arrived at a destination—another town hall, another group of strange faces—with barely enough time to freshen up before speaking for more than an hour. With luck, the speaker could tumble into bed for a few hours before moving on.

Brown soon became accustomed to the lyceum circuit. She traveled to towns and cities throughout New England, New York, Pennsylvania, and Ohio. Although she was not employed by a reform organization, as some lecturers were, she often spoke on abolition, temperance, and woman's rights. Whenever she could get permission, and admission to a church, she preached a Sunday sermon. She discovered that "where I had expected small audiences the novelty of a woman preacher made every meeting whether in a schoolhouse or a church, an unexpectedly large gathering for the conditions under which it was held."[14]

Traveling and lecturing could provide a woman like Antoinette Brown with a knowledge of people and circumstances outside of the normally protected sphere of an unmarried middle-class woman. For example, Brown later recalled one incident:

> Once missing connections when going on westward from southern Ohio, it was found impossible to reach a lecture engagement except by taking a midnight small car called a "caboose" occupied by a construction gang. I found myself at one or two o'clock in the morning seated as comfortably as I could be under the circumstances, but in a somewhat near neighborhood to some dozen and a half of men, generally in working garments, and everyone with a pipe or cigar in his mouth. I am not so opposed to the smell of an excellent cigar.... But this overpowering atmosphere was something hard to bear. Yet who was I who was literally begging my passage, to protest? Accordingly I endured it for some hours until safely deposited at a railroad station where I could go on in the ordinary cars.[15]

Despite the physical demands of the lyceum circuit, Brown found the work satisfying:

> The feeling that all my friends had, that the life of a public speaker would be altogether too hard for me and impossible to realize proved to be entirely a mistake.
> I think it was the general seriousness of my topics and manner of treatment which made me to a certain extent immune from severe and ungenerous criticism. At least this had never met me face to face although I sometimes saw a little of it in public prints. It was never a real trial, not even a hard or difficult thing to face the public with a thought which I really wished to impress upon their attention. From first to last there never was any real self-sacrifice in my chosen work—it was merely self-expression.[16]

Antoinette Brown quickly earned a reputation as a fine public speaker. Many years later an unidentified reporter wrote about her:

> Twenty five years ago no woman was more widely and favorably known as a public speaker than Miss Antoinette L. Brown....[She was] one of the first and most successful on the lyceum platform and in various reform movements.[17]

In part, her fame stemmed from the novelty of her position as both a preacher and a lecturer. In the fifteen years since Sarah and Angelina Grimké had shocked New England's clergy by speaking before mixed audiences, society's opinion had softened somewhat toward women who spoke in public. But Brown and women like her were still unusual and were watched closely, each one a test of what women could do if given the opportunity. One reporter wrote in 1852:

> We venture that, notwithstanding the subject was one upon which nothing had been publicly said, and much conservatism existed in this community, there were scores of men and women who went there filled with prejudice, but who felt these prejudices go down, like frost-work before the clear, steady logic of [Brown's] argument....
> They had before them a living witness of woman's ability and of what woman *can* do, only give her equal facilities with the other sex.... American men instead of indulging in low, narrow, and illiberal prejudices against [Brown

and Lucy Stone] and their cause, will be proud that they,
as well as a score or two of others like them, are *American
Women*.[18]

In the long run, however, her success depended not on
novelty but on her acknowledged competence as a speaker. The
training in rhetoric and public speaking that she had insisted
on at Oberlin served her well. Her speeches often received
favorable notice in the local newspapers:

> Her lecture was sprinkled all over with rich metaphors,
> with graphic figures, and that rare quality of modern
> productions, originality. The ideas expressed were clothed
> in beautiful language, such as none but the finest intellec-
> tual gifts could produce, sentences superbly framed, peri-
> ods rounded with a grace not surpassed by the numberless
> gems of the great English essayists.... There is not one
> that did not leave the hall with the most profound respect
> for the rare mental endowments of the speaker.[19]

Neither the reviews nor her letters include the content of
Brown's speeches; although outright opposition to women
speakers had weakened, the reviewers seemed so surprised to
discover that a woman could use the English language that they
forgot to listen to the points she made.

Even Antoinette Brown's family began to appreciate her
work. She was pleased and relieved:

> When a year or two had passed successfully for me as a
> speaker... the stress of kindly opposition from my family
> no longer existed. I began to make headquarters at the dear
> old home. Both friends and relatives gradually began to
> feel an interest, almost an approval of eccentricities, as
> they still considered them. Still remaining the butt of a
> good many harmless jokes, I felt nevertheless the return-
> ing warmth of a genial neighborhood helpfulness.[20]

During 1851 and 1852, her life revolved around lecture trips,
with time to recuperate in between at her family's farm. She
spent the winter of 1851-52 in Henrietta, resting from her
travels and revising her Oberlin treatise on the position of
women in Biblical texts. In a report to her new friend, a Rochester teacher named Susan B. Anthony, she wrote:

I am tired—have been at home some time, but instead of resting have been performing double duties; up to the ears in sermons & bible arguments during the day & lecturing frequently in the evening sometimes under very exciting circumstances; e.g. giving a lecture at a donation party with a two shilling admission fee on behalf of a minister who would not so much as dream of letting me occupy his desk on Sunday.[21]

In March she left home long enough for a visit to Boston and Concord—famous Concord, home of Henry David Thoreau, Nathaniel Hawthorne, Ralph Waldo Emerson, Bronson Alcott and his daughter Louisa May, and the memory of Margaret Fuller, who had been an integral part of their group until her departure for New York in 1841. Brown reported to Lucy Stone:

Went to Concord—had a nice time, full house and pleasant people. Saw Thoreau there; got acquainted with him some. [He] had a curious, pleasant lecture, unique enough, but conservative in spirit.[22]

She also attended a poetry reading at the Boston home of Dr. Harriot Hunt. But the rich intellectual atmosphere of Boston did not attract her.

When she returned to her home in Henrietta, Brown once again came face to face with death. Her sister Augusta finally succumbed to the tuberculosis that had plagued her throughout the past five years, the same disease that had claimed the other Brown siblings. Brown wrote to Lucy Stone:

My sister Augusta has at last gone from a world of so much suffering to a home where pain and sorrow never come. It was hard to have her leave us, but now I would not bring her back again to this sad sinful earth. Your last letter was put in my hand when we came home from the grave, where we had laid the frail form deserted of its living spirit. I was so sad....[23]

Once again she was confronted with a tragic event for which her childhood faith had few answers; but for the moment, her faith held firm.

As she traveled on the lyceum circuit, Brown was drawn into the assortment of social reform organizations that flourished in the Northeast.[24] Abolition, temperance, and woman's rights were all burning issues. None of them was strange to Antoinette; her parents were firmly committed to the abolition of slavery and the elimination of alcoholic beverages. Now, as an adult, Brown attended many of the conventions held by reform organizations and drew on their principles for lecture topics. Her strength was in clear expression of the values she shared with other reformers, rather than in formulating new ideas. The membership of the various organizations overlapped significantly. Often their conventions were held in clusters in the same city. These meetings served as political planning sessions, outreach to the community in which they were held, and a time to renew and deepen emotional ties among reformers.

From the first, Brown shied away from the tendency within the reform organizations toward fragmentation and doctrinal disputes. Her vision of "progress" was a broad one, encompassing both spiritual and political issues, which to her were all interrelated. She later remarked, "It seemed to me then [1850] ... that we who believe in freedom in religion have no right to refuse to work in any benevolence or in any good cause with whoever is willing to promote that cause."[25] Brown disliked the competition among reform groups, each one feeling that "ours is *the* cause." She wrote to Stone in December of 1850: "Well, let them feel it. The mind cannot from its constitution be so intensely absorbed by all subjects as by one, and of course that one grows larger as it develops itself in all its various phases."[26] For herself, Brown tried to work with all of the various reform groups, not focusing on any one issue for any extended period—a pattern that resulted in a fragmentation of her efforts.

Brown often addressed the topic of temperance, which was one of the most popular campaigns of the pre-Civil War era. The consumption of alcoholic beverages, which by all accounts was commonplace and excessive, was blamed for poverty, crime, irresponsible voting, sexual excess, and domestic violence. It was a topic controversial enough to draw good audiences, but respectable enough to interest solid churchgoing families.

For Antoinette Brown, Susan B. Anthony, and other feminists, the temperance cause was closely related to their concern for women, and particularly to the powerlessness women felt within their own families. It was commonly assumed that drinking was a male problem, with women as victims. William Henry Channing began a resolution at an 1853 temperance convention, *"Whereas,* Women are, of the whole people, the chief sufferers from grievances caused by Intemperance...."[27] Whether or not that image corresponded to reality, it was strengthened by middle-class attitudes toward what were assumed to be the bad habits of immigrant and working-class men. Some of the temperance speeches, however, reveal a deeply rooted fear of sexual assault and domestic violence. In an 1849 speech, Anthony demanded

> [some means] by which our Brothers and Sons shall no longer be allured from the *right* by the corrupting influence of the fashionable sippings of wine and brandy, those sure destroyers of Mental and Moral worth; and by which our Sisters and Daughters shall no longer be exposed to the vile arts of the gentlemanly-appearing, gallant, but really half-inebriated seducer.[28]

The temperance issue also highlighted the powerlessness women felt in attempting to change that reality. At first the temperance campaigns were led by evangelist preachers calling for individual moral conversions to righteous living. In that context, women could play an important role, using their moral influence within their homes to discourage their husbands and sons from drinking liquor.

By the 1840s, however, the cutting edge of the movement was pressure for state laws controlling the liquor business. In 1851 Maine passed a law that prohibited the manufacture or sale within the state of all intoxicating beverages. Reformers in other states hoped to convince their legislatures to copy the Maine law. That shift in emphasis left women in an uncertain position. Brown explained to one temperance group in 1853 why she could not separate temperance from the issue of woman's rights:

> I am reminded that in this Temperance gathering temperance is to be discussed in its length and breadth—nothing else and nothing more, not a word about Woman and her rights.... We have not heard a word either about Woman's right to vote even in favor of the Maine law. Although the world does disenfranchise one half of its inhabitants. ... and although the other half have contributed to leave a [liquor] license to exist in almost the entire world,

> ... still there is not a word to be said here about the right
> of Woman to proper remuneration for her services. Not a
> word about the right of Woman to prevent an intemperate
> husband from taking her earnings and spending them for
> his grog bills and his legal right to do this. ... Why [it is
> said] these belong to woman's rights. What can all this
> have to do with the Temperance cause?[29]

Despite the connection she saw between temperance and improved conditions for women, Brown quickly discovered within the temperance movement itself the same restrictions on women's activities that she and Stone had battled at Oberlin. Many people within the temperance movement, as well as in the antislavery societies, opposed women's speaking to mixed, or "promiscuous," audiences. At the New York State Temperance Association meetings in January 1852, Susan B. Anthony, trying to speak from the floor, was told that women were welcome only to listen. Rather than fighting it out on the floor, a group of women, including Brown, Elizabeth Cady Stanton, and Amelia Bloomer, withdrew and formed a Women's State Temperance Association. Segregation produced only a temporary truce.

In the meantime, the women worked separately. In the winter of 1853 Brown joined Anthony and Bloomer on a lecture tour as agents of the New York State Temperance Association. They began in New York City, where Samuel "Sarsaparilla" Townsend, a wealthy and prominent temperance crusader, arranged a large and profitable meeting in Metropolitan Hall. With the proceeds, Brown was finally able to pay off the last remaining debts from her years at Oberlin. From there the three women traveled to Poughkeepsie, Troy, Utica, Syracuse, Rochester, Buffalo, and many smaller towns and cities across the state.

Her experience on that tour convinced Brown that woman's rights was a concern more pressing than temperance; she said of this transition:

> Our temperance campaign, which was largely educa-
> tional, ... was fairly successful and satisfactory but soon
> we all began to feel that we preferred to devote our work to
> womanhood and its dawning uplift.[30]

Elizabeth Cady Stanton stated the position more vehemently:

> We have been obliged to preach woman's rights because many, instead of listening to what we had to say on temperance, have questioned the right of a woman to speak on any subject.... Let it be clearly understood that... we believe it is woman's duty to speak whenever she feels the impression to do so.[31]

"Woman's rights" throughout the 1850s included debates on a broad range of issues affecting women: marriage, education, jobs, property rights.[32] The right to vote was discussed, but was considered no more important than other reforms. At first, women asserted that voting was a right that belonged to all citizens. During the 1850s, however, speakers increasingly argued that women should vote because their unique feminine interests were different from those of men and needed a separate voice. Brown leaned toward the latter view:

> Man cannot represent woman. They differ in their nature and relations. The law is wholly masculine; it is created and executed by man. The framers of all legal compacts are restricted to the masculine standpoint of observation, to the thought, feelings, and biases of man. The law, then, could give us no representation as woman, and therefore no impartial justice, even if the present law-makers were honestly intent upon this; for we can be represented only by our peers.[33]

But unlike Stanton and other feminists—and despite her identification with the "voting abolitionists"—Brown was disappointed by what she saw of the electoral process itself as a means of achieving reform. In the fall of 1852 Stone persuaded Brown to spend a few weeks helping in the election campaign of Gerrit Smith. Smith, a cousin of Stanton, was a wealthy landowner who was active in many reform causes. His mansion in Peterboro, New York, served as a stop on the "underground railway" for slaves escaping to Canada. The house was also a popular gathering place for liberal people from the entire upstate area; it was there that Henry Stanton had met and courted young Elizabeth Cady some twelve years earlier. A firm believer in using existing political institutions to achieve social reform, Gerrit Smith ran for Congress in 1852 on the abolitionist ticket of the Liberty Party, which he had helped to form. Brown and Stone joined the group of abolitionists who assembled at the Smith mansion to help in the campaign. Their work consisted mainly of organizing public meetings throughout the district.

Although Brown was pleased by the successful outcome of the campaign, she was upset by what she saw of electoral politics. She wrote to Stone afterwards:

> How I should hate to sink so low as to become a common vulgar politician. Let me first be a Garrisonian ten times over. I say, Lucy, I pray you won't get converted to such politics as the world at large advocates. . . . I saw Mr. Smith election morning. Depend upon it he will not even touch the pitch of political corruption and he will not be defiled. He will walk through the fire but there will not be so much as the smell of it upon his garments. But if he does swerve from his own principles I shall give up and say as Sarah Pellett said in the words of the old song,
>
> "There is no faith in man
> No not in a brother,
> Little girls if you must love
> Love one another."[34]

As it turned out, Smith served in Congress for less than two years before resigning. With that introduction, it is not surprising that Brown placed a lower priority on gaining women the right to vote than on changes in women's economic and social roles.

The women's rights movement also attacked issues more basic to women's daily experience than voting. Among these, the question that received the most publicity was costume.[35] The normal clothing of at least middle-class women was both restrictive and unhealthy. Several layers of long heavy skirts and petticoats made traveling, gardening, or even walking upstairs an ordeal, while tight corsets squeezed internal organs out of position. Around 1850, women in the experimental Oneida Community in upstate New York invented a more comfortable outfit, consisting of a loosely belted tunic, a knee-length skirt, and ankle-length pantaloons. Elizabeth Smith Miller, Gerrit Smith's daughter, adopted the Oneida costume and introduced it to other feminists. Elizabeth Cady Stanton found the new outfit "altogether a most becoming costume and exceedingly convenient for walking in all kinds of weather."[36]

It was quickly named after Amelia Bloomer, who publicized it in her journal *The Lily*, and was adopted by many feminists as both a symbolic statement and a practical emancipation.

Brown was one of the few feminists who clung to her traditional long skirts. Stone urged her, "Do take care of your health Nettie—and to that end I wish you would wear a bloomer.... *It is a great deal* the best for health."[37] But Brown disliked both the appearance of the new outfit and the ridicule it provoked.[38] On one trip with some bloomer-wearing friends, she discovered that "we were often followed by a troop of boys and sometimes staring men, joking, but not often making really vulgar comments, though the whole scene was extremely distasteful to us all."[39] Brown herself was often singled out as an example of how women, even feminists, should look; she later commented that "the papers made a good deal of fun of the bloomers, and I, not wearing them, got a good many compliments, almost invariably."[40]

More important, she feared that the uproar over costume would obscure more pressing feminist issues—such as the right to speak in public or to control one's own earnings—and unnecessarily prejudice public opinion against the woman's rights movement. She believed that

> Although the long dress is unhygienic and hampering to the physical powers, it was unwise to put so much stress upon inconvenience when so many greater interests imperatively needed advocating. Appreciating that their stand was made for conscience's sake, I felt that the dress reformers were prejudicing our plea for temperance, and justice to women, and that it would be better to hold steadily to one theory of the wrong done in keeping woman in her servile position.[41]

She pleaded with Stone, "Don't suffer martyrdom over a short dress or anything else that *can* be prevented. Sorrow enough will come and fate itself cannot prevent.... So let every avoidable thing go and good riddance to it."[42]

Within a few years public pressure forced other feminists to abandon the bloomer outfit. Stanton at last conceded to Anthony:

> I hope, Susan, you have let down a dress and petticoat. The cup of ridicule is greater than you can bear. It is not wise,

Susan, to use up so much energy and feeling in that way.
You can put them to better use.[43]

She apparently agreed with Brown that, for the present, other
issues were more important.

At woman's rights conventions Brown also found herself
disagreeing vehemently with other activists, especially about
religion and the institutional church. Although she was quick
to challenge the most blatant forms of prejudice against
women within the church itself, Brown considered her Christian faith a fundamental part of her identity and a source of
personal strength. Far from ready to abandon the church, she
focused her efforts on reinterpreting the Bible and Christian
doctrine to be consistent with a fuller life for women. She found
little support among the most active feminists, and some outright hostility. Stone, Stanton, and many others had left the
church completely; they considered religion irrelevant or even
harmful to the cause of woman's rights. Even Quaker Lucretia
Mott, whose views on religion were probably the closest to
Brown's, stated that arguing about what the Bible said was a
waste of time.

Brown tried unsuccessfully to gain official support for her
views. She proposed that the 1852 National Woman's Rights
Convention adopt a resolution stating that the Bible did not
mandate female subservience. The convention voted her down.
That same year she wrote to Stone:

> There is one thing which I want and have always wanted
> in our conventions—that they should be opened with
> prayer, or at least that there might be some vocal prayer at
> some time during the sessions. I have not felt at liberty to
> propose this because the control or management of the
> matter was not at all in my hands and most of the members
> I supposed did not approve of anything of the kind. . . . I
> think I will write Mrs. [Paulina Wright] Davis about it for it
> really places some members of the convention in a false
> position to have no public prayer during the meeting.[44]

Brown's suggestion apparently was well received; before long,
woman's rights conventions did include opening and closing
prayers. She also served on the business committee that
planned the woman's rights conventions, which met at least
once a year.

All her activity, on the lecture circuit and in reform organizations, nevertheless left Antoinette Brown feeling dissatisfied and lonely:

> What hard work it is to stand alone! I am forever wanting to lean over onto somebody but nobody will support me, and I think seriously of swallowing the yardstick or putting on a buckram corset, so as to get a little assistance somehow, for I am determined to maintain the perpendicular position.[45]

Her dissatisfaction had a number of possible causes—her sister's death, separation from her best friend, the stresses of a transient life-style, the conflicts within reform organizations. But Brown also wished to pursue more directly the goal that had carried her through her Oberlin years: she wanted to be ordained as a minister in her own parish.

Broadway Tabernacle, New York City

↭ Chapter 5 ↮

A MAN-ACKNOWLEDGED MINISTER

As she traveled around the lecture circuit, Antoinette Brown preached as often as she could, usually as a guest minister in the pulpit of a sympathetic minister. She began to look for someone who would break with tradition and ordain a woman. In the summer of 1851 she corresponded with Charles Grandison Finney and President Asa Mahan of Oberlin. She reported to Lucy Stone that

> Finney wrote a long fatherly letter, called me his dear child, daughter, dearest sister, &c. expressed a world of sympathy but said he could not at present act—his wife would if she was a man—but he would examine the subject pray over & consult with the brethren &c. and if he could assist he would.[1]

In July 1852 Brown spent three weeks at Oberlin. It was a much easier trip than in her student days; she could travel the entire distance from Rochester to Oberlin on the newly completed railroad. She enjoyed her visit and came home "hearty and happy," but had been unable to convince the Oberlin fathers to ordain her. She told Lucy Stone:

> I am not ordained yet either, so you may rejoice, and welcome; but what a milksop you must take me for if I can be manufactured over into a "would-be-but-can't priest" by so simple a ceremony as ordination. It is well that certain grave divines should have drawn back just in time for they were on the very brink of the fatal fall over the great wall of custom. A little more and I should have been a man-acknowledged minister, but somebody happened to think that though a woman might preach she ought not to administer the sacraments etc. Others thought this, and so they joined hands, and turning around walked backwards together, and I took up my bundle and walked home.[2]

Brown received more encouragement from Horace Greeley, editor of the progressive *New York Tribune*. Under his

leadership the newspaper, which had a broad circulation in
New York City and throughout the nation, became a forum for
discussions of temperance, vegetarianism, abolition, and
woman's rights. Greeley also enjoyed providing financial assistance to struggling young reformers. Although he often disagreed with feminists, Greeley respected Brown's intellectual
ability and her competence as a speaker. He gave her as much
space as she wanted for articles she wrote, reported her activities
in great detail, and used his influence to help her set up speaking engagements in New York City. In the autumn of 1852,
Greeley and Charles Dana, the *Tribune*'s city editor, offered to
arrange a hall and to guarantee Brown room and board plus
$1,000 salary if she would agree to preach regularly in New
York City for one year. She considered the matter seriously.
Preaching in New York would be exciting and would add to
her growing reputation. The "big-time" atmosphere of the city
would be quite different from the small rural communities—
Henrietta, Oberlin, the towns she visited on lecture trips—to
which she was accustomed. But in the end she rejected their
offer. Her explanation was that "I had the sense enough to
know I was too young and couldn't sustain it."[3] Although she
was twenty-seven years old, with sound theological training
and two years of experience as a speaker, she apparently did not
feel confident enough to commit herself to such a large venture.
Instead, she hoped to find a small parish where she could be a
pastor as well as a preacher, and where she could be ordained.

She did not have to wait much longer. During one of her
tours of central New York state, she visited South Butler, a
village about halfway between Rochester and Syracuse, four
miles north of the new railroad that ran parallel to the Erie
Canal. After hearing her speak, the small Congregational
Church invited her to become their pastor. The poor rural
parish could pay only $300 a year as a salary, and had trouble
finding any minister at that price. A few years earlier they had
hired a Negro minister, which was unusual even for an antislavery community. After thinking about it for several months,
Brown agreed to come.

She moved to South Butler in the late spring of 1853,
finding living quarters in the home of a physician. At last she
had an opportunity to put into practice Professor Finney's
lectures on pastoral theology. She gave two sermons each Sunday, of which one was prepared in advance and the other
improvised. She also had responsibilities for pastoral duties

such as visiting the sick and comforting those who were troubled. After a few months she commented to Gerrit Smith, "The pastoral labors at S. Butler suit me even better than I expected & my heart is full of hope."[4] Later she wrote:

> My little parish was a miniature world in good and evil. To get humanity condensed into so small a compass that you can study each individual member opens a new chapter of experience. It makes one thoughtful and rolls upon the spirit a burden of deep responsibility.[5]

Now that she had a settled home, Brown was eager to have Lucy Stone come to visit, hoping to recapture the intimacy they had shared so briefly six years earlier. "If only you were here," she wrote, "so I could put my arm close around you and feel your heart beating against mine as in lang syne."[6] Stone refused, saying she was afraid her bloomers and radical opinions would hurt her friend's reputation. Brown wrote back:

> You are the biggest little goose and granny fuss, that I ever did see! . . . What nonsense to think of your injuring in any way my success as a minister by lecturing to them. . . . If you don't wish to speak for them more than once, why don't do so—But pray don't get into any such crabbed notions about staying away. If you do we shall quarrel in real earnest, for I never will have a friend that is ashamed of me, or I am ashamed of her, or one that must *keep away from me to preserve my reputation, or ensure my success.* I still have need of you whether you have of me or not. . . . It made me half mad to know you should think so meanly of me, and to see that you fancied my success to be such an exclusive narrow-minded soap-bubble.[7]

It would have been out of character for Stone to turn down an invitation out of fear of adverse public reaction. Stone's refusal fed Brown's fears that their long separations were not simply a matter of two busy lecturing schedules, but rather an indication that Stone's feelings toward her had cooled. She begged for reassurance:

> Lucy darling:
>   It is a long time since either of us has written one such letter as of lang syne. Have you and I grown strangers? God help us then—this is not a world made up of true friends.

> ... God bless you, Lucy! Tonight I could nestle closer
> to your heart than on that night when I went through the
> dark and the rain and Tappan Hall and school rules—all
> to feel your arm around me and to know that in all this
> wide world I was not alone.[8]

At Oberlin they had been friends on a fairly equal basis, bound
together by shared experiences and struggles; now Stone, in her
mid-thirties, seems to have been almost embarrassed by the
younger woman's infatuation. In addition, Stone was busy
lecturing for the antislavery society and organizing the
national woman's rights conventions. Brown had to be content
with seeing her friend only once or twice a year at reform
conventions.

Lucy Stone was, however, concerned about Brown from a
distance. Through her abolitionist activities Stone had gotten
to know Henry Blackwell, brother of pioneer doctor Elizabeth
Blackwell. He fell in love with Stone even before meeting her,
after listening to her fiery antislavery speeches. Now he was
courting her with great persistence, following her on lecture
tours and inviting her to his family's home near Cincinnati.
There Stone had met Henry's older brother Samuel, whom she
encouraged to stop by and visit Antoinette Brown when he was
in the vicinity. Henry Blackwell also encouraged such a visit,
thinking that if Brown was anything like Lucy, she might
make a good match for Sam. Brown knew nothing of this when
Samuel Blackwell arrived at her doorstep in South Butler on
one of his business trips between Cincinnati and Boston. Sam
Blackwell described the visit in his diary:

> She received me very pleasantly, took me to her room, and
> I forgot my drenched boots and the rain and wind without,
> while busily talking with her for three hours.... She is a
> lady of pleasant, intelligent appearance, about 30, strong
> and robust in form, though looking rather pale just
> now.... We had a general confab., commencing with
> "Woman's Rights" and ending with metaphysics and
> theology. She seems to me to be a lady of judgment, very
> kind disposition and with the best principles and high
> aims. She had evidently thought much on the great themes
> of her profession and of the age, and has that breadth of
> sympathy and hearty toleration which are so clear an
> evidence of a magnanimous and cultivated mind. I
> enjoyed the visit exceedingly.[9]

Brown later remembered only that "he stayed perhaps a half a day and had [a] pleasant visit.... His hair had already some gray, but [the] main part was black. [He] was not handsome."[10] Her thoughts were focused on the work ahead of her in her South Butler parish.

As she had hoped, the little congregation was pleased with her work. During the summer of 1853 the church's governing board met and decided to proceed with her ordination, a public recognition of her ministry. The ceremony would not change her role; she already performed all the functions of a minister, including administering the sacraments. But it would be a public statement about a woman's right to preach, and a confirmation of the rather risky step the church had taken. One of the more conservative deacons told Brown:

> If Gerrit Smith will only come here and talk to us about it, it will do us all good. I have not a word to say against your position, and none of the rest of us have; but we are standing all alone so, we need a little countenance in the matter. We shall all feel stronger.[11]

In the Congregational form of government, a local congregation had full authority to choose and call its own minister. No ecclesiastical hierarchy needed to approve its choice, and none had the power to block the choice the South Butler church had made. Nevertheless, Brown explained to Gerrit Smith that the church members "think they have a full right to act in this matter for themselves; but at the same time think that under the circumstances a public meeting will do good."[12]

Smith questioned the propriety of any ceremony at all. He was "a self-appointed minister who built the church [building] and gave religious instruction to friends and neighbors."[13] Brown hastened to reassure him:

> We do not care whether the ceremony is performed in the usual way or not. We only want something done to show the world that we believe in a woman's being initiated into the ministry and something which will answer without questioning as a legal ordination in the eyes of the Law & Public Opinion.... Every person present may express himself opposed to all ordinations & welcome, if he will only be willing in addition to put woman upon the same platform with man, & recognise me as much a minister

as others. I already take part in administering the Sacraments &c.... It will do them good, and me good, & good
to the cause of woman. For this reason we do want you to
talk during the ordination exercises, & then give us a
lecture against creeds & sectarianism in the evening or
any thing else you choose.[14]

With the freedom given him by that message, Smith agreed to
interrupt his duties as a congressman to speak at the historic
occasion.

Usually Congregational clergy from the county association participated in the ordination ceremony. The South
Butler church had trouble finding other ministers willing to
take a public stand in support of a woman minister. Brown
found that a "reaction [was] setting in, people [were] just
beginning to stop laughing and get mad."[15] Ordination would
show that Antoinette Brown meant seriously to intrude into a
male preserve, not merely to poach around the edges. Some of
her friends and supporters, liberal clergy such as Samuel J. May
and William Henry Channing, chose not to attend because they
feared their Unitarian affiliations might call into question
Brown's commitment to the orthodox Congregational Church.
Finally, Reverend Luther Lee, a liberal abolitionist Methodist
from nearby Syracuse, who knew Brown through the temperance movement, agreed to come. He shared Gerritt Smith's
views on ordination; he wrote to the South Butler church,
"Though I should very greatly prefer that some other person
should be called upon to preach the ordination sermon of Miss
Brown, I will do it if the Lord gives life and health."[16] Thus, by
the end of August, the plans were complete.

At the beginning of September, Brown went to New York
City for a series of reform conventions on temperance and
woman's rights.[17] The South Butler temperance society had
selected her as one of its delegates to the World's Temperance
Convention. There were rumors, however, that women would
not be allowed to participate in that meeting. Although the
convention announcement claimed that its invitation was
"unexceptionally broad," several women had been thrust out
of a planning session the previous May because "custom had
not sanctioned the public action of women in similar situations." Horace Greeley, writing in the *New York Tribune*,
feared that the "World's Convention" was in fact intended as
an "Orthodox, White, Male, Adult, Saints' Convention."

Because of this uncertainty, women activists and their male supporters organized a second temperance convention called the Whole World's Temperance Convention. On September 1, more than 2,000 people crowded into the new Metropolitan Hall to hear Rev. Thomas Wentworth Higginson of Boston open the convention by declaring that although this was not a woman's rights convention, it would be "a convention in which Woman is not wronged." Antoinette Brown delivered a speech, as did Lucy Stone and Lucretia Mott. After three days of speeches, 300 of the reformers attended a banquet prepared by the New York Vegetarian Society. Some of them may have gone on to the Broadway Theater to see a dramatization of Harriet Beecher Stowe's popular antislavery novel, *Uncle Tom's Cabin.*

The next morning, Sunday, Brown led a worship service at Metropolitan Hall. Her text was drawn from the fiery prophet Jeremiah: "Oh do not this abominable thing which I hate." Her sermon urged people to respect God's moral law above public opinion. "Let us pass from the mire of sin into the sunshine of God's presence," she told the idealistic group of reformers. She felt confident, almost exuberant, and firm in her faith and in what she was doing.

On Tuesday morning, the original temperance group—dubbed by William Henry Channing the "Half World's" Temperance Convention—took over Metropolitan Hall. The audience consisted primarily of clergymen, with only a sprinkling of women. Brown entered the hall with her friends Wendell Phillips and Caroline M. Severance. The issue of who was welcome at the convention broke out in the open almost immediately. A proposed resolution declaring the meeting open to "all the friends of humanity without respect to age, sex, color, or condition," provoked such an uproar that it was quickly tabled. Despite that ominous action, Brown was determined to speak for temperance as she had planned. Later that morning she was recognized by President Neal Dow of Maine, and began to address the meeting:

> I am interested in the cause of temperance, and have come deputed by two different Societies to represent them in their deliberations and to speak in behalf of a subject on which I feel, and every woman feels a deep and double interest, and in the consideration of her wrongs she has a right to feel an interest. . . .

But she was quickly drowned out by the clergymen, shouting, stamping, pounding on the floor with their canes. When Dow quieted the hall, a resolution was quickly passed that, while women's work on behalf of temperance was appreciated, "the public platform of discussion is not the appropriate sphere of woman." As most of the delegates cheered, Brown left the platform in apparent defeat.

The next afternoon, with full support from friends like Phillips and Quaker James Gibbon, Brown tried again to speak to a question before the meeting, and once again was barred by a general uproar. She described her feelings at that point:

> I feel calm and strong again and sit down until [their] anger has way. "Do you think," says a voice in my ear, "that Christ would have done so?" "I think he would," spoken with a positive emphasis.... I arise, turning away from them all, and feeling a power which may perhaps never come to me again. There were angry men confronting me and I caught the flashing of defiant eyes, but above me and within me, there was a spirit stronger than them all. At that moment not the combined powers of earth and hell could have tempted me to do otherwise than stand firm.[18]

But the convention stood equally firm, and she was not allowed to speak. Horace Greeley, outraged, summed up the proceedings in a *Tribune* editorial:

> First Day — Crowding a woman off the platform.
> Second Day — Gagging her.
> Third Day — Voting that she shall stay gagged. Having thus disposed of the main question, we presume the incidentals will be finished this morning.

Brown left the hall and went down the street to the Broadway Tabernacle, where the Woman's Rights Convention was meeting. Some 1,500 people, about half of them men, had been listening to Lucy Stone recounting the progress made in the five years since the 1848 Seneca Falls Convention, including the greater freedom women had to speak. When word came of Brown's experience at the Temperance Convention, the meeting was amazed and angry.

That evening, when Brown was scheduled to speak, the Woman's Rights Convention had troubles of its own. A huge crowd showed up for the evening session, including people who had clearly come to disrupt it rather than to listen. Brown was almost drowned out by hecklers in the audience, as she analyzed the people who opposed woman's rights:

> Who are they? Persons utterly ignorant of the claims which its advocates advance, ignorant alike of the wrongs existing and the remedy proposed. They suppose that a few mad-cap reformers are endeavoring to overthrow dame Nature, to invert society, to play the part of merciless innovators, to imperil religion, to place all civil and religious freedom in jeopardy.... There is another class, that of genuine bigots, with hearts so ossified that no room can be found for one noble and expansive principle within those little stony cells.... But the most hopeless and spiteful of our opponents is that large class of women whose merits are not their own; who have acquired some influence in society, not by any noble thoughts they have framed and uttered, not by any great deed they have done, but by the accident of having fathers, brothers, or husbands whose wealth elevates them to the highest wave of fashion.... [They dislike] the introduction into the acknowledged rights and duties of their sex, of a new element which may establish the necessity of their being themselves energetic and efficient....
>
> Such are the oppositions we meet; but they are all melting down like frostwork before the morning sun. The day is dawning when the intellect of woman shall be recognized as well as that of man, and when her rights shall meet an equal and cordial acknowledgement.[19]

Public indignation over the Half World's Convention continued for days. Wendell Phillips said it had shown that *men* were not ready for political responsibility. Horace Greeley printed a series of angry editorials in the *Tribune*, in which he appealed to the "upright, intelligent freemen" of the nation to open up public platforms to Brown and other women speakers. For Brown the convention was "a most unexpected advertisement" that provoked numerous lecture invitations, often at the highest lecture-course prices.[20]

The Half World's Convention was a watershed in women's battle for a public voice. People who doubted the

wisdom of women participating in public debates were nevertheless appalled at reports of clergymen shouting gross insults
at an innocent woman. In the aftermath of the convention, it
was generally conceded that women, even when they took on
"men's" roles, were entitled to be treated with decency and
respect. That shift in mores seemed like a small victory, but it
made a big difference. Women younger than Antoinette
Brown, who came to maturity during or after the Civil War,
would have no direct personal experience of being denied the
right to speak solely on the grounds of their gender.

Brown herself had no time to waste on anger, bitterness, or
crusading. She hurried back to South Butler to prepare for her
ordination, now less than a week away.

On September 15, 1853, a large crowd of friends and neighbors braved a violent rainstorm to attend the historic ceremony.
The guests included Dr. Harriot Hunt, a Boston physician,
herself a pioneer in the male medical profession, and a reporter
from the *New York Tribune*. During the ceremony Gerrit
Smith handed Brown a teasing note:

> This pouring rain doth make it clear,
> That silly woman must not teach;
> When will you learn, my sister dear,
> That noble man alone should preach?
>
> So now, Miss Brown, just stay at home,
> Tend babies, knit, and sew, and cook;
> And, then, some nice young man will come
> And on you cast a loving look.[21]

Rev. Luther Lee preached the ordination sermon from the text,
"There is neither male nor female; for ye are all one in Christ
Jesus":

> Without even presuming to discuss, on this occasion, the
> questions of civil and political rights, the text amply
> sustains me in affirming that in a Christian community,
> united upon Christian principles, for Christian purposes;
> or, in other words, in the Church, of which Christ is the
> only head, males and females possess equal rights and
> privileges; here there is no difference.... I cannot see how
> the test can be explained so as to exclude females from any
> right, office, work, privilege, or immunity which males
> enjoy, hold or perform.

Reflecting his view of the meaning of ordination itself, he continued:

> I do not believe that any special or specific form of ordina-
> tion is necessary to constitute a gospel minister. We are not
> here to make a minister. It is not to confer on this our sister
> a right to preach the gospel. If she has not that right
> already, we have no power to communicate it to her. Nor
> have we met to qualify her for the work of the ministry. If
> God and mental and moral culture have not already
> qualified her, we cannot, by anything we may do by way of
> ordaining or setting her apart.... All we are here to do,
> and all we expect to do, is, in due form, and by a solemn and
> impressive service, to subscribe our testimony to the fact
> that in our belief, our sister in Christ, Antoinette L.
> Brown, is one of the ministers of the New Convenant,
> authorized, qualified, and called of God to preach the
> gospel of his Son Jesus Christ.[22]

Gerrit Smith gave the church the encouragement it wanted, saying, "I congratulate you upon your selection of a pastor. You have chosen one who is wise and strong, and good, and faithful, and trusting, and full of love."[23]

Antoinette Brown experienced the day as a weighty occasion: "It seemed to me a very solemn thing when our three deacons and these clergymen all stood around me each placing a hand upon my head or shoulder and gravely admitting me into the ranks of the ministry."[24] The "great wall of custom," as she had once described it to Lucy Stone, had been breached at last.

From the viewpoint of such an observer as Dr. Harriot Hunt, the event was victory, an occasion "monumental to the cause of woman":

> There was something grand and elevating in the idea of a
> female presiding over a congregation, and breaking to
> them the bread of life—it was a new position for woman,
> and gave promise of her exaltation to that moral and
> intellectual rank which she was designed to fill.[25]

Not all the reaction, however, was as favorable. Thanks to the *New York Tribune*, news of the ordination spread. It "called forth a storm of denunciation from press and public and pulpit."[26] In communities that barely accepted the idea of women speaking in public, the thought of a woman minister was unpalatable, if not outrageous. Some denied that the ceremony was a valid ordination. Two years later, when Brown asked Luther Lee for a certificate testifying to her ordination, he refused:

> I do not see my way clear to give you such a paper as you ought to have as I did not ordain you. All I did was to preach a sermon.... I thought at the time there was a want of formality, and raised the question how you was to obtain your certificate, and was replied to that a certificate would be of no use.... I do not make these remarks to suggest a want of validity in the transaction.[27]

In the later decades of the nineteenth century, some historians would question whether Brown actually had the honor of being the first ordained woman minister.[28] But for now, she and her small parish were satisfied that she was their minister.

Whatever its historic importance, the ordination had little effect on the young minister's routine:

> My work through the following winter after my ordination proceeded in the usual way. We had good audiences for the conditions of the surrounding country, and no friction occurred anywhere in the church or the congregation. I did a good deal of outside lecturing and of attendance on other meetings.[29]

Two weeks after the ordination she went to Cleveland for the annual National Woman's Rights Convention. This time, in response to her suggestion, she was asked to give an opening prayer. The *Cleveland Journal* commented only that, "She has one distinction, she is the handsomest woman in the Convention. Her voice is silvery, and her manner pleasing."[30] She also gave a long speech on the Bible's position on women, which provoked a vehement discussion. Stephen Foster apparently spoke for many feminists when he asked:

> What has it [Christianity] done for woman? I am talking now of the popular idea of Christianity.... Are we to depend on a Christianity like that to restore woman her rights? If the Bible is against woman's equality, what are you to do with it? One of two things: either you must sit down and fold up your hands, or you must discard the divine authority of the Bible.[31]

Brown disagreed with Foster and many other feminists, as she believed the Bible was not against equal rights for women. She also feared that the anti-Christian views of some feminists would be seen as the official position of the woman's rights movement, prejudicing public opinion against the push for equality. When she heard Elizabeth Cady Stanton—chair of the Cleveland convention—refer to Paul's epistles as "human parchments," she wrote a strong dissent:

> I am very sensitive about fastening theological questions upon the *woman movement*. It is not that I am horrified at your calling St. Paul's writings "human parchments," but because I think when it is done officially that it is really unjust to the cause. It is compelling it [the woman's rights movement] to endorse something which does not belong to it. When you write for yourself say exactly what you please, but if you write as Cha'n Woman's Rights Con [vention] do not compel us to endorse anything foreign to the movement.[32]

It is not clear whether Brown wished the convention to accept diverse attitudes toward the Bible and religion, or whether—as indicated by her request for opening prayers—she hoped the woman's rights movement would be linked with religion as the abolition and temperance movements were.

Despite these disagreements, Brown enjoyed the convention, as is evident in her report to Gerrit Smith:

> The Cleveland Woman's Convention was a grand and satisfactory gathering. Up to the time I left, the afternoon of the 2nd day, everything passed harmoniously, and I do not think there could have been anything seriously unpleasant at all. . . . It struck me as being as fine a demonstration, and as much calculated to do good, as any Convention we have ever held. The world is going forward "To be better."[33]

In mid-November she performed a marriage ceremony in Rochester, the first time a woman had officiated at a wedding. Again thanks to Greeley's reporting in the *Tribune*, the incident was widely publicized, and Brown found that she "could get any price for lectures after that."[34] At the end of November, she took an active part in the New York State Woman's Rights Convention in Rochester.

After this she set off on a two-week lecture tour, beginning in Providence, Rhode Island, and traveling as far as Pennsylvania. She spoke sometimes on "The Old and the New, or Conservatism and Radicalism," and sometimes on slavery.[35] In February 1854 she attended the New York State Woman's Rights Convention in Albany, where she served on the business committee. Susan B. Anthony wanted her to return to Albany a week later for "the crisis," a series of legislative hearings that would culminate in the passage of the Married Woman's Property Act, giving married women the right to hold property and make contracts in their own names. But Brown had committed herself to a speaking engagement in Philadelphia, and felt "out of a sense of duty" that she had to honor it. She mentioned to Anthony that "I have the blues and feel horribly, that's the whole of the matter."[36] In fact, in the midst of all her bustling activity, Brown was undergoing a serious emotional crisis. Her job as a parish minister was far more difficult in reality than it had seemed as an unrealized goal; its most ordinary demands were causing her intense emotional strain.

A minister's functions were more complicated than merely preaching on Sunday. Church members, the majority of whom were women, expected a minister to be a kind of father figure, sometimes kind and understanding, sometimes commanding and judgmental. The minister was God's representative, and God, too, was "Our Father." The chain of patriarchal authority reached back through centuries of male-centered church history. Perhaps, some time in the distant past, women had been ordained as deaconesses, although no one was quite certain about that; but assuredly Christ and his apostles were all men. In the prevailing state of the church in Brown's day, it would have been difficult, if not impossible, for a woman to be fully successful in a job that was implicitly masculine. Few even wanted to try.

If Brown had been able to rely upon the moral support of her most valued friends and associates, her spirits might nevertheless have lifted under her peculiar burdens. But this support was not forthcoming. On the contrary, Stone, Stanton, Anthony, and many others looked with disfavor upon Brown's formal church affiliation, and viewed with suspicion her desire to expand opportunities for women within what they regarded as the corrupt institutional hierarchy of the church. Few feminists saw Brown's work as a minister as part of a common struggle for a change in the status of women. Other friends and family viewed her choice as peculiar. Once again, Brown felt virtually isolated:

> It was one of my odd experiences to see some of my old intimates of my own age, look at me with a kind of curious incredulity, as utterly unable to comprehend the kind of motive which could lead me to take so peculiar position in life. No attitude of strangers could have affected me half so much....
>
> In that earlier day it must have been more or less difficult for any young minister to meet his familiar friends with exactly the same freedom as he did before he had taken up ministerial duties. For a woman minister the situation was even more estranging.
>
> It was practically ten years after my ordination before any other woman known to the public was ordained. It was therefore doubly hard for me—a young woman still in the twenties—to adapt myself to the rather curious relationship I must sustain either to home conditions or to those of a pastorate. Personally this was more of an emotional strain than the enduring of any opposition that ever came to me as a public speaker or teacher.[37]

Worse still, for the first time she began to doubt the orthodox Christian doctrine she was expected to preach. According to orthodox doctrine, as preached in New England for well over a century, people were essentially sinful, descended from a fallen Adam and Eve, and condemned to eternal damnation unless they were saved by a stern God. Antoinette Brown found that set of beliefs hard to swallow:

> In my mind the question of eternal punishment had long seemed to me to be at least questionable. The exclusive inspiration of the entire Bible began to seem uncertain. Part of the Bible seemed to me to be inspired but other parts definitely not, and discrepancies began to make themselves evident.[38]

Her inquiring mind reached out toward a broader study of books raising similar questions:

> I had a strong bent toward speculative topics. This increased by the habit of reading metaphysical books. When traveling with Miss Anthony I generally carried a heavy volume along some of these lines, studying it as

opportunity offered. During this time I was reading rather
extensively on both sides of questions of religious
opinion.[39]

This questioning was hardly surprising; in fact, it was
virtually inevitable. Although Brown had been formally affil-
iated with orthodox Congregationalism since childhood, her
upbringing had been more liberal than orthodox. She had been
raised on stories of Heaven, not Hell. Charles Grandison Finney, the strongest single influence on her religious beliefs, had
stressed human goodness and the possibility of moral perfection. Oberlin's version of Congregational doctrine was so liberal that some of its graduates had trouble being ordained in
more conservative churches. In her sermons, Brown had always
spoken more freely about Divine mercy and the gradual dawning of a new consciousness than about fire and brimstone. She
may also have been influenced by the theological discussions at
woman's rights conventions, questioning the Divine authority
of the Bible and the image of God as a punishing patriarch.
Within the network of reformers, Brown was constantly
exposed to Unitarians, liberal Quakers, and other nonor-
thodox people who questioned orthodox religion along with
traditional social patterns. That questioning strengthened her
own doubts.

The immediate conflict between her new questioning and
her position as an orthodox minister arose when two children
in her parish died. One was an illegitimate child who died
suddenly of croup. As pastor, Brown "was present to see the last
hard sufferings of the poor little thing, and was forced to preach
the funeral sermon as the custom then was, with some reference
to the mother and the painful conditions surrounding her."[40]
That custom probably was to interpret the child's death as
Divine retribution for its mother's sin in becoming pregnant
outside of marriage. That same winter a young man in the
congregation became seriously ill. His mother asked Brown to
talk with him. Brown later recalled, "She indicated in no
uncertain terms that I was to hold him as supended over the
brink of eternal suffering and in this way to impel him to a
conversion that should bear him in the direction of eternal
happiness." Brown felt that threatening a dying youth was
cruel, and later confessed that "it was impossible to [act] in
accordance with the mother's wishes. I could only do what
could be done conscientiously."[41]

Brown was finding it increasingly difficult to steer a con-
scientious course. The death of children, including the deaths
of her own innocent brothers and sisters, did not appear to fit
the orthodox model of Divine justice. Her youthful belief "that
God was always just as well as merciful and that no wrong
could or would be done" failed to satisfy her emotionally or
intellectually. She no longer found certainty in the authority of
the Bible. Just as she had become the person to whom her
parish looked for an answer to the irrepressible "Why?" she
found that answers had deserted her.

Still, she struggled to continue her parish work. She later
wrote:

> Little by little there seemed to arise a bit of firm ground
> here and there. The belief in practical service, in justice,
> and a few moral principles, never quite forsook me and
> these seemed to make a solid foundation for abstract inves-
> tigation. On the basis of belief in the law of love it was
> possible to go on preaching and lecturing.[42]

But she felt shaky. Her congregation brought their own doubts
and questions to her, and she found that "it was extremely
difficult to satisfy them without troubling my own conscience."[43] She could not provide them with answers that were
both honest and comforting. By spring she was distraught:

> Suddenly I found that the whole groundwork of my faith
> had dropped away from me. I found myself absolutely
> believing nothing, not even in my own continuous per-
> sonal existence. Was I the same entity now as in my child-
> hood? Was I the same even as six months earlier? Was there
> any God? To me, it was the complete downfall of confi-
> dence in anything possible to know or rely on.[44]

In this terrifying state, she was even more frightened at the
thought of revealing her doubts. She wrote to Gerrit Smith,
"What will you say Mr. Smith at my getting more and more
unorthodox? Will you be sorry about the part you took at the
ordination?"[45] Later she recalled:

> To no one was I willing to say anything of the difficulties
> which began to arise.... It was impossible to appeal to any
> of my relatives, who all being still orthodox would only be
> distressed by my doubts....I had so lately received

ordination as a sincerely orthodox believer that I felt as though my sincerity at that time might even be called in question.[46]

She did not expect or look for understanding from her reformer friends, even from women like liberal Quaker Lucretia Mott, who might well have provided guidance.

The only person she felt free to confide in throughout this difficult period was William Henry Channing, the Unitarian minister who was, until his departure for England late in the summer of 1854, pastor of the Unitarian Society in Rochester. She turned to him in a state of childlike confusion, pouring out to him her sense of emptiness and loss. "What means this Night, oh Father Confessor?" she pleaded. He answered like a gentle parent:

> Be patient with yourself, leaning [?] in the nursing arms of your everyday self, that infant angel of your ideal.... Feed it with a mother's hearts-life; watch it slumber, help it to balance itself & walk &c.... Be sure, I would not write this if I did not see clearly that your Spirit is a most lively child, endangered by fever in the brain, rather than by rickety dullness.[47]

Instead of suggesting to her an alternative set of religious beliefs, he told her she would have to discover those beliefs herself.

The immediate outcome of Brown's emotional strain—a combination of intense isolation and spiritual uncertainty—was a breakdown in her physical health. What she called "brain fever" was probably a combination of mental confusion, nervous exhaustion, nightmares, and the like.[48] A few months later, she herself attributed her poor health to "the pressure of severe mental conflict."[49] She badly needed a rest from the pressures of her position, and felt that her religious views had become sufficiently different from those of her congregation that she could not in good conscience remain at her post. In July 1854, less than a year after her ordination, Brown left South Butler and went home to her parents' farm to rest.

Samuel C. Blackwell, ca. 1865

ᴇ Chapter 6 ᴇ

THIS FELLOW SPIRIT, SO WOVEN
INTO HERS

Upon departing from South Butler, Reverend Antoinette
Brown headed for her parents' farm in Henrietta, where she
hoped she could find rest. She wrote to Lucy Stone:

> I am at my own quiet home and have been here more than
> a week.... Rest seemed indispensable so I concluded to
> take it.... Is it not good to rest—to lie still and listen to
> the crickets and grasshoppers.[1]

She carefully explained to Horace Greeley that she did not
intend to retire from public life or even from preaching:

> The only reason for leaving Butler is my *health* and the
> necessity for a few months leisure-time for rest, thought,
> and study; interspersed with lecturing. Preaching with me
> has been deliberately chosen as a life profession and will
> not be lightly abandoned; but I am beginning to feel the
> need of freer surroundings than can be found even in a very
> liberal orthodox church.... I am stout and brave hearted
> and mean to preach the truth as it is revealed to me.[2]

Emotionally her parents' home was not altogether restful
to her; she felt unable to "disturb them with my state of utter
disbelief."[3] The farm was at best a stopping-place, a spring-
board for some new phase of activity.

She remained at the family farm during the summer and
fall of 1854. Slowly, her body responded to rest, sunshine, good
food, and relief from tension. Her health began to return. In the
fall of 1854 she undertook some lecture engagements; she also
remained active in the woman's rights movement. Susan B.
Anthony, whose home was in nearby Rochester, visited Brown
at least once during the summer and encouraged her to put
aside her personal anxieties and help with the ongoing petition
campaign to convince the legislature to change New York's
laws concerning married women. Brown served as secretary of
the National Woman's Rights Convention, now a formal

organization, and was considered for its presidency. But in her uncertain mood she had little energy for those tasks. She wrote to Stone:

> Are you expecting a large convention at Philadelphia? Shall you be there without fail? Does being secretary devolve any duties upon me in the line of sending invitations to anybody? It seems to me every one is at liberty to attend and needs no inviting. If there are any official duties, am quite ignorant of them and am moreover the last person from whom to have expected the discharge of responsibilities.... Everything seems uncertain in these days, since I have "taken to idleness." So please choose some better material for a President.[4]

By mid-November, however, she felt rested enough to commit herself to a series of lectures for the New York Antislavery Society, and sent Horace Greeley an article entitled "Woman an Ecclesiastic" for possible publication in the *Tribune*.[5] At the beginning of January 1855 she set out with Ernestine L. Rose, another woman's rights advocate, on a lecture tour of New England and upstate New York.

But as before her parish job at South Butler, Antoinette Brown was not satisfied with a life of lecture tours and conventions. In the earlier years, she had been drawn on by the dream of being a parish minister; now she was not sure what other choices were available to her. She told Gerrit Smith:

> I can never preach to a regular established church again, let them be ever so reformatory; for I cannot breathe there freely.... Not for months, perhaps years, shall I feel quite strong enough to commence teaching publicly some of the thoughts and beliefs that will come to me.[6]

Although the South Butler experience had taken its toll, by January 1855 she was, in her words, "at anchor again in a calm sea," ready to move forward to a new venture. From Henrietta, Brown wrote to Greeley, hoping that he might help her launch an "experiment" in which she would hire a hall and preach each Sunday—the plan Greeley and Charles Dana had proposed to her three years earlier:

> Of course I can never again be the *pastor of a Church*; but must be *a preacher for the people*.... My present

religion is a free one—all its truths are revelations from Nature's God to the soul; and one must be outside of all sectarian pressure to speak it freely. This can be better done in the city than the country—in NY than in any smaller place.

But of course no one can have confidence in an ability to sustain myself as a speaker, till this is proved to exist. As a lecturer I could never be more than passable; but if I have any talent in this direction, it is of the kind to adapt me to be a free preacher in a free hall, with the whole range of human thought open for investigation, and all human relations ready for the application of perceived principles .... This has always been my ideal—all my thoughts, studies, and preferences have tended to that and except that I then hoped the sphere of labor might fall within the pale of the church proper—now I know that it cannot.... And I shall not fail! There is that within me which gives the assurance of success![7]

Greeley responded with an encouraging invitation. Two weeks later, Brown wrote him from her lecture tour in Newark, New Jersey:

You do not know how sincerely I thank you for the way in which you treat the matter of my going to NY.... I am hopeful and in some things self reliant, and feel sure one can find his level after a while in a great city like yours, so if I have the elements of success in any direction it can develop itself, and if one must prove a failure in life it may as well be done there as any where.[8]

She reported with some satisfaction to Smith:

I am now on my way to N.Y. city. That is to be my home for the future. There are good and earnest people there who will feel an interest in my position, and then every thing seems ready for this. I shall commence preaching there *in a hall*, once on a Sunday, and see what will be the result. Shall try to preach a *free gospel to the people*.

At present I am to do some lecturing, visit prisoners and paupers; and study humanity in all its phases, high and low, as far as may be, and write for the *Tribune* anything which seems worth giving to the Public.[9]

It was undoubtedly Greeley who encouraged Brown to spend some time in New York's growing slums and institutions, and to write about her experiences in the *Tribune*. As an editor he sought out interesting material for his readers; as a person interested in helping other people, he could see that Antoinette Brown would benefit from exposure to a broader range of experiences than her rural upbringing had provided. Ten years earlier he had given a similar opportunity to Bostonian Margaret Fuller, when she was reaching beyond the transcendentalist philosophy that permeated Boston and Concord. Fuller's experience in the slums of New York had pushed her into a radical analysis of the political and economic system, and ultimately led her to Europe, where she became involved in the Italian revolution of 1848. She continued to write for the *Tribune* until her tragic death in 1849. Greeley may have hoped that Brown would find the experience equally invigorating. For Brown, it would at least be an excellent opportunity to sharpen her writing skills, under the tutelage of one of the country's finest journalists; a chance, perhaps, to try out her youthful dream of being a published author as well as a lecturer.

Her new work forced Brown to turn her attention from theological speculation and introspection to a real-life study of poverty and mental disorders, especially among women. She spent long hours with Abby Hopper Gibbons, a Quaker matron twenty years older than herself, who had joined her father in working in prisons. Gibbons took Brown with her to the tenement districts crowded with Irish and German immigrants; to the asylum for poor, delinquent, and handicapped children on Randall's Island; to the huge prison complex known as the Tombs. Social work had not yet emerged as a profession, but the two women, like a number of well-meaning, middle-class women of the period, tried on their own initiative to ease some of the misery they saw. Brown later commented, "When Mrs. Gibbons and I worked together she, of course, was the effective worker, I learning from her example and superior experience the best ways of meeting people and difficulties."[10]

Even with Abby Gibbons's example, Brown felt unable to respond adequately to what she saw:

> In talking with a handsome young woman who had been arrested for the theft of a watch and was awaiting her trial, she told us confidentially that she was guilty. She justified herself, saying that it was right enough for her to

do it under the circumstances. When we tried to point out the way to an honest life and its advantages, she said with a pitiful earnestness, "You can't understand it. You don't know how we women are situated. I have no chance. I can't do anything, any kind of work. I have never been taught and never done anything. I can't even sew. There is no one to help me, and everybody that I know is ready to hurt me." It was all very pitiful and much too true.[11]

She had no way to offer such women the things that might have made a tangible difference in their lives: work that paid enough to feed a family, adequate housing, education.[12] Unable to do anything to ease their misery, Brown found that situation of poor women hopeless and depressing:

The work among the poor and degraded in New York was so pitiful that it was almost too much for healthy sympathy, at least to one whose life had hitherto been so sheltered as mine; and coming not long after the serious religious overturning of my mind at South Butler and before the reconstruction of my positive beliefs, it made the whole world seem a place of shadows and sorrows.[13]

In encouraging Brown to write articles for the *Tribune*, Greeley had told her to write "anyway you choose, only be sure to expose the blackest evils in the severest language, as they deserve."[14] Her essays reflected both the tragedy of her subject matter and her own somber mood. In the first article of her series, entitled "Shadows of Our Social System," she told the *Tribune*'s readers:

Polished, enlightened, civilized Christianized society has yet the black shadow, more or less dense; on its vine-trellised cottages, and its marble palaces, its temples of justice, and its halls of learning; on its costly churches built up as grand houses for God's people to fall asleep in, and on its church spires with their long fingers pointing far up toward heaven.[15]

She then went on to describe the shadow of poverty as she saw it in her daily travels about the city.

She did not, however, explore the causes of the "shadow." Like other sincere reformers, Brown affirmed that human

suffering was the result of human activity. She rejected the view,
advanced by one *Tribune* reader in response to her articles, that
poverty and human misery "came into the world with Sin and
Death."[16] Like most of her contemporaries, she did not grasp
the relationship between economic institutions that caused
poverty. When northern abolitionists heard of the suffering of
black slaves, they looked beyond the actions of individual
slaveholders and condemned the entire institution of slavery.
But when the same reformers saw the suffering of poor people
in northern cities, they failed to see urban poverty as an institution fostered by the technological changes that brought material comforts—progress—to the educated middle class.

Unable to resolve social questions of the magnitude she
encountered in New York, Brown continued her search for
personal truths. One of the men who helped her reformulate
her religious beliefs was Samuel Blackwell, who had visited her
in South Butler more than a year before. She found his friendship comforting and supportive:

> In the midst of the blackness of darkness which was
> around me more or less that year in New York, Mr. Black-
> well's optimism and the fact that he was passing through a
> very similar experience to my own from the orthodoxy of
> his early training and his earlier years, into a more san-
> guine religious phase than my own enabled him to
> become to me a present help in time of trouble.[17]

Unlike her other mentors, such as Gerrit Smith or William
Henry Channing, Sam Blackwell was close to Antoinette's
age—thirty-two years old to her almost thirty—and became a
closer personal friend.

Antoinette gradually came to know most of the close-knit
Blackwell family. They were an unusual group of people,
ranking with the Beechers and the Alcotts as one of the great
nineteenth-century reform clans. The family emigrated from
England in 1832, eventually settling in Cincinnati. Sam's
father, Samuel Blackwell, Sr., spent years trying to manufacture sugar from beets, part of an antislavery effort to reduce
dependence on slave-produced cane sugar. The Blackwell children grew up as staunch abolitionists; they named their
carriage-horses after two of their abolitionist idols, William
Lloyd Garrison and Prudence Crandall.

Samuel Blackwell's five sisters were as proficient in intellectual matters as most women were in housekeeping. Elizabeth and Emily became doctors—despite resistance from male-dominated medical schools—and opened a clinic for poor women in New York City. Ellen and Marian were active in woman's rights and other reform causes. Anna had lived at Brook Farm, Bronson Alcott's transcendentalist commune, but was now working as a newspaper reporter in Paris. None of the sisters ever married; their mother, aided by her husband's mother and four unmarried sisters who shared their household, instilled in all her daughters the attitude that marriage was at best a regrettable necessity.

Samuel Blackwell and his three brothers received a very different upbringing in the same household. Because they were expected to support the family after their father's early death, they had to give up any thought of further education for professional work. Both Sam and Henry, much older than the other two boys, began working as bookkeepers in their early teens. By the 1850s they were business partners in a series of not-very-successful land ventures and a hardware store. They remained active abolitionists; Ohio was a border state between slave and free territory, and there were ample opportunities to help fugitive slaves with money or a place to stay. Unlike their sisters, the Blackwell men had frequent romances, amidst much teasing, but no real criticism from the rest of the family. Not surprisingly, given their sisters' examples, they looked for women who were educated, interesting, and active.

Like other traveling reformers, Antoinette Brown occasionally stayed at the Blackwell home in Cincinnati when she visited the area on lecture tours. She felt as comfortable there as she did at the homes of other reformers. She showed no signs that she imagined or desired a closer attachment to Sam Blackwell; but in the year after leaving South Butler, her feelings slowly changed in ways she did not anticipate.

Within the woman's rights movement Brown was surrounded by a far-reaching and often heated debate about marriage as an institution. Both the legal position of women within marriage and the availability of divorce were major topics for debate at every woman's rights convention during the 1850s. These essentially political discussions were inevitably intertwined with the personal experiences and choices of Brown and her feminist friends.

Many feminists focused on the injustices inherent in marriage as a legal institution in which women lost control over their bodies and their money. In New York state, as elsewhere, a married woman had no legal right to her own earnings or property, to custody of her children, or to her husband's property if he died without a will. She could not legally sign a contract, sue in her own name, or be responsible for her own debts. She had no defense against being beaten or raped by her husband.[18] Even without violent attacks, a woman's ability to exercise control over the frequency of sexual intercourse was often her only defense against repeated pregnancies. Lucy Stone wrote to Brown in 1855:

> It is clear to me, that question underlies this whole movement, and all our little skirmishing for better laws, and the right to vote, will yet be swallowed up in the real question, viz: Has woman a right to herself? It is very little to me to have the right to vote, to own property, &c. if I may not keep my body, and its uses, in my absolute right. Not one wife in a thousand can do that now, and as long as she suffers this bondage, all other rights will not help her to her true position.[19]

Brown agreed that women needed control over their lives—and property—within marriage. She accompanied other feminists in testifying before a committee of the New York state legislature in support of a Married Woman's Property Act, which would enable married women to control their own earnings, make contracts, and own property.

Brown disagreed, however, with feminists—including Stone, Paulina Wright Davis, and Elizabeth Cady Stanton—who advocated easier divorce. Brown accepted the Christian belief that the marriage bond was not merely a human contract, but a sacrament created by God. She believed that in the eyes of God a husband and wife remained responsible for each other's souls, and that even in the most difficult situations, the partner who felt wronged should help the other change, rather than walking out. She wrote to Stone:

> It is said you are in favor of divorce on the ground of drunkenness. So I see is Mrs. Davis. Of course that means you are in favor of divorce whenever the parties want it. That's so isn't it? Well I am not ready for that yet. Let them

have legal separation but not the right of second marriage.[20]

Brown believed that marriage should be strengthened, not weakened; she was critical of those who put public responsibilities—even social reform activities—ahead of family commitments. She proposed to the New York State Woman's Rights Convention early in 1854:

> The family, by men as well as women, should be held more sacred than all other institutions; ... it may not, without sin, be abandoned or neglected by fathers any more than by mothers, for the sake of any of the institutions devised by men—for the government of the State or the Nation any more than for the voluntary association of social reformers.[21]

Brown advocated making men and women more equal by extending to men the obligations and expectations normally reserved for women—those concerning family and home—as well as by extending to women the privileges men enjoyed. In a speech at one woman's rights convention, she asserted that "the cure for the evils that now exist is not in dissolving marriage, but it is in giving to the married woman her own natural independence and self-sovereignty, by which she can maintain herself."[22]

Although she respected marriage as an institution, Brown did not expect that she herself would ever marry:

> It had seemed to both Lucy Stone and myself in our student days that marriage would be a hindrance to our public work. I at least had accepted celibacy as my destiny, and I think she had also at an early day.[23]

She wrote to Stone that she could not envision a marriage that would not interfere with her work:

> In the first place I would never expect to find a man who would sympathize with my feelings and acquiesce in my plans. Such a personage would threaten the overthrow of all or many of my arrangements or else the matrimonial alliance would have to be placed on a different basis from the common; and on the whole it is deemed entirely inexpedient.[24]

Brown also felt that single women could provide an example:

> Let us stand alone in the great moral battlefield with none
> but God for a support & there will be a lesson of truth to be
> learned from our very position which will be impressed as
> deeply on the minds of the people as any we have to teach.
> Let them see that woman can take care of herself & act
> independently without the encouragement & sympathy of
> her "lord & master."[25]

Brown's expectation of remaining single was strengthened
by her friendship with Susan B. Anthony. Anthony, who often
took over responsibility for running Elizabeth Cady Stanton's
household to free her friend for a few precious hours of speech-
writing, was fully familiar with the disadvantages of marriage
and family responsibilities. She had herself decided to remain
single in order to devote her life to social reform, especially
woman's rights. From Anthony's viewpoint, the issue was
simple: Brown was young, active, and eloquent, and her labor
was badly needed.

But both Brown and Stone found that being single had
disadvantages. Despite her strong political views on the injustices of marriage as an institution, Stone confessed to Brown:

> It is horrid to live without the intimate companionship,
> and quiet loving influences which are the constant attend-
> ant of a true love marriage—It [being single] is a wretch-
> edly unnatural way of living. But nothing is so bad as to be
> a *thing*, as every married woman now is in the eye of the
> law. Nette let us get down these laws, and then marry if we
> can .... My heart aches to love somebody that shall be all
> its own.[26]

Given this combination of sentiments, Stone's friends watched
with some interest to see how she would respond to the persis-
tent courtship of Henry Blackwell.

For many months, Henry followed Lucy around on her
lecture tours. By the fall of 1854 he was sure he wanted to marry
her. But Antoinette, still one of Lucy's closest friends, thought
that Lucy would decide to remain single. After a visit to the
Blackwell home, she reported to Susan B. Anthony, "Lucy *was
not* engaged when I left Cincinnati—nor do I believe she will
ever be married to H. B. Blackwell."[27]

By Christmas, however, Lucy yielded and agreed to marry Henry on the condition that he devote his life to woman's rights. Lucy's marriage would, of course, alter her relationship with Antoinette, completing the shift away from a primary and intimate friendship. Nevertheless, Antoinette was delighted; she wrote to Elizabeth Cady Stanton, "I wouldn't be ashamed of 'my Henry' if I had one; but am 'o'er glad' after all that I haven't 'got in love.' "[28]

Lucy herself remained ambivalent about her marriage. As her wedding day approached she wrote to Antoinette:

> "Smiles and tears" follow each other when you think of my "matrimony." Well Nettie dear, the world is full of both, so you are not alone....
>
> If the ceremony is in N.Y. we want you to harden your heart enough to help in so cruel an operation, as putting Lucy Stone to death. But it will be all according to law, so you need fear no punishment. I *expect* however to go to Cincinnati & have the ruin completed there.[29]

Lucy Stone and Henry Blackwell were married in Massachusetts on May 1, 1855. Antoinette found that she was unable to make time in her busy schedule to attend. As part of the ceremony Lucy and Henry signed a joint statement protesting the unjust legal status of married women. Lucy also decided to keep her birth name; the nearly universal custom of a woman assuming her husband's surname seemed to her a vivid day-to-day symbol of a wife's legal disability.

At about the same time Sam Blackwell—perhaps emboldened by Henry's success—proposed to Antoinette. The proposal unsettled her. She wrote him from New York City:

> There is time to say only one thing now and that is that I am feeling some consciencious scruples about allowing our correspondence to continue upon its present basis; but have not had time to settle the matter to my perfect satisfaction and so will just indicate that you may not be surprised at almost any kind of a decision in my next letter.[30]

After a long, frank talk with Susan B. Anthony, she leaned toward breaking off her correspondence with Sam entirely. His next letter must have been less urgent, however, for she wrote instead merely to clarify her feelings:

You tell me there is not need of a "decision," my friend, so I shall make none, but will calmly state facts and leave all the rest to you.

It is very pleasant to receive letters full of kindly sympathies, and sometimes delightful to write whatever one thinks and feels to an appreciating reader. So every line from you was always welcome, dropping like a gleam of sunshine upon the heavy monotony of toilsome days. But I may not be selfish enough to receive friendship under false pretences....

And all this, my brother, is preliminary to saying that our relations, though they might deepen and strengthen by association, could not, I am convinced, ever so far change as to realize a hope which you have sometimes expressed. I should learn to love you dearly, by sharing thoughts, interests, and confidences; as I have loved but few friends ever; but this is all! I could never be more to you than a friend—a sister. Very much of this may arise from my peculiar public position.... Nothing but an unsought all-absorbing affection can make me feel it right to waver in my plan for an untiring life-work of isolation.[31]

But Sam would not accept this answer as final. He wrote back:

Do not talk of an "untiring life work of isolation." Indeed I can't stand that, if you are my sister I shan't let you be isolated. I shall claim to go shares in all troubles and perplexities and shall absolutely demand that you come and tell your brother all about it.... I don't ask you for anything but *friendship*.[32]

Antoinette hesitated. She was not at all sure that she wanted to go on in isolation. She wanted to preach regularly again, but her personal faith was still so shaky that a parish job was difficult to imagine. Whatever Susan B. Anthony might say, it was hard being single. Five years of lecturing, traveling, living out of trunks and boxes, had confirmed Antoinette Brown's feeling that "I can't go wandering up and down in the earth without any home."[33] She had just passed her thirtieth birthday. She began to look with envy at some of the women she knew—Abby Hopper Gibbons, Lucretia Mott, and others—who had homes, husbands, and children, as well as satisfying public work.

At the beginning of December 1855, Antoinette went to Boston for a farewell party for Ellen Blackwell, who was departing for an extended visit to England. She did not tell

Ellen, Susan B. Anthony, or even Lucy Stone that her main reason for being there was to see Sam Blackwell. Later she confessed to Anthony:

> At Boston I own up to hoaxing you & Lucy & Ellen all of you—yet even then the matter was not decided but was just at the crisis where it *must* be decided for weal or woe at once.... After more than a week's visit with him the scales predominated decidedly in his favor.[34]

By the time she got back to New York City, she had decided to marry Sam Blackwell:

> Well Sam there was a stray waif once who belonged no where and to no one. She believed nothing and loved nobody. Then by some strange process her good genius came and pinned this poor lost wanderer closely to another soul till she grew there as a kind of parasite on his sympathies. For good or ill they seem to have grown together. Their destiny was one and the weary little outcast felt more and more ready to nestle quietly into his heart and rest there.... She knew then it was this fellow spirit that had been so woven into hers that nothing could quite tear them asunder.[35]

Later, in a more reflective mood, she explained:

> If I had remained orthodox I should probably have considered marriage out of the question, a hindrance to the best usefulness. But when the early faith seemed wholly lost and the new and stronger belief not yet obtained, there seemed no good reason for not accepting the love and help of a good man and the woman's appreciation of all else that this implied.[36]

She had many lingering uncertainties, however, which she was not afraid to express to Sam:

> I love you Sam; but sometimes I do shrink from that new relation with many mingled feelings; and sometimes wish heartily that it was all over—that we were married and the whole thing settled.[37]

Her chief concern was the impact of the marriage on her public work. During her December visit to Boston, she had met Angelina Grimké Weld, an older abolitionist who had virtually given up her public work after her marriage to Theodore Weld. Antoinette reported to Sam:

> She will remain in Boston to study this winter because she cannot do any thing at that in her own home where there are so many family cares—not very encouraging that is it, to one like me?[38]

Antoinette felt the pressure of other people's expectations; she told Sam:

> No one who knows of [the marriage plan] has much faith in any public duties for the future. The booby Public will triumph in that belief till we demonstrate the opposite.[39]

Yet she seems to have had few doubts that she would continue writing, speaking, and preaching. In the midst of planning her wedding, she undertook to compile some of her *Tribune* essays for publication as a book. Her marriage presented only logistical questions; she suggested to Sam:

> Unless my book can be fully given to the public and accepted or rejected fully before our change of relations . . . it will be best to make arrangements with the friends and publishers, to advertise the book, . . . be married *before* it is issued, and then let it come out directly afterward with the new name.[40]

She also planned a lecture tour for the following February. Sam assured her that marriage would not interfere with that trip. She later commented: "It was entirely understood between Mr. Blackwell and myself that my public work would be as nearly uninterrupted as circumstances would allow."[41]

With Sam's reassurances and support, Antoinette Brown hoped that she could have both her independent work and the love and domestic comforts she had been missing:

> You asked me one day if it seemed like giving up much for your sake. Only leave me *free*, as free as you are and everyone ought to be, and it is giving up nothing. . . . It wil not be so very bad to have a dear quiet own home, with one's husband to love and be loved by with his big heart full of sympathy and an active spirit ready to cooperate in everything good. . . . *You* may sigh for a more domestic wife; and yet to have me merely go into N. Y. to preach Sundays,

or gone on a lecturing tour of a few days or even weeks won't be so very bad, will it?[42]

Above all she trusted that they would be able to shape their life together as they went along:

> Of course we won't mark out the future too rigidly, or take any strict *vows* on the subject or make plans which *must* continue for two or five years. We will be governed very much by circumstances and what seems best as the years go by, but I think, Sam we can be self sovereigns, we can bend everything within & without to our wills, and our wills to our intellects.[43]

Antoinette was convinced that most, if not all, of the inequities of marriage as an institution could be eliminated by careful planning. She outlined to Sam what she considered an equitable way of handling their money and property. She proposed that "Either may act for himself—do business on his own responsibility," a capability only recently open to a married woman. On the other hand, she told Sam that she did not want to keep her own earnings separate—"because it looks so mean to have interests divided in that way"—but wrote instead that ideally "each earns, not for himself, but for both and if there is love in the heart there is a higher and more unselfish pleasure in this than there can be in any form."[44]

Antoinette and Sam did not tell their friends and family of their plans. This secrecy was unusual among the Blackwells, who carried on extensive correspondence and considered that they all had a part in any decision affecting any one of them. The family, which now included Lucy Stone, watched eagerly from a distance. But the secret was well guarded.

The rumor spread around reform circles that Sam Blackwell was planning to marry soon; but no one knew who his bride would be. Antoinette told Sam:

> Everywhere...the Blackwells are most freely discussed. Some people will have occasion to remember some of their comments six months hence. It is quite like being necessitated to play the eavesdropper and is very delightful, much more comical than occasionally provoking.... The feeling of reserve which made me suggest to you not to say much is I think carried almost to excess with me. It grows out of the natural tendency in me to say all or nothing.[45]

Not even Susan B. Anthony, who had spent so many hours
talking with Antoinette, guessed the truth. Finally, in mid-
January, Antoinette confessed to her:

> Will you ever forgive me? ... When you asked me that
> night in Rochester whether I should not "feel bad when
> Sam was married" I came near shaking you on to the floor
> with laughing at the joke for he was in the city there and
> was going up to spend the week at Father's....
> Susan, darling, I love you a little better than ever and
> would ask you to the wedding only that absolutely no
> one is invited my mothers health is so feeble.... You may
> be *sure* of my continued interest and future cooperation in
> our N. Y. movement, and in every other good cause. I go
> right on with the writing, and even lecturing some over
> this winter.[46]

Anthony apparently softened her opposition to Antoinette
Brown's marrying, writing:

> Institutions, among them marriage, are justly charge-
> able with social and individual ills, but after all, the *whole
> man or woman* can and *will* rise above them. I am sure you
> will never be crushed or even dwarfed by them.[47]

In mid-January Sam and Antoinette also announced their
engagement to the Blackwell clan, who responded enthusiastically. Lucy Stone wrote from Cincinnati:

> I congratulate *you* in your rare good fortune, for Sam is
> one of the best men in the world. And *he* may rejoice in the
> fact that he alone of all the men in the world has a *Divine*
> wife![48]

Sam's sister Ellen wrote from London on behalf of the Blackwell sisters, first to Sam:

> I felt that I could not hear of your engagement to any one
> whom I had not known, with anything like the pleasure
> that I should have in welcoming Nettie, for whom I feel
> much love & esteem & whom I have regarded from the first
> as one who might some time be one of the sisters.... Nettie
> is so good, so intelligent, so lovable a person that I am sure
> she will win all hearts & I rejoice & give thanks whenever I
> think of my dear good brother, happy as he deserved to be,
> in the affection of a really noble woman.[49]

After the wedding she wrote to Antoinette:

> It is with the sincerest pleasure that I find myself about to
> write to you as a sister. I have hoped ever since leaving
> America to hear the pleasant news which Sam like the
> excellent good brother that he is sent to me a short time
> ago. Lucy & I have often talked about it & wished it might
> happen, & now behold it has all come about as pleasantly
> & prettily as the winding up of a romance.... What rogues
> you & Sam were to keep even sister Lucy in the dark.[50]

Having shared the news of their engagement with those
closest to them, Sam and Antoinette decided to move ahead
quickly with their wedding. It was to be a small, simple ceremony in the main room of the Brown farmhouse. Antoinette
decided that a fancy wedding cake would "belong very much to
the eating and drinking age of barbarism."[51] She also refused to
wear a wedding ring. She wore a plain dark "sensible" wool
dress—no silk or lace—while Sam borrowed brother Henry's
best suit.

Sam left Cincinnati by train, allowing ample time to get to
Rochester by the wedding day, but was delayed by a blizzard. He
had no way to communicate with Antoinette—the telegraph
line was not yet established—but she easily understood the
reason for the delay. As soon as he arrived, on the day after that
originally set for the ceremony, they were married at once.
Antoinette later remembered:

> It was intended to be entirely a family wedding. We had
> only our own family, an aunt and some cousins. There
> being no opportunity to inform the minister, the cere-
> mony was performed by my father. After the wedding we
> were driven through snowbanks often more than fence-
> high by my eldest brother William to Rochester.[52]

In Rochester they boarded a train for Cincinnati to begin their
married life.

Unlike Lucy Stone, Antoinette Brown was not troubled by
the thought of changing her name. She once said to Sam
Blackwell, "Tell Lucy I like your name better than my own and
have no possible wish against having it added."[53] She later
explained in more detail:

> To me the question of a name seemed of but little account
> compared with other more vital interests. I felt entirely

certain of retaining my own individuality, and reasoned
"what's in a name?" One's reputation good or bad, will
maintain itself if one's integrity of life can be reasonably
maintained. As society decided that I was born in the
Brown family and must remain a Brown until marriage, it
also decided that I must become a Blackwell after marriage. I was content to make my protests against more
unjust vital issues.[54]

For the rest of her life she would be known formally as "Reverend Antoinette L.B. Blackwell."

Antoinette Brown Blackwell with daughter Florence, ca. 1857

A WORLD OF NEW EMOTIONS

For the first few months after her marriage, Blackwell redeemed her pledge to continue working as a public lecturer. In mid-February 1856, after a few weeks of relaxing with Sam at the Walnut Hills homestead, she wrote reassuringly to Susan B. Anthony:

> In 2 weeks I go East. Shall lecture there for a while—and then be a good wife and go where my husband does, though I shall talk a good deal if my throat will allow. One of those long hard coughs you remember of old has tortured me these last six weeks.... but it is nearly vanquished I hope & believe.[1]

She and Sam now planned to move East. He remained in Cincinnati to wind up the hardware business he shared with his brother Henry, while Antoinette began her lecture tour. She traveled first to Philadelphia, where she joined Mary Grew, a gentle but outspoken feminist and abolitionist, and Quaker James Mott. Blackwell later recalled:

> We three held several meetings in the outlying neighborhood around Philadelphia, James Mott taking up the business details and saving us from all manner of outside cares. This journey increased the appreciative friendship with both these comrades.[2]

She wrote to Anthony from New Jersey, apparently thinking about a tour with her later that spring:

> I have been holding a number of meetings lately—am to speak here Sunday evening on Temperance but my throat is still troublesome & I shall venture no more engagements till it is quite well.... The places you name will suit me as well as any, when I am ready to go with you on the lecturing trip. But don't rely on me with *positiveness*. It wont do, & I am a married woman![3]

She did not regret her new status, however; she even teased Anthony:

And for you, Sue, I hear of a number of bachelors making inquiries about Susan B. Anthony. This means something! I shall look out for another wedding before the year closes among our sisternity. Get a good husband, that's all, dear.[4]

Blackwell returned to Cincinnati in mid-April, with a brief visit to her parents' home in Henrietta en route. She felt that her trip had made the homecoming to Sam "more joyous."[5]

By the time she returned to Cincinnati, she must have realized she was pregnant. The child would be born late in the fall. Blackwell left no record of how she felt at the prospect. Probably her feelings were mixed. She had always looked forward to a house full of children, like the family she had grown up in. She told Lucy Stone late in 1849—long before she had any thoughts of marrying—that she wanted to adopt seven homeless children: "I need a pleasant happy home to rest in and some pleasant happy children there to keep me from becoming a misanthrope."[6] On the other hand, a child would mean substantial changes in the pattern of her life, much more than marriage had. She must have wondered how she could manage to continue her public work once the baby arrived. Pregnancy would also alter her relationship with Samuel. The four months since she had agreed to marry hardly gave her time to absorb all her new feelings.

Lucy Stone, hearing the news, warned her sister-in-law of the difficulties of pregnancy itself:

How do you do? With your new experiences and new hopes and fears? Don't feel obliged to answer one of these questions only be sure, dear Nettie, that I sympathize with you and respect the moods, silent or otherwise, which these months will give. I am glad that you are so well. Don't blame yourself, Nettie, if you find that all the original sin seems to try and manifest itself in you for even Margaret Fuller with all her strength and philosophy says she was "never so unreasonable and desponding." Blame the circumstances, though may be the Furies will not haunt you, as they often do the very best. I hope that everything will go pleasantly, and that another new year will find your heart made glad and warm and large by a mother's love. For myself I almost despair. Will you give me one of your seven?[7]

There is no indication that Antoinette Blackwell had either emotional or physical problems during her pregnancy. She was thirty-one—much older than most women during their first pregnancy—but was in good health, active, surrounded by the Blackwell family, and secure in her husband's love.

She had plenty to do while she waited for the baby. Not only she and Sam, but also the entire Blackwell clan was preparing to move East, leaving the Walnut Hills house that had been their home for twenty years. They spent many hours crating or selling rooms full of furniture, and sorting through mountains of books deciding which to keep and which to donate to nearby Lane Seminary. By early summer, Antoinette and her mother-in-law, Hannah Lane Blackwell, were ready to leave for Henrietta for an extended visit with Antoinette's parents. Antoinette found that "Mrs. Blackwell was a cheerful old lady with a very social disposition who made herself at once at home in my family and the neighborhood which gave various entertainments in her honor."[8] Samuel went ahead to New York City to look for a job. In August the entire family was reunited in New York, at the home of Samuel's older sister, Elizabeth Blackwell. "Dr. Elizabeth," and her associate, Dr. Marie Zakrzewska, ran a clinic for poor women and children on East Seventh Street, which later became the New York Infirmary. They had purchased a townhouse on Fifteenth Street near Union Square, a large open park. Sam and Antoinette remained through the winter at the townhouse.

By October Sam found a permanent job as a bookkeeper at the excellent salary of $1200 per year. Antoinette largely eschewed public speaking or other public work that fall; her own need to focus on the emotional and domestic drama that now held center stage reinforced the taboos that may have existed against middle-class women appearing in public noticeably pregnant.

Antoinette and Sam's daughter was born early in November, with both "Dr. Elizabeth" and "Dr. Zak" assisting. Antoinette later remembered it as "a pretty hard birth."[9] The baby was born with a black face, and Dr. Zakrzewska slapped her until she began breathing. Sam and Antoinette named her Florence Brown Blackwell, deliberately using both surnames. Either by choice or medical necessity, Antoinette did not nurse Florence. Hearing this, Horace Greeley, wary of store-bought milk adulterated with chalk and other substances, brought them fresh

milk every day from his farm north of the city. For the first time
in six years, Antoinette missed the annual National Woman's
Rights Convention, held within a few weeks of Florence's
birth. She did write a long letter suggesting that all state legislatures be sent a demand for woman suffrage.

Antoinette and Samuel considered Elizabeth Blackwell's
house a temporary home until they could save enough money
to buy land outside of the city. New York City was a difficult
place to live. Fires broke out frequently in the crowded wooden
houses that used coal or wood for heat and cooking. There was
no public fire department, and when a fire occurred it was not
uncommon for two rival private fire companies to fight each
other instead of extinguishing the blaze. Riots often erupted
against antislavery speakers, or in protests over rising food
costs and low wages. Epidemics of yellow fever and cholera
were common. It was hardly an ideal place to raise a family.
Antoinette hoped for a rural home, with plenty of space for a
garden. Samuel's bookkeeping job limited them, however, to
areas he could reach by commuter trains or ferries. Greeley
offered to show them several lots near his home in Westchester
County, warning:

> You need to look a month before you buy. Most of our
> people buy a home as hurriedly as an Arab pitches his tent,
> but that is not the way.... Do not mind those who will tell
> you, "here is a rare place going very cheap, which you
> must secure now or lose." There will always be nice
> places.[10]

The Blackwells finally settled on New Jersey, rather than
Westchester County. New Jersey was Sam's boyhood home,
and land was cheaper there. Even so, they could not afford the
farm that Antoinette wanted. Their first real home was a small
house in the middle of Newark. She later recalled:

> It was a curious place, a tiny house of three stories, a
> basement, two rooms on the second floor and two above,
> with some land around it and a little shrubbery, and a
> charming outlook. The Newark of that day was about as
> different from the solidly built up city of the present day
> [1909] as might be. We were delighted with this first little
> home.... This little house we called "The Pepper-box"
> because of its shape—as tall as an ordinary house and very
> narrow in proportion.[11]

Although they would move from town to town many times in the coming years, New Jersey was now the Blackwells' permanent home. They were surrounded by family and friends. Samuel's mother and sister Marian found a house nearby. Antoinette later remembered:

> My little daughter being the first grandchild in the Black-well family was regarded by them as a treasure and almost daily the mother, who liked a walk for her constitutional, made us a visit. She was an enthusiastic lover of children and made herself a daily brightness in the household.[12]

Henry Blackwell and Lucy Stone moved to Orange, about five miles away. Lucy, thirty-nine years old, was at last expecting a baby. For the first time in nearly ten years, Antoinette's and Lucy's lives could be connected on an almost daily basis, although without the emotional intensity of their shared years at Oberlin.

In their country home, focused on their own family, with Samuel's steady salary, the Blackwells were insulated from the worst of the social and economic strains of 1857. Large manufacturing plants increasingly dominated the economy; Henry Bessemer's process for refining iron into more durable steel provided a foundation for heavy industry. Railroad lines now extended to the Mississippi River, and telegraph wires all the way to the Pacific Coast and under the Atlantic Ocean to Europe. The economic boom was unstable, however. In July 1857, all the banks in the nation were forced to close to stem a financial panic brought on by too many speculative investments, especially in railroads. In New York City thousands of unemployed people rioted, demanding food, until armed troops restored an uneasy order. During the same year the United States Supreme Court ruled in the Dred Scott case that a Negro slave who entered a nonslaveholding state did not become a free citizen—a major setback for abolitionists like Blackwell who hoped to end slavery by working within the government.

Antoinette Blackwell absorbed her new role as wife and mother with no sign of regret or mourning over her freer days as a single traveling lecturer and preacher. She wrote to Susan B. Anthony in September 1857:

> I am getting invitations to Lyceums occasionally. Florence is getting teeth & is cross enough, & really sick besides,

some days.... I am very well and in good spirits & of course
very busy.[13]

To Anthony's dismay, the National Woman's Rights Convention scheduled for the fall of 1857 had to be canceled because too
many of its leaders were absorbed by childbearing. Lucy Stone's
daughter, Alice Stone Blackwell, was born in September of that
year.

By the fall of 1857, Antoinette Blackwell was pregnant
again; the new baby was expected in the spring, a year and a
half after Florence. It is not clear whether Antoinette had the
information to control either the number of children she would
bear or the spacing between them.[14] Given her desire for a large
family—and her age—it is unlikely she would have chosen any
different childbearing pattern.

Antoinette and Samuel's second daughter, Mabel, was
born in April 1858. Antoinette reported to Anthony, "My new
baby is a strong stout girl.... I am very well."[15] The news
provoked a reproach from Anthony:

> Now, Nettie, *not another baby*, is my *peremptory com-*
> *mand, two* will solve the *problem* whether a *woman can* be
> anything *more* than a *wife* and *mother* better than a half
> dozen or *ten even* .... I don't really want to be a *downright*
> *scolder*, but I can't help looking after the married sheep of
> the flock a wee bit. I am sure it is folly for any human being
> to follow too many professions at the same time.... I am
> glad you are getting on so finely. Mrs. Stanton sends love
> and says "if you are going to have a large family of chil-
> dren, go right on and finish up at once, as she has done.
> She has only devoted *18 years* out of the *very heart* of
> *existence* here to the great work." But *I say stop now*,
> once and for all. Your life work will be arduous enough
> with two.[16]

Along with her teasing, Anthony was afraid that motherhood
and domesticity would keep Blackwell away from what
Anthony considered the more important work of politics. She
lamented to Elizabeth Cady Stanton:

> Those of you who have the talent to do honor to poor—oh!
> how poor—womanhood, have all given yourself over to
> baby-making; and left poor brainless me to do battle

alone. It is a shame. Such a body as I might be spared to
rock cradles. But it is a crime for you and Lucy Stone and
Antoinette Brown to be doing it.[17]

Stanton, who had just given birth to her seventh—and
last—child, was much more encouraging. Like Blackwell,
Stanton was committed to carrying on both public work and
childrearing, unwilling to give up either. She wrote to Blackwell in the spring of 1858:

> I was so happy to hear that you had another daughter. In
> spite of all Susan's admonitions I do hope you and Lucy
> will have all the children you desire. I would not have one
> less than seven, in spite of all the abuse that has been
> heaped upon me for such extravagance. Just as soon as I
> can summon the courage to enter my cold garret and
> overhaul the trunks of winter clothing, you shall have all
> that remains of my baby-wardrobe.... Can we depend
> upon you for a speech at our coming Anniversary?[18]

Although Blackwell was not emotionally as close to Stanton as
to Anthony or Lucy Stone—often disagreeing vehemently with
Stanton on issues such as religion and divorce—she must have
appreciated Stanton's support for her choice of roles.

During 1858 Antoinette and Samuel moved from Newark
to a farm near Millburn, New Jersey, with their two daughters
and a "good-natured Irish girl" who helped with the cooking,
cleaning, and child care. At last Blackwell had the rural tran-
quility she wanted, as well as space for a garden:

> The quiet life there was extremely restful and delightful.
> Our home was an old farmhouse near the road, then very
> little traveled.... We had a wide and fine view of the
> surrounding country with hills above rising still higher. It
> was a new and fascinating experience to watch the coming
> up of storms, the clouds with their lights and shadows and
> the evenings with their moonlight or their wealth of stars.
> Even the smoke and slight sound of the railroad trains as
> they wound their way along in the valley had their own
> attraction.... The quiet village of Millburn and the scat-
> tered farmsteads gave a pleasant and civilized aspect to the
> landscape which in other parts was of a much wilder
> type.[19]

Antoinette and Samuel both relished the new experiences of parenthood. She described watching young Florence learning to talk:

> She had not yet begun to put together sentences when one day as she sat on the floor playing with toys, a large heavy cat came along and seating herself on the child's dress, calmly went to sleep. The child occasionally stroked the cat, evidently enjoying its quiet presence. After a time she wished to get up and tried to rouse the cat. Then she tried with her whole little strength to push the cat away. I watched her curiously to see what she would do, trying to keep my eyes on a book I was reading so that she might not appeal to me too quickly. To my astonishment she burst out with her first full sentence, "Up a daisy, naughty pussy!" This incident led Mr. Blackwell and me to reflect upon the stimulating effect of outside conditions upon language as well as upon other acquirements.[20]

At the same time, Antoinette Blackwell had no intention of retreating entirely from writing, speaking, and preaching. She wanted both the challenge of her own intellectual work and the richness of family life, and was determined to have both. She tried to remain active in the woman's rights movement, which meant primarily giving speeches at conventions. She wrote to Anthony shortly after Mabel's birth:

> I see that you have advertised your Convention and list of speakers. Though I especially requested you to consider me as one expecting to take part in the meeting, you choose to quite ignore me.... The public has nothing to do with my babies or my home affairs. It may take care of its own personal interests as best it may and I will do the same but since I fully expect and intend to take part in a public anniversary I do not [see] any particular reason for setting to work the inquiry why I am not working in that direction.[21]

Anthony enthusiastically corrected the list of speakers, writing back to Blackwell that "no one elucidates great fundamental principles better than Antoinette Brown, with grand illustrations of life."[22] Blackwell did speak at the Ninth National Woman's Rights Convention in New York City in May 1858. Later that spring she went with Samuel to Boston for some antislavery meetings, and did some lecturing on the way home. She felt that she could combine marriage and childrearing with lecturing and conventions.

Soon, however, a new crisis arose. In July 1858, three-month-old Mabel developed an infection with a high fever. Elizabeth Blackwell came out from New York City to care for her, but with no success. At the beginning of August, Antoinette wrote to Lucy Stone, "Our hearts are vacillating between hope and fear.... What a world of new emotions and experiences has come with these children!"[23] Within a few weeks, the baby was dead.

Antoinette was overcome with grief. She confided to Lucy Stone that losing a baby "is almost like losing something of one's own life."[24] It was hardly her first encounter with the death of loved ones, but this affected her more intensely than the deaths of her siblings. She found it "hard... to quite rally from the unexpected blow."[25]

Despite her grief, she wrote to Anthony sometime in August to suggest that the two of them, plus Stanton, plan a lecture tour of New York state for the coming winter. Anthony was delighted; she wrote back early in September, "Your 'pet plan' is worthy [of] 'Napoleon' herself—Your proposal fills me with new hope and new energy to rush into the battle."[26] Blackwell was deeply disappointed when Anthony's own poor health forced her to call off the trip:

> You will never know what a sharp twinge of disappointment came also until you have nearly abandoned the platform for years and then think of stepping on again in a long free talk of at least a month. I did long for a chance to pour my heart all out in this great woman question once more and could see and can see no way to do it but in a series of Conventions.... Lecturing is neither my natural nor education fort; still it is, and is to be an incident of life.... Yes, I will speak in your course at Rochester if you wish it and on the day you name if that is fully decided upon; but if you *can* fix the date positively I should like it, for then I may try to arrange for some other meetings on the way.[27]

Anthony suggested, as an alternative to the lecture tour, that Blackwell begin preaching regularly again. Blackwell was less enthusiastic about that idea than about lecturing on woman's rights:

Now you will ask will your advice be followed, the hall
taken and the preaching commenced? Not just at present. . . . The public has forgotten me entirely and has no
wish to have its memory quickened. If it were, there would
arise the dim phantom of an orthodox young clergywo-
man whom some people watched as they would a newly
discovered insect to see how soon it was going to burn its
wings in the candle and which finally disappeared somewhere and was reported to have fallen into the grave of
matrimony. It is the *unorthodox* reserection that I dread. I
may preach any number of occasional sermons; but to take
a hall and let it be a fixed thing that I have begun lecturing
again must call up either disagreeable criticism or silent
contempt.[28]

What Blackwell feared was that her growth away from
orthodox Congregational doctrine would be seen as evidence
that her ordination had been almost a hoax, that she was not
serious about preaching the Gospel. In fact, she felt more secure
about her own religious beliefs than she had when she left her
South Butler parish nearly five years before:

Marriage when I was in a state of unbelief, and the hope-
fulness and advancing confidence of my husband in his
own religious transition from Presbyterianism as he
grounded his belief upon the love of God and men, and the
helpfulness of the little children when they came had
saved me from despair, and gradually built up for me a far
firmer and more confident belief in God as the all-in-all of
mind and spirit and as the creator of the universe by the
limitation of his own power in the limited individual
units of his creation.[29]

Blackwell planned eventually to return to a pastoral job; she
ended one of her letters to Lucy Stone, "Much love to Henry.
Thank him for offering to be one of the Deacons of my church.
He may have a chance yet."[30]

Despite that security, Blackwell was questioning her ability to speak and to draw audiences, although she had been a
popular speaker only five years earlier. She wrote gloomily to
Stone in April 1859:

The world has voted me dead long ago. I have been coolly
told over & over again that the time was when I stood first

as a preacher but now a host of women mostly spiritualists have "gone ahead" of me.

But in all soberness I often doubt whether I can ever do anything worth while publicly. I am not a popular speaker. My subjects are metaphysical & not well adapted to the masses. . . . I am too poor to attempt anything & also too much oppressed with a consciousness of my own deficiencies to strike out boldly.[31]

She later explained:

My religious views were rapidly crystalizing after the several years of loss of faith; but they were not really well and consistently formed in all of the many-sided directions into which speculation and investigation had carried me. The many home duties and interests, while of real value to my personal growth even in the direction of theology, had not afforded time for a really consistent harmonizing of various many-sided questions.[32]

But unlike Anthony, Lucy Stone could offer no encouragement. Since her marriage, Stone herself had withdrawn from public speaking, overcome by severe migraine headaches and the awesome responsibility of childrearing. She wrote to Antoinette:

I wish I felt the old impulse and power to lecture, both for the sake of cherished principles and to help Harry with the heavy [financial] burden he has to bear—but I am afraid, and dare not trust Lucy Stone. I went to hear E.P. Whipple lecture on Joan d'Arc. It was very inspiring and for the hour I felt as though all things were possible to me. But when I came home and looked in Alice's sleeping face and thought of the possible evil that might befall her if my guardian eye was turned away, I shrank like a snail into its shell and saw that for these years I can be only a mother— no trivial thing either.[33]

It was a sharp contrast to Stone's initiative and assertiveness at Oberlin, when she had persistently prodded Antoinette Brown not to "settle into something less than you ought to be."[34]

Anthony's suggestion caught hold, however. In the winter of 1859 Antoinette Blackwell began to plan a "New York experiment," hoping to rent a hall and preach every Sunday

evening for an extended period. The most pressing obstacle was
money. Once she began preaching, she would be taking in
some money from collections; but before she could arrange for
a hall, she needed a down payment securely in hand. In 1852
Greeley and several others had stood ready to underwrite just
such a venture. Now, Anthony warned, it would be more difficult to find outside funding except by drawing on Samuel
Blackwell's capital:

> I am glad you will go forward in faith that the end will
> come. It is due yourself to try the experiment and those
> who love you most will I am sure feel it is a pleasure to lend
> a helping hand financially.... I can see how you must
> shrink from drawing heavily upon the finances of the one
> you most love & cherish—and I can see too, that to aid you
> in carrying to success your long cherished ideal would be
> the most precious blessing to his soul. I expect it will be
> more difficult to get men to open their purses in aid of any
> project for *Mrs. Blackwell*, than it used to be for *Antoinette
> Brown*—for now the query first suggested to every man's
> mind is, "Where's her husband, why doesn't he help her?"
> ... But notwithstanding all the mountains in the way, I
> cannot but feel that if you are ready *spiritually*, mentally &
> physically, strong all round, to begin your *great world
> work*, you should do so—even though no human being
> should promise to share the burdens—five or six hundred
> dollars out of your own and loved ones little all, would be
> most profitably invested, and would yield far richer har-
> vests to you than added houses & acres.[35]

Anthony did not realize that, although Samuel Blackwell fully
approved of Antoinette's endeavors, they had no "little all" to
draw on. Antoinette complained to Lucy Stone:

> To take a $20 hall upon uncertainties is out of the question
> while we owe more than $7000 dollars of debts, and have
> nothing to pay with but real estate which is eating us up
> with taxes instead of being of any service at present.[36]

Antoinette Blackwell hoped to draw on a special fund set
up to promote woman's rights by underwriting publications
and lectures. She knew that its trustees, Susan B. Anthony,
Lucy Stone, and Wendell Phillips, all supported her work. She
asked Stone:

Do you think you could conscienciously contribute something from the Woman's Rights Fund towards defraying
the expenses of a Hall for me in New York during six
months of next winter. You would pay a lecturer say $10
dollars per week. Now I believe that I should really do
more good to the cause of woman by speaking there once
every sabbath, *sermons carefully prepared*, than by 4 lectures up & down the country every week.... It does seem to
me $250 of that fund could not be better or more legiti-
mately applied.[37]

Stone readily agreed, but she was outvoted by the other two
trustees; most likely they did not believe that Blackwell's
preaching would directly aid woman's rights.

Antoinette Blackwell knew of no other means to earn
money than by public speaking. After several months of correspondence, she and Anthony decided to embark on a three-
month lecture tour of upstate New York. Blackwell's primary
goal was to raise funds for her preaching venture. She wrote to
Lucy Stone:

I [am] out on this tour almost for the sole purpose of
making the poor 12 or 15 dollars per week that I may have
something to begin the N.Y. experiment with this winter.
Of course the subject, political rights for woman, is a
grand one & has my fullest sympathies.... This will say
that I am alive again; it *may* bring some Lyceum invitations; but I wish most to begin my proper work & to be able
to carry it on, while I still have the home & its goods also.[38]

Blackwell left Florence, by now almost three years old, with her
adoring grandparents in Henrietta for the summer. She did not
worry about leaving Samuel for such a long time:

The truth is I fall in love with you anew every time we
separate.... If we are to know just how much we are to
each other, it seems decidedly well to separate now and
then to test the matter. I suppose lovers quarrels have
something of that character; but as we never quarrel, taking a trip somewhere for a few days answers the purpose
very well.[39]

The two women went mainly to Saratoga, Niagara, and other
summer resorts. Blackwell reported to Lucy Stone:

I have never known so cordial an earnestness on the part of
the people before. It is the thinking earnest people who
come to hear. The rest stay away. The fashionables do
their best to ignore us; but the people are awake and eager
to hear. I think I speak better than I have ever done
before—I know I do.[40]

By the end of the summer, Antoinette Blackwell had regained
her self-confidence about speaking, and had earned enough
money to begin the New York experiment. Upon returning
home, she began at once to combine public preaching with her
domestic responsibilities. She reported to Susan B. Anthony:

Fancy me spending four mortal days from morning till
night tramping up and down New York streets and stairs,
interspersed with omnibus rides, in search of a suitable
hall to preach in; then fancy me sitting down in the midst
of it all to write an appropriate introductory sermon,
going in by the Sunday afternoon boat, preaching it, and
coming home to breakfast and to a dressmaker next morning...[The hall] was packed with a good listening
audience and many turned away.[41]

Through the winter and spring of 1859-60, Blackwell
made the trip to New York to preach every Sunday evening. She
also took at least one longer trip, a visit to Antioch College in
Ohio to speak with the women students about her life and work
as a minister. That visit inspired one of the students, Olympia
Brown, to persevere in her own desire to become a minister; she
went on to theological school and was ordained in the Universalist Church in 1863.

By the spring of 1860—her thirty-fifth birthday—Antoinette Blackwell had apparently succeeded in reestablishing
herself as a minister. But her venture was short-lived. She found
it difficult to preach regularly in addition to her responsibilities at home. Even with Bridget, the hired maid, helping with
cooking and cleaning, the work required to maintain a household was overwhelming. Blackwell wrote wearily to Anthony
after their lecture trip:

So you wonder at my unaccountable silence. Poor child!
Then listen, pity "a poor married woman" and forgive.
The ordeal which I have passed through!...

Remember that a little three year old is capable of growing out of everything it wears once in three months, just the time of my absence, and fancy me set down in a *very* dirty house, just on the outside edge of cold weather with a child minus one decent or comfortable winter suit, a husband whose garments as well as himself have been deserted the whole season, and one's own wardrobe the worse for wear. Then there is the whole winter store of coal and provisions to be taken in, a garden to be covered up from the frost, seeds to save, label and put up for spring, bulbs to store away, and shrubs to transplant.... This, Susan, is woman's sphere![42]

The preaching venture eventually foundered on financial problems, not domestic ones; she could not continue indefinitely when the donations she collected did not even pay for renting the hall. After six months, Wendell Phillips paid off the accumulated debt from his own pocket, and the experiment was over. By the time she gave up the New York venture, Antoinette Blackwell was pregnant again; another daughter, Edith Brown Blackwell, was born in December 1860. For all practical purposes, Blackwell's work as a minister and lecturer was at a standstill. To many people—including, undoubtedly, Susan B. Anthony—it looked as if Antoinette Brown, minister and public figure of the 1850s, had buried herself in domestic responsibilities.[43]

Antoinette Brown Blackwell, ca. 1870

PRIVATE AND PUBLIC INTERESTS

Soon after Edith Brown Blackwell's birth, events outside the Blackwell homestead put an end to any possibility of renewing the preaching experiment. The debate between abolitionists and slaveholders finally erupted into open civil war. On December 24, 1860, in the wake of Republican Abraham Lincoln's election to the presidency, South Carolina voted to withdraw from the United States of America. In early February, before Lincoln's inauguration, representatives of seven southern states formed the Confederate States of America. On April 12, 1861, confederate troops opened fire on Fort Sumter, South Carolina. President Lincoln called up 75,000 men for military duty and declared a naval blockade of the entire southern coast.

At home in the quiet New Jersey hills, Antoinette Blackwell complained to Susan B. Anthony:

> The war news occupies my whole thought.... I cannot write on anything else and do not feel equal to sermonizing on those topics. I fully planned to give several sermons this spring in New York but it is utterly useless to speak on any other topic than that of the times, and with all my cares I am not equal to the emergency I fear.[1]

The organized woman's rights movement, like all the prewar reform groups, suspended its activities during the war; the last Woman's Rights Convention was held in February 1861.

The Civil War had surprisingly little direct impact on the Blackwell family. Antoinette later explained:

> When the Civil War broke out and the newspapers brought us constant rumors of calamity, it was almost impossible in the peace and quiet of our surroundings to credit them. On the Fourth of July 1861 Henry Blackwell and Lucy Stone with their little Alice spent the day with us. The two brothers wandered far away over the hills. The sisters went up to the summer house placed just at the edge of the mountain rise. To sit there talking of private and public interests more personal to ourselves while the children played on the grass, little Alice and Florence running

hither and thither gathering treasures and appealing to us
as happy children do, it seemed impossible that cruel
slaughter and a Civil War that might wreck our country
itself could be in active progress.[2]

The closest reminder of the reality of the war was the
continual call for volunteers for the Union Army. Henry and
Samuel Blackwell, along with many others who had long
supported the abolitionist cause, felt torn between two ideals.
As abolitionists, they wanted to aid the cause of freedom for
black slaves; but they were also pacifists. Antoinette wrote that
the family "all abhorred the thought of war, although they
realized it was in this case inevitable."[3] In 1863 President Lincoln introduced conscription to fill the Union Army, touching
off violent riots in many northern cities. Even so, none of the
Blackwell men was forced to fight. Like many others who could
afford to do so, Henry and Samuel both avoided what
Antoinette called "the painful business of the draft" by paying
$300 each for someone to fight in their places.[4]

Northern women were asked to support the Union's fighting men in traditional ways, such as knitting and sewing. But
the women who had been working vigorously on the lyceum
circuit and in reform organizations were not content to sit at
home rolling bandages and waiting for the war to end. Many
played important administrative roles in the institutions that
emerged in response to the war. Dorothea Dix, Clara Barton,
Mary Livermore, and Dr. Elizabeth Blackwell took the lead in
organizing the Sanitary Commission, similar to the Red Cross,
which provided nursing and relief services to the army.

Other women, looking for ways to advance the cause of
women as well as that of abolition, focused on political action,
demanded that women participate in the ongoing political
discussions and decisions. Elizabeth Cady Stanton remarked to
Antoinette Blackwell at the beginning of the war, "Have not
the Lords of Creation clearly proved their incapacity to govern.
I wonder if black men and [all] women could do worse."[5] In the
spring of 1863, Stanton, Susan B. Anthony, Lucy Stone, and
other leading feminists called a meeting in New York City to
organize the Women's National Loyal League. They drew in
antislavery veterans such as Angelina Grimké Weld and Lucretia Mott, as well as women who simply wanted to help the
Union cause, many of whom had little interest in what they saw

as a separate issue of political rights for women. Stone came out of her self-imposed retirement to preside over the meeting.

The Women's National Loyal League embodied one of the most vital roles northern women played during the Civil War, that of inspiration and ideological support for the war effort. According to common stereotypes, women were considered innately peace-loving and gentle. Prior to and during the war, however, women produced a flood of propaganda that was anything but conciliatory. From Harriet Beecher Stowe's *Uncle Tom's Cabin* to Julia Ward Howe's "Battle Hymn of the Republic," they portrayed slaveholders as evil incarnate and military victory for the North as a victory for truth, democracy, and Christ. Their powerful rhetoric cloaked the war effort with legitimacy, and made it easier for Union politicians and generals to maintain the emotional commitment of their soldiers— "troop morale"—that made it possible for brother to kill brother for four long years.[6]

Antoinette Blackwell participated in this propaganda effort. Although she had not given an antislavery speech for some years, she spoke eloquently at the Loyal League meeting in 1863, linking the slavery issue to the democratic ideals she had learned from her parents:

> The consent of the governed is the sole, legitimate authority of any government! This is the essential, the peculiar creed of our republic. That principle is on one side of this war; and the old doctrine of might-makes-right, the necessary groundwork of all monarchies, is on the other. It is a life-and-death conflict between all those grand, universal, man-respecting principles which we call by the comprehensive term democracy, and all those partial person-respecting, class-favoring elements which we group together under that silver-slippered word aristocracy.... A nation proclaiming to the astonished world that governments derive all just powers solely from the consent of the governed, yet in the very fact of this assertion enslaving the black man [sic], and disfranchising half of its white citizens, besides minor things of like import and consistency —do you wonder that eighty years of such policy culminated in rebellion?[7]

The Women's National Loyal League was intended for action, not merely speeches. Anthony and Stanton, among others, pushed the organization into political involvement. They knew that, for many politicians, the central issue of the war was the South's secession, not slavery. President Lincoln's Emancipation Proclamation of January 1, 1863, had freed slaves only in the southern states. Congress was considering a constitutional amendment that would abolish slavery throughout the nation. Although women could not vote, they could certainly make their views known by petitions. Once before, in 1837, the Women's Anti-Slavery Society had organized such a petition campaign, and learned that many women found collecting signatures a comfortable style of political work. The tight-knit organization that grew out of the 1863 Loyal League meeting resolved to collect one million signatures—five percent of the population of the northern states—on petitions asking Congress to pass the Thirteenth Amendment. It was an ambitious goal, requiring long hours of work by more than the handful of dedicated women who had run woman's rights conventions. Anthony, working out of a tiny New York City office, coordinated the efforts of about 2,000 women around the country. On February 9, 1864, after fifteen months of intensive work, the petitions were presented to Congress with close to 400,000 signatures. In February 1865, Congress submitted the Thirteenth Amendment to the states; it was ratified within a year, abolishing slavery and involuntary servitude throughout the nation.

If Antoinette Blackwell helped at all in the 1863 petition campaign, it must have been in only minor ways. Blackwell's strength was enunciating broad principles; she left to others the tasks of translating those principles into specific campaigns. Even if Blackwell had the temperament for the details of political organizing, in the 1860s her circumstances made full-time public work virtually impossible. The women who ran the Loyal League were largely free from family and household responsibilities. Lucy Stone's only daughter, Alice Stone Blackwell, was rapidly developing into a teenage assistant to her mother. Elizabeth Cady Stanton's youngest child was born shortly after Antoinette Blackwell's oldest. Throughout the 1860s, Blackwell, in contrast to these close associates, was largely absorbed in her growing brood of little girls. In 1863, Florence turned seven, and Edith was almost three. A third daughter, Grace, was born in July 1863, in the middle of the Loyal League petition campaign. Antoinette's next pregnancy, the only male child she conceived, ended in a premature still-birth early in 1865.

Blackwell therefore did not share in the political transformation within the feminist community. Through the Loyal League petition campaign, Anthony and other feminists learned to administer an efficient political organization quite different from the loosely structured prewar conventions. When the war ended, they meant to use their new skills to gain political rights for white women as well as for newly freed black women and men.

On April 9, 1865, the Civil War officially ended with General Robert E. Lee's surrender at Appomattox, Virginia. A few days later, President Lincoln was assassinated. Congress proceeded with the reconstruction of the country—North and South—including amending the Constitution to help the newly freed slaves.

Antoinette and Samuel Blackwell's life, however, was affected more by their personal needs than by these external events. During the summer of 1865, Sam became ill after an unsuccessful attempt to climb Mount Washington in New Hampshire during a snowstorm. His doctors advised him not to return to work for at least several months. Instead of trying to stretch their meager savings, he and Antoinette decided to sell their Millburn farm to one of her Oberlin classmates. They took their three children for an extended visit at Antoinette's childhood home in Henrietta. Joseph and Abby Brown, both more than seventy years old, welcomed their grandchildren to the farm. When Samuel felt rested, he and Antoinette left the children and Bridget, their servant, at the farm and took a ten-day drive alone. It was their first vacation in the ten years they had been together. Antoinette later remembered:

> We drove first to Rochester and then followed the shore of Lake Ontario, stopping to rest as often as we chose in the shade of the luxuriant trees of the region, and taking our noon-day luncheon either in the carriage under some pleasant tree or in the shelter of a rock. At night we often stopped at some farmhouse which more than willingly opened its doors to us and provided the next day's luncheon. We carried a supply of books, one of us often reading aloud as the horse walked on at a leisurely pace. It was now the early fall and in this apple-growing region the trees were already bending under burdens of red and yellow

fruit, and glimpses through them of the blue of the lake
made a long series of charming pictures such as I have
never seen in any other region. It was altogether one of the
pleasantest outings of our joint lives.[8]

When the Blackwells returned from their trip, they decided
to rent an apartment in New York City for the winter, to spare
Sam the strain of commuting to his office. They left two-year-
old Grace with Bridget in Henrietta, and arranged for Florence
to live with Elizabeth Blackwell on Fifteenth Street and to
attend the new Friends Seminary a few blocks away. Only Edith
remained with her parents. Antoinette was grateful for the
reduced responsibility:

> Our families on both sides always came heartily to the
> rescue in any and every family emergency. This is a sug-
> gestive opening for the way in which women who take up
> public business may have the necessary help from inter-
> ested and affectionate relatives.[9]

By the summer of 1866 the Blackwells, reunited with all three
children, had bought a house in Somerville, New Jersey, a
small village near Newark, and were expecting another baby.

In New Jersey, Antoinette's primary community was the
extended Blackwell clan. Henry Blackwell, Lucy Stone, and
their daughter Alice lived close by, as did "Mother" Blackwell
and two of her adult children. The entire clan spent long
summers together on Martha's Vineyard, five miles off the
southern coast of Massachusetts. Henry, Lucy, and Alice visited
the island first. In 1866 Sam and Antoinette rented a small
cottage in the quiet "up-island" village of Chilmark. Antoinette later recalled their first trip to the Vineyard:

> We crossed from New Bedford in a small packet which ran
> semi-occasionally, landing on the north side at Menemsha
> Creek and waiting for an hour or two until the tide was
> favorable for sailing in through the ponds very close to the
> neighborhood of our home. We met a friendly greeting.
> Captain Flanders, who brought us over from the main-
> land, proved very approachable and glad to confide his
> reminiscences, and knowing that we were coming to a
> place where supplies were not easily procurable, he pro-
> posed to take us fishing on Squibnocket Pond. When we

arrived at the little rented cottage we found that our land-
lady had left us a delightful wild strawberry pie.[10]

Martha's Vineyard was inhabited for generations by
Algonquin Indians and Yankee whalers. Beginning in the
1830s it became a popular summer resort. Its first attraction was
a Methodist outdoor camp meeting, whose pavilion could hold
up to 10,000 people. Gradually, those who came to hear the
evangelical preaching came to enjoy the sun and ocean as well.
The tents at Oak Bluffs gave way to row upon row of small
summer cottages, filled with families who wanted to escape the
city but could not afford the fashionable older resorts such as
Saratoga or Newport. After the Civil War, summer vacation
homes became fashionable among a wide range of people, and
land prices on the island skyrocketed.

The Blackwells shunned the "Cottage City" at Oak Bluffs,
and in 1871, just before the real estate boom, bought a house on
a peninsula known as Quitsa. It was covered with neat farm-
houses, quiet hills, and sheep, with very few other summer
people. Nearby down the beach were the spectacular Gay Head
cliffs where the Algonquins still lived. Antoinette found it an
idyllic setting for writing, bathing, or walking, "less than a
quarter of a mile from the ocean with an easy walk, and a
charming row or sail through the ponds into Vineyard
Sound."[11] Eight or ten households of Blackwells bought houses
on the peninsula: Samuel, Antoinette, and their daughters;
Henry, Lucy, and Alice; and several of Samuel's sisters with
their assortment of adopted children. Antoinette's older
brother William Brown and his family later joined them.

Despite the idyllic setting, the Vineyard summers and the
continual presence of the Blackwell clan in Antoinette's life
were also a source of stress for her. Although Elizabeth and
Emily Blackwell, both physicians, were strong women pursuing nontraditional roles, they did not appreciate Antoinette's
intellectual work. In a rare display of bitterness, Antoinette told
Alice Stone Blackwell some years later, "I think Aunt Elizabeth
thought I was a failure, and in her book she never mentioned
me, though she spoke so often and so kindly of Lucy."[12] Elizabeth and Emily—both of whom had adopted children—
believed that Antoinette and Sam were too permissive with
their growing daughters, feelings that intensified as the children approached adolescence. Lucy Stone, closer to the

Blackwells than Antoinette was, maintained a warm friendship with Antoinette but did not provide strong affirmation of her professional work. In that context, it must have been difficult indeed for Antoinette to maintain a positive image of herself in other than domestic pursuits.

Similarly, Antoinette found little encouragement among active feminists. Although she must have had ample opportunities to meet with them, especially during the year of 1865-66 when she lived in New York City, she had only a limited involvement in the organized woman's movement.

After the Civil War, feminists organized one woman's rights convention like those of the 1850s, which was held in New York in May 1866. Antoinette Blackwell was one of the featured speakers, a role in which she excelled and felt comfortable. She discovered, however, that the intense political work that had been going forward over the past five years now made obsolete the old format of speeches and resolutions on a wide range of issues. The convention voted to form a more structured organization called the American Equal Rights Association, which would work actively for more political rights for both white women and newly freed Negroes. As with the Loyal League petition campaign, Blackwell found it difficult to participate in this new push for political implementation of feminist goals.

The Equal Rights Association quickly focused on the right to vote as a symbol of human dignity and full citizenship as well as a means of obtaining other rights through legislation. At first, Susan B. Anthony, Elizabeth Cady Stanton, and other leaders of the association believed that the Republican Party would thank women for their contributions to the war effort by allowing them to vote. They were astonished when the Fourteenth and Fifteenth Amendments were drafted so as to enfranchise male Negroes but not women. Suddenly woman suffrage, one of a long list of demands of the prewar woman's rights conventions, became the central issue around which the Equal Rights Association coalesced. For the next four years, many of Blackwell's friends lobbied intensively for the inclusion of woman suffrage in the postwar constitutional amendments. By early 1870, however, both federal amendments were ratified without enfranchising women.

Despite these setbacks, many feminists believed that, with a concerted effort, nationwide woman suffrage could soon be achieved. A sixteenth amendment giving women the right to vote was introduced into Congress in March 1869. Feminists seriously underestimated the opposition to that one simple demand, and the decades of difficult work it would consume. Some efforts were also made to achieve woman suffrage in individual states. In the spring of 1867 Lucy Stone and Henry Blackwell traveled all the way to Kansas to campaign vigorously—but unsuccessfully—for passage of a state woman suffrage referendum. Many feminists attributed the defeat, at least in part, to the silence of influential liberals—especially newspapers, including Greeley's *New York Tribune*—who feared that discussions of woman suffrage would jeopardize passage of the parallel Negro suffrage referendum.

The Kansas campaign brought out the growing tensions among those who favored woman suffrage. There were tactical and ideological differences in how women viewed the drive for Negro male suffrage. There were disagreements about whether to focus on a federal amendment or to work in individual states, and about whether advocacy of other reforms such as liberal divorce laws would jeopardize the suffrage cause. These political disagreements were exacerbated by personal conflicts among the women who were the movement's acknowledged leaders.

The Equal Rights Association soon developed two opposing camps.[13] Stanton and Anthony led one faction, often considered the more radical one. They encouraged women to oppose the Fourteenth and Fifteenth Amendments unless woman suffrage were included, and advocated other reforms, including pressing for more liberal divorce laws. They welcomed alliances with anyone who supported woman suffrage, including the notorious Victoria Woodhull and a wealthy and eccentric Irish revolutionary named Francis Train. Train poured in money for speaking tours, and provided financial backing for Anthony's longtime dream, a nationwide feminist newspaper, on the condition that he would have some space for his own views. The first issue of the *Revolution* was published in January 1868 with the motto, "Principle, not policy: Justice, not favors. —Men, their rights and nothing more: Women, their rights and nothing less." From its inception, the *Revolution* was Anthony's paper, reflecting her opinions and priorities.

Instead of unifying feminists, the newspaper only further antagonized those who disagreed with it. Lucy Stone, Henry Blackwell, and Julia Ward Howe, the center of a developing

Boston faction, refused to write for the *Revolution* or to be associated with it. The Howe-Stone-Blackwell group included many old-guard abolitionists, both men and women, who considered rights for male Negroes at least as pressing as woman suffrage. They firmly supported ratification of the federal Negro suffrage amendments even though women were not included. Their views on marriage and organized religion were closer to the American middle-class mainstream.

At first, the disputes resembled arguments among siblings within a close-knit family. Stanton wrote to one friend:

> I received your kind note and hasten to say that I fully agree with you as to the wisdom of keeping all our misunderstandings to ourselves. No word or pen of mine shall ever wrong or detract from any woman, especially one who has done so good a work for woman as Lucy Stone.[14]

She confessed to Antoinette Blackwell, "I wish so much that all petty jealousies could be laid aside, for all that our cause needs now for a speedy success is union and magnanimity among women."[15] The conflict could not be so easily resolved. The formal split came in May 1869, after a stormy meeting of the Equal Rights Association. One attender, Mary Livermore, described the same meeting as "more resembling a Tammany Hall than a Reform meeting."[16] Antoinette Blackwell was one of the speakers at that meeting, but she minimized the depth of the group's dissension. After the meeting, she wrote to one friend, "I too was worried with the Convention quarreling .... But we must bear and forbear, and not expect too much magnanimity in a miscellaneous world."[17]

The next night a small select group met in the *Revolution* office to organize a National Woman Suffrage Association (NWSA), with Elizabeth Cady Stanton as president. The new association said that it welcomed all suffrage workers. In fact, the group's weekly meetings in New York City limited its geographic scope, and it was dominated by the ideologies and personalities of Stanton and Anthony.

Lucy Stone and Julia Ward Howe, who had not been invited to the NWSA organizational meeting, saw the new group as a deliberate attempt to cut out the more conservative wing of the suffrage movement. In response, they formed a rival organization, the American Woman Suffrage Association (AWSA). Men were welcomed as full members of AWSA; Henry

Ward Beecher, a popular minister, was chosen as its first president. AWSA conventions were held at various locations around the country, and were composed of delegates from local suffrage groups to ensure nationwide representation. Early in 1870 Lucy Stone and Henry Blackwell started a second nationwide feminist newspaper, the *Woman's Journal*. With a firmer financial base and a less radical editorial policy, it soon outstripped the *Revolution* and circulated widely among middleclass and professional women. It provided a forum for news about women in traditionally "masculine" occupations and for discussion of issues like dress reform, in addition to woman suffrage.

Antoinette Blackwell refused to ally herself definitively with either faction. Her views, especially her support for organized religion and for marriage, were closer to those of the American Association. Her personal loyalty to Lucy Stone and Henry Blackwell also drew her to AWSA. Despite those ties, however, she remained a close friend of Stanton, Anthony, Lucretia Mott, and others in the National Association.

Blackwell's aloofness reflected in part her distaste for political conflicts. As they concentrated on the single tangible goal of suffrage, other feminists discovered that effective social reform work involved making choices, choosing allies and enemies, and narrowing issues. In this sense, the suffrage split marked the coming-of-age and the growing sophistication of the feminist movement. Blackwell failed to participate in that coming-of-age, partly because of family commitments that prevented her from joining in the day-to-day work, but also because of her own temperament and philosophy. To those who were active in one or the other suffrage organization, it appeared that Blackwell removed herself from the political arena simply to avoid making the difficult choices that maturity demanded. In this judgment, however, they were mistaken.

Blackwell viewed the suffrage movement as only one small aspect of the transcendent moral progress of the universe. The decision to focus on suffrage was not unanimous. Quaker Lucretia Mott, the seventy-four-year-old godmother of the movement, questioned the value of the electoral process itself.[18] Blackwell, although she believed heartily in suffrage and the democratic political process, considered other issues more central—women's education, for example, or opportunities for work outside the home. She regarded squabbles over tactics as matters that were too petty to be fretted over. For her the key to freedom—for women and everyone else—was moral reeducation, not suffrage, nor even the entire process of political decision making. Given that underlying approach, it is hardly surprising that in the 1860s, as in the early 1850s, she chose to concentrate her energy on a predominantly individual search for universal truth. She was not alone; other feminists were more concerned with divorce, health care, alcoholism, or the social problems of poverty than with suffrage. Her choices during these years reflected the intellectual strength and creativity of Antoinette Blackwell more faithfully and fully than any amount of organized political work she might have done.

"Lunch in the Grove," an illustration from
Antoinette Brown Blackwell, The Island Neighbors

ℐ Chapter 9 ℛ

A FRESH DIP INTO METAPHYSICS

The year 1869 brought two milestones in Antoinette Blackwell's life: the birth of her last daughter, and the publication of
her first book. The first forecast the eventual lightening of her
household responsibilities. The second, a birth of a different
sort, announced that, although Blackwell rarely appeared in
the ranks of the women who commanded public attention in
political battles, she had not retired into the kitchen and the
nursery. She later explained that she had changed her mode of
self-expression to one that did not require traveling:

> As the responsibilities of family life increased the extended
> trip[s] for lecturing and preaching were naturally super-
> ceded to a great extent by writing which easily coincided
> with family duties.[1]

Blackwell had always defined her work to include writing
for publication as well as for speech making. As a young girl
she had dreamed romantically of becoming an author, perhaps
a poet. At Oberlin, she told Lucy Stone that she expected to
divide her time between writing and public speaking:

> Much is to be accomplished in reforming the world by
> writing; more persons are accessible by this means than by
> any other and it seems to me that almost any one can
> accomplish more by both methods than by being confined
> to either.
> I know a person needs to be talented to write any thing
> which is worth reading and yet the truth even if plainly
> told will produce an effect and the novelty of many of my
> subjects will ensure a reading for a time at least. Then I
> love to write and by taking great pains—more than I have
> ever done yet, shall I do believe do passably well.[2]

In the decade of studying since 1859, Blackwell had
focused her attention on what would be her central interest for
many years: a broad abstract vision of the nature of the universe
and the place of God and humanity in it. She read extensively,

especially books and articles by philosophers and, increasingly, scientists.

It took Blackwell many years to digest the concepts she read and to express them in her own way. Aside from the sheer difficulty of the questions she addressed, her studying was carried on in the midst of managing a household and raising five young children, a situation with which professional scientists, mostly men, rarely had to contend. She must have done much of her thinking while she washed dishes, planted flower bulbs, canned vegetables, and did a hundred other tasks. Those mundane details of daily life crept into her thinking, so that her writings on the most abstract topics were punctuated by analogies to concrete events:

> A negative belief, a belief based upon nothing except the bare fact that it is "necessary to one's comfort" has no more solidity than a girl's fancy that her doll is enjoying a delicious breakfast.[3]

During these years, Blackwell returned to writing primarily as a means of resolving issues: "As my views matured, naturally I began to write them down as a better method of clearing my own thought."[4] Preparing essays for publication apparently came later. Blackwell chose to write a series of relatively brief essays. She explained to her readers:

> My aim has been to make each article as complete and distinct in itself as the nature of the topic would allow; and yet to connect them all in a progressive series of thought.[5]

Undoubtedly this format suited her working conditions, which preluded long stretches of uninterrupted writing.[6] *Studies in General Science,* a compilation of essays, was the first published fruit of that process, and it shows that by 1869 Blackwell had developed a solid philosophical base that would remain intact for the rest of her life.

Metaphysics, the branch of philosophy that covers the fundamental causes and processes in the universe, was of interest to more than a few stuffy academics. Philosophical discussions were as much a part of everyday life among the educated middle class as they had been in upstate New York during Blackwell's childhood. Only the terminology had changed. In the 1830s the talk had been of damnation and righteousness; by the late 1860s it was full of startling new concepts: evolution, natural selection, the struggle for existence. A philosophical revolution was under way, not only in the disciplines of botany and geology that had given birth to the new theories, but more broadly in the ways ordinary people viewed the world. The transition would extend well into the twentieth century. Blackwell, motivated at first by her need for a personal religious faith to replace the orthodox beliefs shattered during her year at South Butler, found herself in the midst of the great debate between science and religion.

By the 1860s the debate was focused on the work of two Englishmen, Charles Darwin and Herbert Spencer.[7] Darwin began his inquiry with empirical data, not, as a theologian might, with sacred texts or abstract principles. On an extended sea voyage to South America and islands in the Pacific Ocean, he observed diverse—but obviously related—species of plants and animals. He began to question the prevailing view that each species had existed forever, immutably, in its present form. In *Origin of Species*, published in 1859, Darwin proposed that the variety of plants and animals, each adapted to its own particular environment, resulted from an evolutionary process in which organisms changed over time, the sturdiest and best suited organisms in each generation surviving the ravages of nature and predators. Even human beings, he theorized, had developed gradually from more primitive species, rather than being created initially in human form as described in the Bible. *Origin of Species* quickly gained a wide audience among intellectuals on both sides of the Atlantic; in twelve years it ran through six editions. By the late 1860s, its philosophical and theological implications had virtually overshadowed its scientific ones, which awaited later discoveries of the mechanisms of genetic inheritance.

Darwinism challenged many cherished tenets of orthodox Christian faith. If the theory of evolution was true, the creation story in Genesis must not be—a direct challenge to the Divine inspiration and literal truth of the entire Bible. Darwin himself was aggressively agnostic and stated plainly that the Bible was worth no more than the beliefs of any barbarian, a view that shocked most Americans. Second, if, as Darwin proposed, evolution happened more or less mechanically by natural selection and adaptation, there was no room in the universe for Divine guidance and design. Third, the cruelty of the evolutionary process, the wasteful deaths of millions of organisms who failed to adapt or were consumed by predators, contradicted an image of God as compassionate as well as omnipotent. Finally, Darwin's hypothesis implied that human beings were merely one rather accidental outcropping of the animal world, not beings specially created in the image of God. Victorian America, already shaken by a fratricidal war and enormous changes in its economic and social structure, reeled with uncertainty and insecurity in the face of these threats.[8]

The remainder of the philosophy that was known as "Darwinism" came from the writings of Herbert Spencer, a self-educated school teacher who applied the concept of evolution to human societies. In his books, *First Principles* and *Principles of Biology*, Spencer described the entire universe, natural and human, as integrated and coordinated in all its parts and progressing in predictable ways from simple to complex, from chaos to integration. In the absence of scientific data to the contrary, Spencer and many of his contemporaries assumed that all characteristics that an organism acquired during its lifetime—physical, moral, or intellectual—could be passed on to its offspring; any moral lapses or degenerate living would, therefore, endanger the vitality of future generations. Spencer used the term "survival of the fittest" to describe the process by which both animals and human beings progress. Like the liberal philosophers of the seventeenth century, Spencer believed that although Ultimate Reality is unknowable, the perfection of God is revealed in the observable phenomena of matter, motion, and force. The path to God, according to Spencer and his followers, was not mystical experience or study of sacred texts, but scientific study of the natural world.

Blackwell encountered the new theories within a few years after her own disaffection with orthodox Christian doctrine. She probably read both Darwin and Spencer's books as soon as they were available, and set out to reconcile them with her own developing beliefs. Blackwell's background in science was scanty. Like others who had gone to college prior to 1870, she had studied "natural philosophy," a generalized study of the physical universe but not science as such. Her principal exposure to the "scientific method" of testing hypotheses by controlled experimentation was the primitive experiments she and her older brother Samuel had conducted in their teens. She had no way to challenge or verify the empirical data, drawn largely from the study of animal species, upon which the new theories were based. Nevertheless, she quickly adopted the belief that the new science would provide solid answers to her philosophical questions. She opened *Studies in General Science* by affirming the possibility of finding God through His Creation, echoing the writings of Herbert Spencer:

> The Author of the moral universe, first writing his record in things, may or may not afterwards explain it in books, or by the mouth of inspired teachers; but the point to be made now is... where are those truths to be found at first hand, if one has power to discover or verify them for himself.... The direct exercise of one's own Perceptive Force is held to be the only mode by which he can obtain a knowledge of anything.[9]

The essential difficulty, which Blackwell never directly addressed, was that the same data could be explained in ways that indicated quite different moral lessons.

In the essays that make up *Studies,* Blackwell examined the most important points of dispute between the new science and traditional Christian doctrine. She specifically rejected the most extreme elements of Darwin's theory. For example, in "Different Types of Mind," she reaffirmed the unique place of humanity in the Divine scheme:

> But if we are akin to all inferior sentient beings, we are yet almost infinitely removed from them all, by the possession of powers which must make us kindred also with even Diety himself! Man alone, among all of earth's inhabitants, gives evidence of intellectual comprehensiveness enough to entitle him to be called a *rational* being.... Man alone, therefore, among them all, is a responsible moral agent!... Man alone possesses discriminations broad enough to enable him to distinguish between the intrinsically right and wrong, the true and the false, the beautiful and the ugly; and as his volitions and sensations are commensurate with his perceptions, he only can intelligently make his own and other lives more and more desirable, by a closer conformity with all established coordinations. He alone can enter upon a course of unlimited improvement—of unending progress.[10]

In her later writings, Blackwell would reaffirm her faith that human society and morals were evolving toward increasing good, beauty, and cooperation.

In an essay entitled "The 'Struggle for Existence,'" Blackwell addressed the apparently Godless cruelty and wastefulness
of the natural world, which Darwin and Spencer assumed was
the mechanism for evolution:

> If the highest animals feed upon the more lowly, yet
> the highest of all, man himself, his organism once fallen
> into decay, becomes food for the very lowest, the plant.
>   Here, then, is a cycle of perpetual change—a most
> complicated system of economy for the utilization of mat-
> ter.... To be thus socially related, through our bodies as
> well as our minds, is but another evidence of the unity of
> the whole rational plan of creation. By no other conceiv-
> able scheme could so many living beings, who can attain
> to active sentience only through the cooperation of matter,
> have lived and enjoyed at all....
>   The more we give our attention to this subject, the
> more and higher evidence shall we find that the seeming
> cruelties and sufferings incident to the existing organic
> scheme, are only *seeming* cruelties, and that the highest
> beneficence has ordained them all.... No one can intelli-
> gently doubt that a larger number and a higher type of
> sentient beings may exist under the present system of
> interchanging organisms, than by any other which can be
> devised....
>   At any rate when the cat seems to be torturing her
> prey, or when we watch the spider who has been so beauti-
> fully instructed in the art of entrapping her flies, remem-
> bering how excessively ignorant we are, we need not in our
> hearts accuse God of malevolence!... The struggle for exis-
> tence, then, regarded in its whole scope, is but a perfected
> system of cooperations in which all sentient and unsen-
> tient forces mutually co-work in securing the highest ulti-
> mate good.[11]

Unlike Spencer, who saw in the natural world support for a
philosophy of rampant individualism, each organism or person scrambling to advance and survive at the expense of its
competitors, Blackwell viewed the same process as a sign of
cooperation and unity—each reading the facts so as to support
his or her political outlook.

In another essay in the book, Blackwell indicated her
disagreement with the social and political implications
Spencer drew from his theories. The "survival of the fittest"
was used throughout the nineteenth century to justify amoral
competition and individual profiteering in social and eco-

nomic decision making. Spencer himself proposed that unemployed persons—presumably those discarded by the labor market as unfit—should be allowed to starve.[12] That notion was naturally repugnant to a dyed-in-the-wool reformer like Blackwell. Her essay on "Social Progess" recalls the vision of gradual moral perfectibility expounded decades earlier by her mentor Charles Grandison Finney, and Blackwell's own sermons from the 1850s looking toward the dawning of a new moral order.

Blackwell did not completely reject individualism, or the prevailing economic view that each individual's pursuit of personal profit would lead to progress for the community:

> The mere love of personal gain may lead to the coordination of winds, waves, steam, or electricity to machinery, and thus to human control; but the result inevitably quickens the progress of the race many fold. A world spanned with telegraphs and railroads is impelled on in intellectual and moral advancement by the simple correlation of forces. The scheme of the universe so binds all things together that a forward move in any direction enlarges all other capabilities. This has been beautifully illustrated in almost every department of science.[13]

Blackwell did not consider the possibility that advances in one area, such as industrial production, might be balanced by deterioration in another, such as the stability of close-knit communities. She apparently had forgotten the "shadows of our social system" that had preoccupied her in New York some fifteen years earlier.

Unlike Spencer, however, Blackwell was not satisfied to let political and economic events unfold separate from moral decisions. In the same essay she stressed the connection between morality and true progress:

> All movements which combine the cooperative energies of many persons, and thus closely bind together the interests of the community, point to a new era of progress.... The code of social amenities has always been refined and elevated in common with other branches of science, however strong may have been the popular inclination to dissociate all higher morality from business relations, and from every-day life. Laws of qualitative value have been found so personally distasteful and self-subjugating when applied to quantitative affairs, that the world will not yet

believe that they are bound together from an inherent
unity in the general scheme embracing both; and not till it
fairly grasps this thought as a fixed reality, and applies it
to practice, shall we have entered on an era of progress
which can at all realize the ideal, ultimate good which
humanity is yet destined to attain. When the masses can
perceive that it is an unvarying fact, established in the
whole coordinated nature of things, that every mind must
learn to subject all quantitative values to the sublime law
of the qualitative, or suffer grievously in default of so
doing, then we shall soon progress into a literal earthly
millennium.[14]

In the final essay in *Studies*, entitled "The Creator," Black-
well linked her world view to her private religious experience.
The essay reflected a sense of the immediacy and presence of the
Divine, comparable to that which had supported Blackwell at
Oberlin and then apparently disappeared:

There are wrongs which a good man cannot right,
and they burden his soul! The more noble he is, the more
he suffers from a sense of his own incapacities, and the
boundless need of a Beneficient Helper.... To be assured
that there is an Almighty Arm and a Sleepless Omniscient
Eye, able to see all things and to reach everywhere, cannot
fail to bring its own comfort!
... The beautiful coordinations of things become too
self-evidently adapted to the highest well-being of all sen-
tient experience not to reveal the intelligence which coordinated them—the beneficence which was the underlying
element of the whole creative scheme.... Deity... must of
necessity be to us incomprehensible in the fullness of his
perfections. If we cannot altogether fathom the nature of
the bird or the insect, because they are so far removed from
our own experiences, and their capacities so unlike ours, it
must be hopeless to reach immeasurably above and
beyond our own powers.... We may as well, with our
present powers, hope to find the outermost world and the
pure space beyond in which all existence ceases, as to find
the mental conditions or limitations of the Infinite, Creative Mind. We know Him only as He is revealed in his
works![15]

In *Studies*, Blackwell largely accepted Spencer's philosophical
views, but reformulated in her own way the social and moral
implications of the natural world.

Studies in General Science received favorable notice in the popular press. The *New York Tribune* called it "a great work within a narrow compass."[16] Another reviewer hailed the book as signaling Blackwell's return to public life:

> We had lost sight of the once noted Miss Antoinette Brown beyond the fact that she followed the law of nature and became Mrs. Blackwell.... Why should a young woman who has had a careful education abandon study and continued culture from the moment of marriage?... We honor Mrs. Blackwell for putting her matured thoughts on paper and giving them to the public in a book. It is more womanly than preaching in our judgment.[17]

An anonymous reviewer for Susan B. Anthony's feminist paper, the *Revolution*, described the book as

> A very handsome volume of 350 pages, showing the author to be a diligent and perhaps promising student in her subjects but hardly ready yet to ascend the tripod as an oracle. Indeed the author says in her preface she makes no pretension to a practical, scientific knowledge of the subjects treated.... The tone of the book denotes rather a patient, careful habit of study of the investigations and conclusions of others than any new discoveries or explorations of its own. Still, it is a valuable addition to the class of literature to which it belongs, and the young women especially would do well to exchange all their Lady's Books, Fashion-plates, and most of their Novel and Newspaper reading, until they have mastered it.[18]

Despite these acclamations, Blackwell herself was unsatisfied with *Studies.* At the time it was published, she wrote to one friend:

> The orthodox world cannot approve it, and the philosophy of this country is so very largely orthodox, and the work itself in so unpopular a class of topics, that I am not over sanguine as to its reception. Not many, I suppose, can give much credence to the wisdom of a woman who chooses to go off on so many tangents.[19]

Her characterization of the topic as "unpopular" contrasts with the intense interest otherwise reported in Spencer and

Darwin's writings and the debates they generated. The same
letter reveals, however, the book's more serious flaw: Blackwell
was all too aware of herself as a *woman* writer, and therefore an
inadequate one. In the Preface to the book itself, she under-
mined the strength of her ideas by explaining apologetically
the process by which she arrived at them:

> The more metaphysical portions were the special
> studies of early youth, when everything pertaining to
> mental philosophy was eagerly devoured; with such
> imperfect digestion as youth has for abstract theori-
> zing. The theological and moral topics, though the
> constant food of childhood, yet pertain more especially to
> early womanhood, in an Orthodox Theological Semi-
> nary, and subsequently, as Pastor of an Orthodox Congre-
> gational Church; bound to the discharge of the usual
> duties of that position, in addition to the more general
> demands of the lecturing field,—a period in which, while
> trying with reasonable faithfulness outwardly to meet the
> just expectations of others, for myself, I studied first to
> reconcile revealed and natural religion, and afterwards to
> learn what the basis and the doctrines of the one absolute
> religon really are. The remaining more generally scien-
> tific portions of the work, with the labor of grouping and
> harmonizing the whole, were carried on in mature life; but
> while those earlier studies were hindered by duties which
> few women attempt to shoulder, the later ones were
> impeded (perhaps in both cases I should say aided) by
> duties which no man ever performed—those which
> devolve on the mother of a young family, all of whom are
> still in childhood.
> All these things are stated not in egotism, but yet
> frankly, as friend might speak to friend, to that generous
> public upon whose indulgence I must rely in its judgment
> of the many deficiencies and faults which must necessarily
> appear in the present volume.[20]

This Preface reveals an insecurity within Blackwell that eroded
her ability to write clearly and unselfconsciously. It probably
owed something to the general disregard of women's thought
and writing on topics other than domestic management. As a
younger woman, however, Blackwell had spoken out forcefully
and without apology, despite substantial opposition to a
woman studying theology or preaching the Gospel. Her self-
deprecation, a continuing problem in her later writing, seems

to have stemmed in part from the particular circumstances under which she worked.

Blackwell chose to work in relative isolation from other intellectuals. In part, the nature of her inquiry dictated isolation; William Henry Channing had warned her many years before that the search for religious truth was of necessity an individual pursuit. But Blackwell's deliberate choice of a rural home intensified her isolation, separating her from live interchange with other intellectuals. She insisted that she did not regret the choice; she wrote to one friend in the spring of 1869, "With a husband, four children, and ten times more than enough to do, one cannot well be lonely even in the deep country."[21] Nevertheless, if she and Sam had chosen to live in New York City, closer to Sam's office, or perhaps in Boston, she could have had considerably more face-to-face contact with other philosophers, scientists, and reformers, with the opportunity to test her ideas and arrive at new syntheses through bracing dialogues such as those she had enjoyed in the debating societies at Oberlin, or in the close fellowship of the lyceum circuit. She recognized the value of that interaction:

> A single hill of corn won't always do well in a garden all by itself, it wants for a whole cornfield round about it sometimes, just for sociability's sake. I find that old blood and young blood both begin to race through the veins a little more briskly for coming into company where every body is alive.[22]

She did not, apparently, take steps to follow her own advice. Instead, virtually all of her ideas came through reading, and her writings went out to a faceless audience. Her writings from the 1860s on have the aura of someone who has been talking to herself for so long that she does not know whether her words have meaning for anyone else, and rather fears that they do not.

Her family, even the intellectually vigorous Blackwells, could not provide the challenge she needed. Lucy Stone, earlier a trenchant critic, no longer played that role; once she and Henry Blackwell moved from New Jersey to Boston in 1868, her relationship with Antoinette was dominated by the details of family matters rather than arguing about religion or politics. Sam Blackwell encouraged Antoinette, but apparently without significant criticism. Antoinette later told her niece, Alice Stone Blackwell:

Uncle Sam thought all I did was right—read all I wrote,
and it was [the] most unselfish thing he could have done,
for that kind of writing wasn't in his line, yet he always
took the greatest interest in it, and gave me his advice.[23]

But Sam's attention was not enough. Antoinette needed
the reactions of people in her own field. She tried to elicit
responses from people she respected, not her peers as much as
older men like the clergymen who had lent their support in the
early years of her ministry. In 1869, for example, she asked
Gerrit Smith, the now-elderly reformer who had assisted at her
ordination, for his evaluation of her work:

I have taken the liberty of sending you and Mrs. Smith my
"Studies in General Science," which probably you have
received before this.... If you could find time and inclination to review the book or to make any comments you
choose upon it in any way that suits you, I should be
greatly obliged.... I shall be equally grateful for commendation or criticism from yourself.[24]

She also sent copies of her books to others she respected, including Charles Darwin, regardless of whether they were personal
acquaintances.[25] Presumably what she hoped for was some
response, some reassurance that her work was correct and
valuable.

After publication of *Studies*, Blackwell decided to try her
hand at writing fiction. The market she hoped to reach was the
popular world of *Harper's Bazar*. The *Bazar*, founded in 1867 as
a women's counterpart to *Harper's Monthly*, ranked with the
Atlantic Monthly as a forum for the best new fiction by American and English writers. Its pages also contained serialized
versions of the flood of novels of varying quality by women
writers—the ones that Nathaniel Hawthorne referred to as
"that damned mob of scribbling women."[26] Mary Louise
Booth, the *Bazar*'s editor, was herself a successful historian,
author, and translator. She seems to have encouraged Blackwell to submit whatever she wrote to the *Bazar* for possible
publication.

Blackwell's reasons for shifting away from the scientific
and philosophical studies that constituted the core of her intellectual work are not altogether clear. She wrote to Mary Louise
Booth in December 1870:

> Having taken up stories, I am determined to write it out on
> that line till the attention of the public is secured; which
> sometimes seems to be effected by quantity rather than
> quality. Yet to write nothing but fiction, must be about as
> objectionable as to read nothing else; and with me it is
> rather a means to an end or to several ends.[27]

Perhaps her youthful dreams of becoming a well-recognized
author led her to seek acceptance by a wider audience. She may
have hoped, too, that fiction would sell more briskly than
philosophy, enabling her to contribute to her family's support
as she had promised to do when she married. But money alone
could not have been much of an incentive. In an unpublished
essay, Blackwell lamented that women were poorly compen-
sated for their writing:

> Our American women are not generally ranked among
> first class authors. Then why? From mental inability to go up
> higher or because they have allowed themselves to be
> steadily dwarfed by the all pervading law of literary supply
> and demand? . . . It is claimed that the profession of letters
> makes no distinctions of sex in its rewarding of merit, but
> practically this is immensely untrue. . . . There has been
> but one Margaret Fuller. Yet if the inducements offered to
> women for solid literary work were comparable to those
> always offered to young men it would be possible to
> mention a dozen women who might fairly compete with
> our one Margaret in subtlety of critical analysis, in depth
> and comprehensiveness of thought as in vigor and finish
> of expression.[28]

Blackwell may have thought that writing fiction would
require less effort than her philosophical writing—an attractive idea to a woman with family responsibilities and fragmented work time. According to popular belief, analytical
writing took disciplined effort, which women were thought to
be either incapable of or unsuited for. Novels—at least popular
"women's novels"—were supposed to run from the writer's
pen in a more or less effortless overflowing of emotions, like a
stream bubbling over. Blackwell in fact described her own
fiction writing as "a little recreation now and then"; she wrote
to Mary Louise Booth, "To write a story now and then is as
much rest for me as to read one."[29] Unfortunately, the quality
of Blackwell's fiction reflects that rather casual approach.

In 1871 Blackwell completed a novel, *The Island Neighbors*, based on the Blackwell's summer visits to Martha's Vineyard, which she submitted to *Harper's Bazar*. They found it "too quiet" for publication as a magazine serial.[30] Harper Brothers did agree to publish the book as part of their "Library of Select Novels."

As fiction, *The Island Neighbors* was no worse than thousands of other obscure novels of the period. It can be identified with the emerging "local color" story in American fiction, an offshoot of the realistic, regional literature that arose following the Civil War and flowered in the work of regionalists such as Mark Twain, Sarah Orne Jewett, Bret Harte, and Mary E. Wilkins Freeman. The plot consists of a rambling series of vignettes of summer life on the island: fishing expeditions, picnics, a carriage ride to Gay Head cliffs, a visit to the camp meeting at Oak Bluffs, viewing an eclipse of the sun as the Blackwells themselves had done in 1869. Through these activities the island's year-round residents, primarily an elderly couple, try to rouse the visiting Warner family from their lethargy and chronic illness, with varying degrees of success. The Warners' governess, Margaret, falls in love with Alfred, a local fisherman. Their courtship consists of daily silent long-distance glimpses, several warnings from Margaret's employers that Alfred is not a suitable husband, many imagined rebuffs, and one heroic rescue after Margaret falls off a fishing pier. The Warners' opposition to the match disappears when Alfred rescues their young children from a cave during a violent storm. The Warners then return home, while Margaret comes back a month later to marry Alfred.

Blackwell claimed that she had no desire to inject any moral message into the novel. In yet another apologetic preface, she wrote:

> [This book is] the normal outgrowth of a restful mood—the fruit gathered in the leisurely moments of a long play-day when there seemed nothing better to do.... There is no more thought of a moral in it than there is in the plays of children and the friskiness of all young animals; or in the unreckoning content of comfortable, everyday enjoyment in our maturer years.[31]

She barely touched on current events, such as the controversy over Darwin's theory of evolution and the recruiting of soldiers to join Cuba's Nationalist revolt for independence from Spain, which would have been familiar to her readers. On the other hand, the narrative is frequently interrupted by abstract philosophical and personal comments by the author, which preach her opinions rather than illustrate them.

The book does reveal the kind of person Blackwell admired. She contrasted Captain Giles, a vigorous seventy-nine-year-old islander, and his neat, trim, warm wife, with Mr. Warner, a wealthy depressed chronic invalid, and Mrs. Warner, an overly fastidious, "pleasant, polite, middle-aged, rather pale and languid woman."[32] The author applauded when the Warners' grown-up son pursued with interest the wholesome activities Captain Giles offered, and when their twelve-year-old daughter, an "old-fashioned" child, "delighted to turn over the sheets and blankets in the same deft and clever way that [Mrs. Giles] did."[33] Through Captain Giles, Blackwell, in her preaching mode, condemned the Warners for being overly concerned about differences in class or breeding, especially when that prejudice caused unnecessary strains between Margaret and her beau. She did not, however, portray any direct confrontations among her characters.

Margaret, the central character, embodied Blackwell's ideals. She is described as quick-witted, vivacious, patient, sympathetic, thoughtful, robust, and sensible. She takes her place next to the men to help free a boat that has gone aground; she arranges for all the family's physical needs with considerable ingenuity; she cheerfully brings the invalid Warners endless blankets and cups of tea, without complaining about her servant role. But Margaret also illustrates some of Blackwell's unresolved ambivalence about women's roles. Instead of challenging the Warners' views of her lower-class beau, she goes off by herself to sulk. When Margaret finally tires of being a servant, she considers starting out on her own, perhaps as a typesetter, one of the occupations newly opened to "respectable American women." Instead, she finds happiness and fulfillment by marrying the right man, without any signs of conflict. Blackwell recognized that in the novel she had avoided "strong situations," that is, the human conflicts and growth that make good fiction more than just light entertainment.[34] The book fits her characterization of it as "a handful of wayside flowers gathered in pleasant moments."[35]

After publication of *The Island Neighbors*—an achievement for its author, although hardly a major literary event—

Blackwell wrote several other stories, none of which seems to have been published. She wrote to Mary Louise Booth in the fall of 1871:

> I am half afraid to send you any more manuscripts but here is a little sketch eager to speak for itself, and to which you are at liberty to say "no." . . . I am not convinced yet that story writing is in my line. You can help me to decide.[36]

Her attention, however, was returning to philosophy; in another letter she reported:

> I would have replied sooner and would say much more now; but I am taking a fresh dip into metaphysics so that when I do get an hour to spare it is so fascinating to go up there into the clouds, that everything else is sent adrift.[37]

Blackwell seems to have decided that philosophy was, after all, her forte, and determined to go ahead with it, whether or not it was less "womanly" than fiction. As the decade continued, she was to find growing recognition for her intellectual efforts, both among other women scholars and among other scientists and philosophers.

Letter, Antoinette Brown Blackwell to Mary Louise Booth,
July 18, 1876

THE IRREPRESSIBLE
WOMAN QUESTION

In the early 1870s Antoinette Blackwell wrote a series of articles directly addressing the position of women in American society. She focused on the issue closest to her own experience: how could women like herself combine intellectual work with the responsibility for a household and children?

By 1870 Blackwell had demonstrated her determination that marriage would not cause her to abandon her work. In 1869 she wrote to Rev. Phebe A. Hanaford, "I think that nothing but marriage should take the precedence of the *vocation* and we should *all* try how far the two can be made compatible."[1] In the early 1860s, Blackwell wrote to young Olympia Brown, who wanted to follow her into the Christian ministry:

> Doubtless the mother of a family can attend to professional duties; but she cannot absorb herself wholly in professional life.... Women must bend the professions to themselves and their capacities; and do as much or as little as they find consonant with higher duties.[2]

Her own circumstances forced Blackwell to consider how, as a practical matter, women could carry on professional work. At first she did her reading and writing in the middle of family activity. She later recalled:

> While my children were all small, generally one or two were playing about me as I carried on reading, thought, or writing. The habit was acquired of turning from the practical needs of others to my own individual work.[3]

As soon as space permitted, however, Blackwell moved her books from the common rooms to a solitary study, the proverbial room of her own:

> With a locked door I soon almost forgot the ease with which I had been wont to turn from one interest to the other. At my Somerville home outside my room was the

roof of a veranda and while I was working intently I
would sometimes look up to see little faces peering in at
me from the window that looked out on this roof or hear a
tap upon the glass and some beseeching voice begging for
some privilege which the mother alone could grant.[4]

What made it possible for her to absent herself from the
family circle at all was an unusual family. Blackwell had
written to Lucy Stone in 1850 that if she married, "the matri-
monial alliance would have to be placed on a different basis
from the common."[5] She married an unusual man, distinctive
less in his public role than in his private one. Most importantly, Samuel Blackwell shared in the work of the home will-
ingly and without argument. After his death Antoinette wrote:

> Mr. Blackwell, who was engaged in business and might
> have fewer hours to give to home occupations, declared
> himself more than willing to help me with home duties.
> This promise he generously more than redeemed for
> almost fifty years.[6]

"Home duties" included caring for their five daughters, who in
1870 ranged in age from one to fourteen.

The Blackwells' experience seems to have been unique,
even among liberal reformers. Elizabeth Cady Stanton, for
example, wrote in her autobiography, "Mr. Stanton announced to me, in starting, that his business would occupy all
his time, and that I must take entire charge of the housekeeping."[7] Susan B. Anthony wrote indignantly to Antoinette
Blackwell about the Stanton household:

> [Mrs. Stanton] will be able to lecture however up to January,
> provided she will only *make* her surroundings bend to
> such work—but her husband, you know, does not help to
> make it easy for her to engage in such a work.... Mr. Stan-
> ton will be gone most of the Autumn—full of *Political Air
> Castles*—and so soon as Congress sits, at Washington
> again—he was gone *7 months* last winter—the whole
> burden of home & children, therefore falls to her, if she
> leaves the post all is afloat.[8]

Blackwell's vision extended far beyond shared housework.
Buried in her essay on "Social Progress" in *Studies in General
Science* was the seed of a new order in which men and women
would share both outside work for pay and household tasks:

When we become nobler as individuals we shall find better modes of co-working for mutual assistance; for the best good of one is the best good of all. Woman must become a broader and more rational worker; more self-forgetting, remembering the well-being of the whole community; while man must equally learn that charity begins with the necessary, unending, small details of home and its inmates.[9]

Four years later she elaborated:

Wife and husband could be mutual helpers with admirable effect. Let her take his place in garden or field or workshop an hour or two daily, learning to breathe more strongly, and exercising a fresh set of muscles in soul and body. To him baby-tending and bread-making would be most humanizing in their influence, all parties gaining an assured benefit. . . . We need a general reconstruction in the division of labor. Let no women give all their time to household duties, but require nearly all women, and all men also, since they belong to the household, to bear some share of the common household burdens.[10]

It was a startling proposal. Although women had begun to move into traditionally male wage-earning positions—as factory workers, office clerks, even doctors and lawyers—no other writer proposed publicly that men should share "feminine" jobs such as child care and cooking.[11] Most available jobs demanded that workers work ten to twelve hours a day, six or seven days a week, a schedule that left little time for either childrearing and housework or for individual pursuits. Workers' pleas for an eight-hour day were considered so radical as to border on revolutionary anarchism. Meanwhile, working women continued to shoulder domestic burdens as well as working long hours outside the home as best they could. Blackwell's vision did not touch the vast majority of American families.

Nevertheless, in the 1870s the Blackwells themselves attempted to translate that vision into experience. They chose it as a way of meeting their own needs, not as a symbolic statement or a model for others to follow. Samuel Blackwell worked at an office job only because they needed the income. He hoped that eventually he could earn enough from real estate investments to maintain the family while leaving more time free for writing. By 1871 Sam decided he could afford to give up his job and earn money exclusively from supervising the building and selling of houses, which he could manage from their home. Antoinette told her friend Mary Louise Booth:

> [We] are proposing to coax the village out here by opening streets, buildings, etc. This is Mr. Blackwell's business—not mine—and yet it is likely to interest and occupy us both a good deal for a year or two possibly.[12]

It was a fulfilling time for Antoinette, a satisfying resting place at the midpoint of her long life. She later described their home, a "fine old white farm house with its long verandas and red barn":

> Our home on the side of Watchung Mountain had ... an outlook upon a wide plain varied by the towns of Somerville and Raritan and a more or less settled high-lying and attractive region.... It was an excellent place for the young growing family. There was a good little country school for the younger children and very fair private schools for the older ones who were driven down daily to their studies.... This Hillside home left in the memories of my children the impression of a veritable paradise. It was the family gathering place on Christmas and other holidays.[13]

Antoinette wrote a newsy letter to her teenage niece, Alice Stone Blackwell, describing the family's activities one evening:

> Floey [age 16] is pouring over her *latin* here at my side, looking sleepy and not too amiable. She has taken a long walk this afternoon and is more fond of learning to skate than plodding on in lesson books.... We have just heard from Edie [age 12, visiting her grandparents in Henrietta], who asks when papa will come and bring her home—her chief anxiety being, apparently, to see baby whom she supposes to be rapidly growing into a large girl. Miss Baby [Ethel] herself is not well at present, having her first hard cold. She can walk now, but has declined to do so the last few days. Grace [age 7] goes to school and is growing very rapidly. Agnes [age 5] plays and reads a little now and then.... Your uncle Sam is sedately reading at the table, and wishing, I have no doubt, that the days were twice as long as they are, he finds so little time for himself.[14]

Antoinette herself found their arrangements satisfying. She later wrote:

> For a time the plan worked extremely well. Houses were built and sold and we both did a great deal of writing.... Mr. Blackwell wrote poems and articles for the press on topics of the day.... I had also published one or two books and was still much absorbed with the writing and the study it necessitated while still speaking in public occasionally as opportunity offered and attending various conventions as in the older days.[15]

The Blackwell's household arrangements were made easier by their ability to hire servants to do some of the housework. Bridget, a young Irish woman, worked for the Blackwells from the time they first moved to New Jersey until at least the end of the Civil War. She helped with the endless cleaning and cooking, and occasionally cared for the babies. As the children grew older, they were under the supervision of a series of governesses. The Blackwells called in a dressmaker and other specialized workers as they were needed. Only ten percent of American households could afford that amount of domestic help.[16] Newspapers of the time carried lengthy discussions about the difficulty of finding competent servants so that middle-class women could give elaborate dinner parties. The Blackwells, like Elizabeth Cady Stanton and other publicly active women, used for writing and study the time that was freed for them by servants' work.

Not surprisingly, in numerous essays and speeches during the 1870s, Antoinette Blackwell chose to address the problems of women undertaking intellectual work. She focused primarily on the processes of study, both psychological and practical, rather than on the results. For example, she wrote to editor and author Mary Louise Booth:

> It is your work and your methods of working—not the events of your life, except as they bear on these, that I wish to record.... I should like to say definitely what [you] have done; but also to give something of the conditions under which the work was done. To give the names and dates of your books, would be of little general interest by itself merely; but to know that one book followed another in a certain time; to see how much you could steadily accomplish...etc., would make the whole graphic and

impressive. In my mind, you represent ease and rapidity of
work more than any one other quality.... The world does
not yet know that women can work on steadily—that they
often must work from sheer inward impulse. That is why
exceptional women now must be held up as types and
examples.[17]

Blackwell's writings and speeches focused primarily on
practical concerns of women like herself. During the early
1870s, most of her writings concerned, in her words, "The
Relation of Woman's Work in the House to the Work Outside." These writings, primarily articles published in the
Woman's Journal, were designed to encourage other women to
take up the study of serious topics and to participate in public
affairs. They reveal, however, an unfortunate defensiveness,
perhaps reflecting Blackwell's need to justify and gain
approval for her own unusual position.

The prevailing ideology in the 1870s was that motherhood
was the primary—if not the only—sphere of interest for
women. The ideology was more than a simple expectation that
women, in the natural course of events, would bear children
and care for them. Maternity had become a prescriptive norm,
an obsession, a fitting topic for floods of rhetoric, precisely at a
time when a declining birth rate, household technology, and
expanding opportunities for education and paying jobs threatened to allow women options other than kitchen and nursery.

Blackwell's first public speech on this issue did not directly
challenge the ideology, but largely shared its sentiments:

There is one dogma, I believe, which has been taught and
accepted universally. It asserts that the paramount social
duties of women are household duties, avocations arising
from their relations as wives and mothers, and as the
natural custodians of the home. I make haste to endorse
this dogma; fully, and without equivocation. The work
nearest and clearest before the eyes of average womanhood
is work within family boundaries—work within a sphere
which men cannot enter; surrounded by a still wider area
of duties and privileges that very few of us desire to relin-
quish. I yield to none in the earnestness of my faith that
to women preeminently has been committed the happiness, the usefulness, and the dignity of the homes of
Christendom.[18]

Yet in the same paper she proposed that men could and should share in "baby-tending and bread-making." Declaring that women had a right and even an obligation to involve themselves in public life, she continued:

> If women devote their energies to preparing bread only, the race must starve miserably for want of proper nutriment....
>
> So far from admitting that women have occupation enough in their family duties, I maintain unqualifiedly, that every woman, rich or poor, not actually an invalid, confined to one room, is in imperative need of a daily distinct change of thought and employment. The change of mere recreation is not sufficient....
>
> Women need a purpose; a definite pursuit in which they are interested, if they expect to gather from it tone and vigor, either of mind or body.[19]

Blackwell's apparently inconsistent position was similar to that taken by virtually all other feminists, who hastened to reassure an uneasy public that increased opportunities for women would not detract from their more traditional responsibilities. Blackwell asserted that outside interests could be smoothly integrated with domestic duties. In an 1874 speech on "Work in Relation to the Home," she told the New England Women's Club:

> It should be easy to turn aside from bathing the chubby limbs of babyhood, and clothing them in the pretty white frocks which all mothers love... —easy to put aside all this to deposit one's vote in the ballot box, or to spend a few hours eagerly poring over newspapers to gather, from the whirling current of events, some fact which may be of national or cosmopolitan importance. A home-nest, with the young birdlings in it, has warmth enough to shed the influence outward upon the maternal heart, go where it may; and the active womanly brain, which has sufficient breadth to appreciate the widest human interests, and to work to promote the welfare of the race, stimulated by its deeper affections can have no difficulty in applying itself also to the loving details of the home regimen.[20]

Such sentiments as these scarcely needed to be defended. The more critical question was how women could effectively

carry both domestic duties and responsibilities beyond the
hearth. Blackwell's public writings and speeches on that subject are unsatisfactory. She spoke little about women with
paying jobs or other obligations that physically removed them
from the home. Instead, she directed her comments to women
like herself, who remained at home but who might direct their
attention to the world outside by thinking, and perhaps writing, about public issues. In an 1874 speech she asserted:

> Almost every mother can learn to take up intellectual work
> profitably, even in the midst of her little noisy group of
> children. It need not be fatal to the highest continuity of
> thought to stop every now and then to answer some of the
> endless suggestive questions, to kiss a little bumped head,
> or to settle some of the inevitable small disputes. The well
> balanced woman with a limited income, can learn to live
> in her kitchen, ready to watch the boiling pot, to superin-
> tend the elder girl's sewing or dish-washing, and to send
> maternal cheer now and then into the distant corner where
> the little ones are at play; and yet, alternated with much
> housework, she can accomplish an immense amount of
> reading, of thinking, and of connected severe study in any
> department in which she is thoroughly interested.[21]

Aware, perhaps, that her advice did not ring completely true
even to her own experience, Blackwell conceded that practical
difficulties might interfere:

> Children are disturbing elements, more fickle in their
> impulses than the weather.... Servants are not automa-
> tons.... Every housekeeper knows that cook, laundress,
> seamstress, maid of all work, everyone of them has a free-
> will of her own, full-grown and resolute after its kind.
> Kitchen utensils, and the black cooking stove itself, have
> taken some share in the evils which resulted from the fall
> of Adam's wife. From the dust we came, and under the ban
> of dust must abide the mistress of every household, in spite
> of old silk handkerchiefs and feather-dusters. But life
> would be tame enough if there were no trials in it—insipid
> enough with nothing to conquer.[22]

She did not raise with her audience the question of why women
who wished to do serious work should have to endure constant
interruptions, while men were free to leave the house or shut
themselves into a study for hours at a time.

Privately, Blackwell admitted that with all the interruptions, "I do a little of a hundred things every day and not much of anything."[23] Yet in her speeches and articles, she did not discuss the actual arrangements that made her own work possible—Sam's assistance, financial security, servants, a locked study. In a passage that sounds autobiographical, she projected a "superwoman" image:

> I know of a woman, who, not long ago, kept house for some months with no other assistance than that of her own five children,—the oldest about sixteen and the youngest three—with other occasional help in washing, or when there was company. During this time she regularly prepared an article each week for a weekly journal, wrote one or two papers for a magazine, and carried on a continuous study while writing upon a topic in which she was interested. The children all did some habitual study and reciting, and the house was as orderly as usual, visitors coming and going, yet knowing nothing of the unusual internal arrangements.[24]

One wonders why it was so important that visitors not be aware of the woman's intellectual work.

In the process of trying to blunt antifeminist criticism, Blackwell succeeded too well, blunting also the force of her more radical vision. Yet despite their shortcomings, her speeches and essays drive home Blackwell's insistence that women should not be forced to choose between family life and the work they might do beyond the family, an assertion she was determined to illustrate in her own life.

The question whether women should engage in serious intellectual work was widely debated in the 1870s. Opportunities for higher education for women were expanding. Many state land-grant colleges admitted women from their inception, as did some private colleges such as Swarthmore and Boston University. Several new women's colleges such as Swarthmore and Boston University. Several new women's colleges opened with high academic standards and ideals: Vassar in 1865, Wellesley and Smith in 1875. Even staid Harvard was to organize an "Annex" for women in 1879. Growing numbers of women chose to prepare for and enter formerly male professions. Some male professionals and intellectuals perceived these women as a threat, and confronted them with a barrage of arguments that set the terms of debate for many decades.

In the 1840s, public work for women was challenged as being contrary to God's plan. By the 1870s, scientists and physicians, rather than clergymen, led the assault on "advanced" women. Drawing on the new theory of natural selection, they argued that women had an obligation to contribute to human progress by bearing superior children. Women were to avoid any activity that might injure or interfere with their delicate reproductive organs. Instead of looking at the debilitating working conditions in factories, or living conditions in urban slums and rural shacks, these writers focused on the dangers posed by too much studying and mental exertion.

In 1873 one of the strongest statements of this position became a best-seller. *Sex in Education, or a Fair Chance for Girls,* was written by Dr. Edward Hammond Clarke, a minister's son, distinguished Boston physician, and professor at Harvard Medical School. In keeping with the prevailing views, he insisted that he was not opposed to educating girls as such, but only against methods of education that would interfere with girls' delicate "female organization," which he termed one of "the marvels of creation." He wrote:

> The problem of woman's sphere ... is not to be solved by applying to it abstract principles of right and wrong. Its solution must be obtained from physiology, not from ethics or metaphysics.... [It] will be decided by her [physical] organization. This limits her power, and reveals her divinely-appointed tasks....
>
> Much of the discussion of the irrepressible woman-question, and many of the efforts for bettering her education and widening her sphere, seem to ignore any difference of the sexes; seem to treat her as if she were identical with man, and to be trained in precisely the same way....
>
> Appropriate education of the two sexes, carried as far as possible, is a consummation most devoutly to be desired; identical education of the two sexes is a crime before God and humanity, that physiology protests against, and that experience weeps over.[25]

Dr. Clarke's central theory was that "undue and disproportionate brain activity exerts a sterilizing influence," especially upon girls. He warned that if girls attempted to ignore or overcome their physiological limitations and engage in "masculine" studying, they would suffer from menstrual problems, hysteria, vaginal infections, and general weakness. Instead of trying to master intellectual work, which would drain energy away from their developing ovaries, young women were advised to nurture "the fine instincts and quick perceptions that have their root in the catamenial [menstrual] mechanism."[26]

Criticisms of Dr. Clarke exploded from all directions. In Boston Julia Ward Howe quickly compiled a volume of rebuttals by leading feminists from Elizabeth Stuart Phelps to Thomas Wentworth Higginson. Many passed over Dr. Clarke's medical arguments to address the essentially political issues underlying his theories. One unidentified woman wrote, "This physiological scare is the most insidious form under which the opposition to the higher education of women has yet appeared."[27] Eliza Bisbee Duffey, author of dozens of popular books on marriage and household management, wrote an entire book attacking Dr. Clarke's conclusions:

> *Sex in Education* is a covert blow against the desires and ambitions of woman in every direction except a strictly domestic one. The doctor has chosen to attack co-education as a representative of them all. . . . He knows if he succeeds in carrying the points which he attempts, and convinces the world that woman is a "sexual" creature alone, subject to and ruled by "periodic tides," the battle is won for those who oppose the advancement of woman. . . . If women can be persuaded to become unreliable on principle, there is an end to the competition between the sexes in every department of employment. . . . [This book is] the last, the most desperate struggle of the advocates of fogyism against the incoming new order of things.[28]

Antoinette Blackwell also responded to Dr. Clarke's book, which directly challenged the propriety of her own lifelong work. On the specific question of women's capacity for studying, Blackwell heartily disagreed with Dr. Clarke:

> The every-day question is, does study, a few hours of regular daily application to mental work, impair or tend to impair the vigor of the feminine constitution? Are the daily lessons which are fitting and healthful for a school boy so exacting that they must draw the blood to nurture the brain of the school girl to the detriment of her appropriate womanly growth? Does moderate study, on any day and at any period of a healthy woman's life, tend to

exhaust her natural strength, or to produce a reaction so
violent that is must become a direct promoter either of
weakness or of disease?[29]

Blackwell's answer, as one would expect from her years of
experience at Monroe Academy and at Oberlin, was no:

> Any school girl of fair ability... can maintain a standing
> in her class equal to that of boys of her own age, and yet
> leave all her womanly functions quite unimpaired.... She
> is not porcelain to be easily broken.[30]

For Blackwell, however, the inquiry did not end there; she went
on to a more detailed discussion of female physiology and
psychology.

Blackwell approached the question of gender differences
as she had that of women's authority to preach, by careful and
protracted study of the books and articles available to her. In
addition to her earlier scientific study, she undoubtedly read
Charles Darwin's *Descent of Man and Selection in Relation to
Sex*, published in 1871, and Herbert Spencer's *Principles of
Biology*, which appeared in two volumes in 1870 and 1872. She
subscribed to *Popular Science Monthly*, a new journal founded
by Edward Livingston Youmans, which carried serializations
of Spencer's books as well as articles on topics as diverse as
"Science and Religion" and "Women and Political Power."
Although Blackwell suspected that "there must be some
unconscious masculine bias in the theoretical portions of many
sciences,"[31] she relied on the work of those male scientists.

Blackwell explained her position in a series of essays, first
published in the *Woman's Journal* and in *Popular Science
Monthly* and, in 1875, compiled into a book, *The Sexes
Throughout Nature*. In those essays, Blackwell largely accepted the terms of debate set by Dr. Clarke and other scientists.
In 1848, surrounded by clergymen, she had based her argument
for female equality on a scholarly exegesis of a Biblical text. By
the 1870s, Blackwell shared the common view that "it would be
as futile to expect the Bible to settle [women's] position in the
community as to expect it to settle the details of domestic
service."[32] Instead of considering women's rights as an ethical
or political question, however, Blackwell affirmed that "the
'Woman Question' must be met just here, upon a comparative
physiological and psychological basis."[33] Science was the new

authority and source of legitimacy for the whole society. Scientists claimed that they were replacing the old inadequate religious faith with knowledge grounded in objective facts and logic. They fostered the hope that the same scientific method that led to the development of railroads, telegraphs, and a host of other technological wonders would provide unshakable answers to social and moral questions such as the proper role for women.

Blackwell largely accepted the scientific method, as she understood it, as the appropriate process for finding truth:

> Every educator of either sex... must ask whether existing inequalities are "accidental and removable," or whether they are "radical and permanent, and belong to the very constitution of the sexes." Data enough must be accumulated on one side or the other to fully determine whether or not Nature has entailed on one sex disabilities which are not offset and equalled by similar disabilities in the other.... This [question]... can be settled only by the most careful and extended chemical tests.... It requires a deeper reading of facts, a reconsideration of all the old data, from the bottom upwards; in a word, a new science— the science of Feminine Humanity. For this we must rely largely upon facts, to be slowly and carefully gathered, and to be still more slowly and guardedly lived, if there are not to arise some very painful mistakes.[34]

She also shared Dr. Clarke's premise that men and women are different, both physically and mentally:

> I have a sincere appreciation of the excellent service done [by Dr. Clarke] in calling attention seriously to the more complex, more highly organized, and therefore more, easily harmed and disarranged feminine organism with its added rhythmical complexity of functions, which cannot be too carefully or continuously guarded from disturbance....
>
> It is currently known that the emotional and intellectual processes in woman are *more closely in relation* than in man.... Women's thoughts are impelled by their feelings. Hence the sharp-sightedness, the direct insight, the quick perceptions; hence also their warmer prejudices and more unbalanced judgments, and their infrequent use of the masculine methods of ratiocination.[35]

Those sentiments could easily be used to bolster attempts to keep women out of jobs or other positions where "unbalanced judgments" would be a distinct liability. Blackwell, however, maintained that these differences did not render women inferior. She challenged "the accepted theory that the male is the representative type of the species—the female a modification preordained in the interest of reproduction."[36]

> I maintain that men and women as classes are held in perpetual equilibrium, and are compelled to remain virtual equivalents physically, mentally, and morally; constrained by fundamental underlying laws of nature to rise and fall together in the scale of attainments; superior endowments of muscle and muscular vitality in the one being transformed to superior feminine functions in the other.[37]

In a long essay on "Sex and Evolution," Blackwell set out to illustrate her theory that men and women are different but equal, using the cross-species data collected by Darwin. She believed that her task was one "of pure quantity; of comparing unlike but strict measurable terms."[38] She then set forth what appear to be her own conclusions from the data:

> It is claimed that average males and females, in every species, always have been approximately equals, both physically and mentally. It is claimed that the extra size, the greater beauty of color, and wealth of appendages, and the greater physical strength and activity in males, have been in each species mathematically offset in the females by corresponding advantages—such as more highly differentiated structural development; greater rapidity of organic processes; larger relative endurance, dependent upon a more facile adjustment of functions among themselves, thus insuring a more prompt recuperation after every severe tax on the energies. It is claimed that the stronger passional force in the male finds its equivalent in the deeper parental and conjugal affection of the female; and that, in man, the more aggressive and constructive intellect of the male, is balanced by a higher intellectual insight, combined with greater facility in coping with details and reducing them to harmonious adjustment, in the female.[39]

She even included a table of mathematical equivalents to support her belief in the biological equality of males and females.

Blackwell used gender differences as support for her thesis that women must be allowed to discover and develop their own unique skills and strengths:

> Evolution has given and is still giving to woman an increasing complexity of development which cannot find a legitimate field for the exercise of all its powers within the household.... That she is not [the peer of man] in all intellectual and moral capabilities, cannot at least be very well proved until she is allowed an equally untrammelled opportunity to test her own strength.[40]

This "different but equal" argument reflected a subtle shift in feminist thinking. Until the Civil War, feminists frequently argued that women had a right to vote and to take on any work they felt drawn to, because they were citizens just as men were. By the 1870s, however, many feminists conceded that women differed from men in significant ways, but argued that women should be allowed broader public responsibilities so that their special insights, moral influence, and sensibilities could be brought to bear on problems in the community. They had little leverage, however, for responding to those opposed to increasing opportunities, who argued that the difference demanded separate spheres of work and interest—the home for women, the marketplace for men.

Blackwell felt self-conscious about her lack of formal scientific training, and feared that the scientific community might dismiss her work as amateurish. In the middle of her argument she wrote:

> I do not underrate the charge of presumption which must attach to any woman who will attempt to controvert the great masters of science and of scientific inference. But there is no alternative! Only a woman can approach the subject from a feminine standpoint; and there are none but beginners among us in this class of investigations.[41]

Formal scientific training might not have aided Blackwell substantially. Even the best educated scientists of her day based their sweeping conclusions on a rudimentary understanding of evolution and heredity. It was widely believed that characteristics acquired during an organism's lifetime—muscle strength, intellectual facility, drunkenness, moral virtue—would be passed on genetically to its offspring. This hypothesis overemphasized the impact of a person's habits on the genetic characteristics of future generations. Most people, including Darwin, also assumed that each organism inherited characteristics primarily, if not exclusively, from the parent of the same gender, so that men and women constituted virtually separate species. Blackwell sensed that that theory was erroneous, but did not have information proving it; empirical proof that each child inherits genetic material from both parents did not exist until the 1880s.

The more significant limitation in Blackwell's work was her acceptance of the premise that the oppression of women was caused by a lack of factual information. An extensive and essentially favorable review of *The Sexes Throughout Nature* in *Popular Science Monthly* outlined the problem:

> Considered as an original scientific argument, we fail to see that Mrs. Blackwell has advanced or altered the position of the question she has taken up. She undertakes to prove that throughout all Nature the sexes are equal. We will not say that this is an impossible task; but if it be attempted in a truly scientific spirit we have no hesitation in saying that even the proximate solution of her problem belongs to the very distant future. For what she proposes to do is nothing less than to reduce the whole organic world, with all its vital and psychical characters, into exact and demonstrable quantitative expression....
>
> Mrs. Blackwell seems to us to be quite oblivious of the difficulties of the task here undertaken.... Certain important physiological constants have been determined with some accuracy of general expression.... But, when we rise to more complex organic manifestations, to the functions of the nervous system, to feeling and thought, and those proportions and combinations of characters which distinguish classes and individuals, nothing whatever has been done toward their quantitative elucidation, and we can only say that the phenomena are vaguely comparable as more or less.[42]

In other words, Blackwell had attempted to prove scientifically something essentially impossible of exact quantitative proof, because it concerned human character and values. Blackwell proposed that the qualities she attributed to females—endurance, intuition, gentleness—were as valuable as those attributed to males—strength, logic, speed. That evaluation was, however, a matter for moral and political debate, not one resolvable by scientific fact-finding.

Nevertheless, *Sexes Throughout Nature* was probably Blackwell's most important book. In it she offered some radical suggestions for a "natural" division of work, including the suggestion that cooking, as "indirect nutrition," was properly a task for men. She recognized the complexity and depth of the debate about women's roles, commenting that, "The 'irrepressible woman question' is broader and more radical in every direction than most of us have been accustomed to think."[43] She sought to integrate her own experience into her analysis of women's strengths; for example, in describing "the sympathy of the average woman for all of her own sex . . . the sympathetic aid which women render each other," she referred to the support she had received from the girl students when she was a young insecure teacher.[44] The requirement that observers separate their personal experience from scientific facts— discrediting their own perceptions—was one of the hallmarks of masculine intellectual culture, and especially of science.[45] It would be a century before feminist scholars would attempt on a broad scale to restructure intellectual disciplines and revise accepted dogma concerning evolution and gender differences.

In the meantime, Blackwell continued to insist that both society and women themselves should encourage women to undertake intellectual work. In a speech in the fall of 1876, she said:

> It is impossible to judge of the relative ability of the sexes from an impartial *historical* basis. The outside limitations have always been unequal—so unequal that the feminine intellect has been virtually check-mated from the beginning. . . . Woman is taught to suffer her mind to drift hither and thither without a rudder, borne on passively by every current of outward suggestion. . . . Nothing is lacking but courage, perseverance, resolution applied as diligently in the new higher direction as it has been applied century after century to endless petty needle and lace-work.[46]

Her own endeavors, and especially the Blackwell's experimental household arrangements, were, however, impeded by outside events. In September 1873, following a cycle of uncontrolled speculation, Jay Cooke's Philadelphia brokerage firm closed. In the next few weeks many banks collapsed, and the country swung from prosperity into deep depression. The real estate market, on which the Blackwell's livelihood depended, stagnated, with prices falling and few buyers; they found that their crop of little houses only ate up money in taxes. Blackwell later recalled:

> Then came the financial stress of 1873. The first firm of importance to fail held very much of our always too-limited savings. There were now five little daughters in the family group. For a time we resolutely carried forward our chosen pursuits, even trenching upon the remaining capital with the hope of making good our plans.[47]

They trimmed household expenses; Antoinette even tried her hand at making her daughters' dresses until one unfortunate attempt pushed her to tears. The Blackwells were forced to sell the remaining land and houses at a substantial loss, including the Somerville farm that Antoinette had come to love. She dreaded moving again, but had no alternative. They moved to smaller houses, first in Somerville itself, and later in the village of Elmora, now part of the city of Elizabeth. Sam once again accepted a bookkeeping position in New York City. Antoinette's vision of a more equal sharing of household responsibilities and money earning, with time free for writing, would have to await more favorable economic conditions.

Rev. Antoinette Brown Blackwell, ca. 1880

ᔐ Chapter 11 ᑫ

THE CROWN AND SUMMIT

As Antoinette Blackwell approached her fiftieth birthday in May 1875, she looked forward to expanded opportunities for intellectual work. A quarter of a century had passed since she left Oberlin, nearly twenty years since she had married Samuel. They had been good years, full years. Now, with her children growing up, she wanted to reach beyond to new challenges and new satisfactions. She told one audience of women like herself:

> Fifty or fifty-five should be but the prime—the very crown and summit of a woman's life. Thenceforward she should aim at vigorous personal achievements with a reach beyond the household.[1]

Many of the opportunities Blackwell pursued were within women's organizations. While the decades following the Civil War have often been described as an era of rampant individualism,[2] this characterization may only reflect the experience of men, particularly wealthy entrepreneurs. Antoinette Blackwell and other women of her general social class experienced instead a growing spirit of interdependence. Perhaps as an outgrowth of cooperative efforts during the Civil War, numerous women's clubs and organizations were formed in the years that followed it: missionary societies, literary clubs, the Women's Christian Temperance Union, state and local suffrage societies, and many more. These clubs were particularly important to educated middle-class women like Blackwell, who had both the leisure to devote to them and a desire to use their intellectual talents in creative ways. These organizations provided a supportive social context within which women could work and participate in the political life of their communities.

Blackwell saw the potential value of women's collective efforts both as a way for women to affect society and as an outlet for creative energy. In an 1875 speech entitled "Marriage and Work," she explained why the question of opportunities for active, educated women had taken on particular importance. It was, Blackwell said, a direct outgrowth of the increased numbers of women who had access to postsecondary education:

For many years, as class after class of girl graduates completed courses of study broad enough and solid enough to
fit them for some of the higher work of the world, many of
the oldest advocates for a wider field of occupation for
women waited anxiously to see what would be the result.
Year after year went by; the women thought and felt and
waited. And then, as if impelled by a common impulse, ten
thousand women at once quietly took up some broader
work, each in her own line, associating together, and by an
almost unconscious widening of methods, all these and
many other growing organizations are the result.

She gave credit to the many women who found ways of working in their own communities, particularly in women's
organizations:

To-day, it is not simply exceptional women who feel
impelled to put their woman's shoulders to some of the
lagging wheels of social revolution. There are multitudes
who can no longer comfortably shake off the burden of
their direct responsibility.... Women belong to humanity; they must work, then, for the human weal.

Blackwell recognized that not everyone would choose the
same tasks, and welcomed the diversity:

The harvest fields to-day are many. The same work is not
for all. Personal ability is the limit of personal responsibility. The highest work for each is that to which she is most
drawn in heart; that to which she is most nearly connected
by the circumstances of her position and by the fitness of
her special talents.

She listed some of the many ways in which women were contri-
buting to the common good:

What is the [temperance] movement to-day, in its
organizing efforts to effectually crush the dominion of
alcohol?...It is womanhood awakened to a sense of its
own most solemn responsibilities; reaching out after the
most practical and effective methods of compassing its
ends....
Why have the farmers' granges, the out-growth of
modern civilization, found a practical working position

on all boards for women? They saw and comprehended the fundamental fact that the women of the country, and more especially farmers' wives and daughters, whose homes are comparatively isolated, needed and desired to be healthfully active and useful....

What women did in the war, the whole country can remember. It was then that multitudes of them put on the spirit of real work for the Commonwealth, a spirit which never again can be suppressed. What have women done, and what are they doing, for the Centenniel? Giving it effective aid and comfort at every stage of its progress. Their effort is another great co-operative manifestation of the growing imperative need in women to identify themselves with the honor and the well-being of their country.

Blackwell saw—correctly—that one of the significant changes after the Civil War was the association of local groups into larger nationwide organizations. Economic enterprises were increasingly centralized. Railroads, heavily subsidized by the federal government, crisscrossed the continent and made it possible for fresh and canned food, natural resources, manufactured goods, and people to move quickly from New York to California and back. Telegraph lines paralleled the railroad, providing almost instantaneous communication throughout the country. Families like the Blackwells, in rural New Jersey, could purchase Swift or Armour beef from Chicago slaughterhouses, Pillsbury flour from Minneapolis, Singer sewing machines, or a multitude of manufactured goods from a new mail-order business called Montgomery Ward's. The major industries—steel making, oil, meat packing—were increasingly controlled by large nationwide conglomerates. Blackwell noted that the same trend could be seen in charitable organizations:

The millions of local, benevolent, and church associations have long been an outlet for the quickened energies of many women. Now these are associating themselves more and more widely. Women's benevolent enterprises are becoming national. Missionary boards have their auxiliary female societies reaching to the ends of the earth. Church associations every year admit their women to a wider and more active co-operation in almost every church enterprise.

As in her other writings on women's work, Blackwell carefully denied that work in the world would require women to abandon their domestic responsibilities. "It is time," she asserted, "that we utterly repudiate the pernicious dogma that marriage and a practical life-work are incompatible." In fact, she told her audience, working women would better fulfill their traditional role:

> The majority of all these eager workers are wives and mothers! Their homes are better kept, their children are more wisely guided, and their husbands are more honored among their townsmen, because this energy of the soul has found expression and toned the whole nature to the broader harmony.

Blackwell ended her speech with an exhortation, particularly directed toward upper-middle-class married women, who formed the majority of her audience:

> Why, then, appeal particularly to married women to enter the lists as workers for the age in which they live? ... First, because of the lingering prejudice that wifehood and maternity are all-sufficient, life-long occupations for women. Not at all....
>
> Second—the temptation to absorb all of one's powers in home affairs is specially strong with mothers. It is they who most need warning against this influence....
>
> The third reason for particularly calling on the matrons of this country, earnestly and in singleness of purpose to take upon themselves the world's highest work, is that in their ranks we shall find the only existing, considerable American leisure class.... In our civilization it is the rich married women, the childless wives and the "old wives"—classics in the earlier days, despised and set aside as croning retailers of senseless fables—who now, in the normal progress of human events, are ordained to become standard-bearers of a higher culture; disinterested pioneers in every needed enterprise; careful and conscientious investigators into many of the marvelous but open secrets of the universe.
>
> ... The time has come for women of leisure, for all they who need neither toil continuously for the bread they eat, nor spin a thread of raiment which they wear; it is time for these steadily and persistently to take up the higher intellectual work of which they are capable. It is time for

all women to begin fairly to test themselves and their capacities.[3]

Unwittingly, Blackwell now applauded an essentially elitist view of a natural aristocracy of leisured women, a marked contrast to the fervor with which she had condemned the aristocracy represented by the southern cause during the Civil War. She did not pause to consider whether the leisure and wealth that enabled a small group of women to engage in creative community activities was made possible by the same economic structures that caused the problems that those creative women were bent on solving.

Blackwell looked to women's organizations as a forum for her own talents as a public speaker. She was invited to speak at meetings of both rival suffrage organizations. Despite any disagreements over political issues, Susan B. Anthony remembered and respected Blackwell's abilities as a speaker. Blackwell had regained the self-confidence that had faltered during the late 1850s. After returning from speaking at a meeting of the National Woman Suffrage Association in 1874, she reported to Lucy Stone:

> I wrote the N.Y. speech on "Evolution applied to the Woman Question" and gave it in Susan's Convention, first because I had something to say, 2nd because they are anxious now to be respectable and proper, and I am desirous they should and would like to help them. Some of their elbows were apparently quite ready to give me a poke; but if they did, it was not hard enough to hurt; and it was really a good meeting.... This speech *was good*.[4]

At Stone's urging, Blackwell served as a vice-president of the New Jersey State Suffrage Society, organized in 1867 to try to reestablish the voting rights that women had exercised in the state from 1776 to 1807. The suffrage associations were, however, too narrowly focused on a single goal to satisfy Blackwell's desire for a broad-reaching exploration of women's roles.

In the spring of 1873, Blackwell received an invitation to the first meeting of a new organization, the Association for the Advancement of Women. The AAW's announced goal was to foster cooperation among women and "to receive and present practical methods for securing to Woman higher intellectual, moral and physical conditions, and thereby to improve all domestic and social relations."[5] The public call, or advertisement, for the first AAW Congress stated:

> The necessity of fellowship and concerted action among women interested in the advancement of the race and more especially of their own sex, is so apparent, that we do not hesitate to assert that by far the larger portion of our efforts in that direction are fruitless, because they are solitary and isolated.
>
> Thousands of noble and beneficent women, scattered all over our country, are to-day thinking, writing, and speaking the truths which all women need, and many are waiting to hear, and which would at once be a renovating force in the land, if the believers could, in a congregated body, unite upon practical methods for their incorporation into government, business and social life.[6]

Antoinette Blackwell immediately asked that her name be added to the list attached to the call, and enthusiastically attended the Congress, held in New York City in October 1873.

The membership of the AAW included active suffragists such as Elizabeth Cady Stanton and Frances Willard. Through the AAW, Blackwell also met women professionals from a wide range of disciplines, including Dr. Mary Putnam Jacobi, ministers Phebe A. Hanaford and Celia Burleigh, writer Julia Ward Howe, and the AAW's first president, Maria Mitchell, professor of astronomy at Vassar College.

Over its twenty-year lifetime, the organization served as a forum for many issues that suffrage associations considered marginal, such as education, science, dress reform, and religion. Its format of annual congresses, consisting of sets of prepared papers, allowed Blackwell to contribute her strongest skill. The AAW also spoke to her firm belief—perhaps naive—that the issue of women's role in society could best be resolved by rational discussion and education. She wrote, "In this country, all questions must come for final settlement to the people. Let them take up this; discussions will penetrate to the truth."[7]

Blackwell made it clear that in affiliating herself with the AAW she was in no way dissociating from the suffrage movement. In 1875 she discovered that her membership in the American Woman's Suffrage Association had lapsed, and quickly wrote to Lucy Stone:

> I never withdrew through intention; it is simply from neglect to pay the annual dues at a time when I was not

present at an annual meeting. . . . Now let me in again, as I have no desire to be counted out from the Suffrage movement when the papers are saying that the women of the [AAW] Congress are giving up suffrage.[8]

Women's organizations had one serious drawback: they provided no money for the work that women did. In fact, they drew on the resources of their members for expenses such as postage and travel to meetings. Blackwell commented to the AAW in 1888:

It is a curious, an interesting, and a characteristic fact that while organizations abound; though they reach from the babies and their kindergartens to the aged who need shelter and home; though they extend a chain of helping hands to nearly every class and every land, yet there has been almost no organized effort to obtain money values for the workers.[9]

It was an ongoing problem for volunteer organizations, reflecting in part the low value placed on activities that were seen as extensions of the tasks of mothering and housekeeping that women had performed within their own homes without pay.

By 1875 Antoinette Blackwell herself was looking for work that would earn money for her family, as well as provide a broader scope for her creative energies. In the wake of the financial collapse of 1873, she hoped to contribute to the family income, as she had promised to do at the time of her marriage. Blackwell turned once again to the ministry, the profession she had abandoned more than twenty years earlier. During those twenty years of studying, thinking, and living, she felt she had resolved the theological uncertainties that had precipitated her departure from her South Butler parish. In 1876 she published a synthesis of her philosophy, entitled *The Physical Basis of Immortality*. In it she addressed the question that had pursued her since adolescence: "Is my life immortal life?"

More than ever the soul cries out: Give me a positive assurance that my present conscious life is so deeply grounded in the very constitution of Nature that while this existing order of Nature remains unchanged, I also shall continue unchanged in true personal identity! . . . True personal identity in the present and in the future, is the vested kingdom of all religious aspiration! Continuous individual rectitude becomes impossible otherwise.[10]

She sought, in other words, a definitive answer to the question of whether an individual personality survived the death of the body. Blackwell turned to the new scientific disciplines for the answer, as she had for an authoritative description of gender differences. She hoped fervently that the scientific method of reasoning from established facts would at last provide a definitive answer to the question of human immortality:

> If the foundations of religious belief are to be shaken ever so slightly in the name of Science then the first work for Science must be to search diligently for other foundations which are laid firmly in the unchanging Constitution of Nature.... [To me] life and immortality have both seemed waiting to be brought into the light of established science. They have been waiting to be proved as admitted facts in nature which could be known to us through a mass of cumulative evidence, all converging toward the truth that the ultimate elements of Universal Nature are all simple and indestructible.[11]

In *The Physical Basis of Immortality*, Blackwell used as evidence the indestructibility of matter on the molecular level, and of motion-energy, both of which were accepted principles of physics. She then reasoned that the human personality must display the same physical endurance:

> Granite is durable; a metal is to us indestructible; the great worlds which shine out nightly in space are slow to break asunder; every organism is tenacious of its continuous maintenance. Is the mind-unit likely to be the only exception to this physical instinct, to the innate attraction, which is always seeking for permanent alliance? What is more probable than that, co-acting with its ever changing organism it is able to steadily provide itself with allies which shall outlast the perishable form with which it is temporarily associated.[12]

Although her proof may not be adequate to convince skeptics, Blackwell presented her ideas in a straightforward manner, without the apologetic tone found in her earlier writing. On the contrary, the book's Preface shows that she anticipated a favorable reaction:

> [Since 1869 this] subject has become more and more familiar to me. In the meantime there has been a remarkable

growth of public thinking; and scientific discussion has been tending strongly in the same general direction.... The possibility that a writer on this class of subjects may gain a hearing is much greater than even a few years ago.[13]

As Blackwell expected, *The Physical Basis of Immortality* was widely and favorably reviewed. A reviewer in Burlington, Iowa, wrote:

> The author of this work is well known in the world of writing and reading people, as one of the advanced thinkers of the age. There is a womanly power in her strength and depth of thought, and her investigations of the truth are so earnest and sincere, that the very force of her earnestness and sincerity is well nigh sufficient to carry home the conviction that she has found the truth, even unaided by the profound knowledge of her subject which she evinces and the completeness with which she anticipates every objection, and the readiness with which she answers and refutes opposing arguments, almost before they have been offered.[14]

A Boston newsman concurred:

> The subject is a vast as well as a puzzling one, but Mrs. Blackwell's method of dealing with it shows that she has studied it thoroughly and deeply. The volume is one that will be eagerly read by all those who have a taste for philosophizing upon such subjects.[15]

One criticism came from Albany:

> The book embodies her best thoughts, but while it affords very creditable evidences of her scholarship, it is quite too abstruse in its arguments and language to be of any material service to the great mass of American readers. If the idea of immortality must remain in abeyance until its reality can be scientifically demonstrated, mankind are to be pitied.[16]

What Blackwell did not accept was that some facts might be outside the range of scientific empirical proof, and that her attempts to find scientific certainty provided merely an additional set of metaphors through which the philosophical truth about the human condition could be grasped.

Having clarified her religious beliefs to her own satisfaction, Blackwell began looking for a religious group in which she could feel comfortable. For the past twenty-five years, since leaving her South Butler parish, Blackwell had deliberately avoided any affiliation with a religious sect, out of fear that she would once again feel hemmed in and restricted. She warned young Olympia Brown, when the latter was studying for the ministry:

> Do not unite with any church organization unless you see your own way quite clear.... I know how sorely you will need every help; but first and surest of all you need to stand upright in your own convictions—not in any other persons. I think I only intended to caution you against doing any thing prematurely; and perhaps I had a feeling that what *must be* for me, *might be* for you also—that the time might come when you would find something "cramping" in all Christian organisations; but to refuse present cooperation with those who are really with you in belief would be a sad mistake, especially to any one who is trying to occupy an exceptional position.[17]

By 1878, however, Blackwell experienced the disadvantages of her self-imposed isolation:

> [H]aving grown up in the midst of those who shared common beliefs, aims, sympathies and work religiously, I have greatly missed the moral support which that class of associations can give. In studying others, I am more and more convinced that many become lax and inefficient if not hopeless from need of the same bracing influence.[18]

Not surprisingly, Blackwell was drawn toward the Unitarian Church. Samuel Blackwell and three of his sisters had earlier joined the Unitarian Church, and they must have had an important influence on Antoinette's religious faith and affiliations.

The Unitarian revolt that had split New England congregations early in the nineteenth century involved much more than the official dispute over whether God had one part or three. The new liberal faith defended human freedom and reason instead of stressing the sinfulness of human pride and moral depravity. The liberals envisioned God as a benevolent father rather than an angry tyrant, and Jesus as a moral example who would show people how to be good. Unitarianism was, in fact, quite similar to the liberal Congregational theology of Charles Grandison Finney that Antoinette Blackwell had absorbed as a child and as a student at Oberlin. Her early familiarity with the writings of Ralph Waldo Emerson and her association with William Henry Channing had introduced her to similar ideas.

In New Englnd, at least, the Unitarian churches attracted well-educated middle- and upper-class people, interested in social reforms. They included many of the people Blackwell had worked with over the years in suffrage, temperance, and abolition organizations, as well as many of the ministers who had supported her when she was a young struggling speaker. There were few Unitarians in New Jersey before the Civil War, because the Congregational churches there were generally so liberal that no split occurred. By 1878, however, there were several new congregations around the state, including churches in both Montclair and Newark, near the Blackwells' home. Antoinette Blackwell visited Unitarian churches in New York City as well; both she and her husband turned for spiritual guidance to Robert Collyer, the new pastor of the Unitarian Church of the Messiah.

Blackwell was looking for both religious fellowship and possible opportunities to preach. In the spring of 1878 she wrote to several of her Unitarian friends to ask if they thought Unitarianism would suit her. All four letters were forwarded to Rev. R. R. Shippen, Secretary of the American Unitarian Association. In response to his questions, Blackwell then wrote directly to him:

> Rationalism or Natural Religion may mean Theism, Atheism, Comptism or any phase of reasoned morality. To me, it means the class of views indicated by my brief synopsis. I very much desire to know whether or not average Unitarians, . . . can cordially fellowship that phase of Rationalism. . . . I [cannot] well judge unaided whether my present views, my past orthodox beliefs, or my womanhood, any or all of them, would tempt the cold shoulder rather than the warm one from average Unitarians today, or from the Denomination as such.[19]

Blackwell apparently received a satisfactory reply, for she decided to join the Unitarian Fellowship and asked to be

recognized as a minister. In October 1878, the Committee on
Fellowship of the American Unitarian Association acknowledged her ministry. They warned her, however:

> You are of course aware of the feeling that exists in many
> of our established churches in regard to the propriety of
> women appearing in the pulpit. I do not understand that
> the Committee share this feeling. I simply refer to it to
> remind you that no word of ours will remove any such
> difficulty or indeed touch upon any other matter than that
> referred to us, viz. the antecedents of the person applying.[20]

In a fortuitously timed decision, Oberlin College, in 1879,
recognized Blackwell's professional status by awarding her an
"honorary" master of arts degree, which she had in fact earned
during her three years of study in the Theological Department
nearly thirty years before.[21]

With her new credentials, Blackwell set out to find a permanent position as a parish minister. She advertised in the
Woman's Journal and other publications. She told Lucy Stone:

> If nothing turns up before, my plan now is to go on to
> Boston May meetings, and from there begin actively to
> push my way into pulpits and other places; and see if I can
> get an opening after a while which shall have more of
> permanence.[22]

The environment into which Blackwell ventured in 1879 was
quite different from that of 1854, the last time she had held a
parish job. The liberal theological views that had been unorthodox, if not heretical, in the 1840s had become entirely
respectable. Blackwell had no need to fear that her "unorthodox resurrection" would arouse public criticism.[23]

The other major difference was that Blackwell no longer
stood alone as a woman minister. In 1864 Olympia Brown,
inspired by Antoinette Blackwell's speech to her class at Antioch College, was ordained as a Universalist minister; she served
full-time in parishes in Massachusetts, Connecticut, and Wis-
consin. By 1880 close to 200 women had been formally recognized as ministers, and many held full-time parish jobs. Phebe
A. Hanaford, pastor of a Universalist Church in New Haven,
Connecticut, declared in 1873, "Woman in the pulpit is no
longer an experiment, it is an established success."[24] Sarah

Perkins reported to the Association for the Advancement of Women in 1875:

> We all know that women are succeeding beautifully in the pulpit, and the common people hear them gladly, and woe be unto him who would thrust them out of the clerical ranks.[25]

Julia Ward Howe, a lay minister as well as a writer, established an association of women ministers to provide mutual support for their work. Blackwell did not join the group—for reasons that are not clear—but must have felt strengthened by their presence.

Within feminist organizations there was also encouragement for women like Blackwell who were looking for creative jobs. Opportunities were limited, especially for highly educated women. Only one married woman in twenty worked for pay outside her own home.[26] Of these, the vast majority were domestic servants, and the remainder mostly clerical workers, seamstresses, mill workers, and teachers of small children. Nevertheless, feminists felt excitement and hope as women pushed into new fields. Maria Mitchell, professor of astronomy at Vassar College and president of the AAW, said in her opening address to the 1875 AAW Congress:

> Our next duty should be to bring together women and the work for which they are fitted.... We must not only be ready to help women into new occupations, but we must make women willing to enter them. Finding, as we must when we have our statistics, gifted women whom the world has not known, and failing to find a place in the world's workshop for them, we must be ready to make one.[27]

Given that encouragement and the enthusiasm, persistence, and resourcefulness that Blackwell herself had shown earlier in her life, one would expect that she would have been able to find, or create, a suitable position. She did act as guest or "supply" preacher on occasion, as she had when she first left Oberlin. She preached several times that year in the church in Brooklyn, Connecticut, that she had visited in 1851 at the invitation of William Henry Channing. She told Alice Stone Blackwell many years later that the church had offered her a permanent position, which she refused; the church records, on the other hand, show that its pulpit was occupied from 1877 through 1881 by Rev. Caroline R. Jones.[28]

There was at least one suitable position open not far from the Blackwell's home. The newly organized Unitarian Church of All Souls in Newark was in dire need of a pastor. The New York Local Conference reported in 1878 that the congregation was "in a state of suspended animation, and without positive assistance cannot survive."[29] The All Souls parish would seem to have been ideal for Blackwell, enabling her to remain in the same geographic area while ministering to the needs of this struggling congregation. Blackwell left no record of having applied for the position. It is possible that the Newark congregation had no money to hire any minister, or that they were not bold enough to consider hiring a woman.

By December 1879 Blackwell was feeling discouraged by her inability to find a position. She wrote to Lucy Stone, "I must speak more or less somewhere. My gifts, such as they are, evidently lie more in that direction than any other."[30] The same letter reveals that Blackwell had mixed feelings about taking on a full-time permanent position, a reluctance that may have affected the intensity of her search:

> If I can get back into the lecture field and also preach as opportunity offers, that will, under the circumstances, be really best of all because I can be a good deal at home and look after the children and see to the general running of affairs; as well as give and take some home comfort.[31]

Despite her advocacy of work outside the home, Blackwell was not sure she personally would welcome the severe dislocations that full-time outside work might cause.

Blackwell also had less than wholehearted support from her husband. Samuel Blackwell, who supported and encouraged Antoinette's solitary studying and writing, was less enthusiastic about more controversial efforts. After his death, Antoinette told Alice Stone Blackwell that Sam "was always ready to do everything in his power to help me in my public work [and] to give money for long journeys." Like his doctor-sisters, Emily and Elizabeth, who refused to have their medical college named "Blackwell College," Sam was, Antoinette felt, "just a little too diffident about pushing his own fortunes, even properly... for himself and also for me."

[This diffidence is the] only respect in which I have felt a little freer since he was gone, because although I was never good at pushing I could do things that would have offended his taste. I think we should never seek praise, but if people want to do things for you, let them, if there is no harm in it. He believed more in woman's work than I did, if possible, yet if I was to lecture on suffrage where I should have everybody against me he did not like me to be criticized and would rather I went somewhere else.[32]

One can only speculate whether Antoinette would have been more aggressive in her job search had Sam's ambivalence not affected her.

Blackwell did not seriously consider any jobs other than preaching. She might have found a comfortable niche teaching at one of the increasing number of coeducational or women's colleges, which provided a stimulating community for some talented women.[33] Maria Mitchell wrote to Blackwell in 1878, perhaps in jest, "How gladly would I have had you for our Pre[siden]t at Vassar!" Blackwell did not follow up on the comment, writing to Stone that it "of course may mean very little, yet it is rather pleasant to have her say it."[34] It is possible, however, that Mitchell was seriously suggesting an academic position for Blackwell.

Most of the women in academic jobs were single or widowed, like Caroline Soule, who, finding herself at twenty-seven with five children to support, turned to teaching "as a barrier between me and cold and hunger and nakedness."[35] It would have been quite unusual for a married woman with five daughters still at home to take a full-time teaching job. Yet in the 1840s and 1850s Blackwell had not been deterred by the uniqueness of her situation. It seems more likely that she was not sufficiently involved in the academic community to consider it seriously. Blackwell's lack of formal training, especially in science, would have restricted the positions open to her. In addition, she may have been deterred by her early teaching experience and her strong aversion to becoming a "chronic teacher."[36]

By 1880 the Blackwells' financial problems were eased in the traditional manner when Sam took a regular job again. Antoinette later explained:

When the sudden illness of someone important in the Mexican and Central & South American Telegraph

Company occurred and the firm of Grinell and Minturn
with which Mr. Blackwell had been connected recommended him as a temporary supply, he gladly accepted the
situation; and conditions finally induced him to continue in the employ of the same firm for about twenty-five
years.[37]

For the rest of her life, Antoinette was free to pursue her own
studies, traveling, and other activities without worrying about
earning money.

This solution did not, however, respond to her equally
pressing need for an expanding sphere for her energies. Instead
of being a peak in her life, her fifty-fifth year was one of
depression. She complained to Lucy Stone:

> I am half sick and cannot get over it. Nerves, I think, and
> dullness too dense for ordinary humanity. Hope that will
> fly away under excitement.[38]

It is possible that her usually excellent health was disrupted by
menopause. It is more likely, however, that as in South Butler
her physical condition stemmed from uncertainty, perhaps
from despair.

At fifty-five Antoinette Blackwell felt she had explored—
and exhausted—all of the limited options open to her. She
found none that would utilize her education, her skills in
writing and public speaking, and her years of careful research,
while allowing her to continue to care for her children, her
garden, her home. As a younger woman she had possessed the
energy—and the audacity—to create a position for herself that
no one else had thought possible. Now she was tired, perhaps,
or at least subdued; her fighting days were over. Having created
in the abstract a vision of a better world for women, she could
not find or carve out a satisfactory place in the present one for
Antoinette Brown Blackwell.

Left to right: Edith (seated), Agnes, Sam, Ethel (seated), Florence,
Antoinette Brown Blackwell (seated), ca. 1880

Chapter 12

A WORLD OF INEFFECTUAL WORRY

While Antoinette Blackwell was engaged in public debates about appropriate education for young women, she did not seek to impose her ideas on her daughters. By 1875 her oldest daughter, Florence, was almost twenty years old; the two youngest, Ethel and Agnes, were six and eight, with Grace and Edith in between. Their care was divided among Antoinette, a nursery governess, and Samuel Blackwell. Sam took an interest in his children that surprised even Antoinette:

> He was both father and mother. The children are always more enthusiastic over what he did for them than what I did—it was so unusual for a father to be so motherly.[1]

Absorbed in her writing and her efforts to find a steady professional preaching position, Antoinette was largely content to allow each of her daughters to find her own way.

Florence was an awkward teenager. She showed signs of turning out all wrong, at least by the standards of her unusual Blackwell aunts. She did poorly at her school lessons, had no interest in college or a profession, and was preoccupied with boys. Antoinette seems not to have been alarmed by these signs. The rest of the Blackwell clan, however, were appalled.

Elizabeth, Ellen, Emily, and Marian Blackwell had each adopted at least one child, and all had strong ideas as to the right way to raise children. By 1874 Elizabeth, already respected as a physician, was writing a tract called "Counsel to Parents on the Moral Education of Their Children."[2] The Blackwell sisters apparently hoped that Samual and Antoinette's daughters would follow their own Blackwell pattern, eschewing romantic involvements and seeking out training in some useful profession. Despite—or perhaps because of—her own pioneering efforts as a physician, Elizabeth Blackwell believed that women's primary work was domestic. When she wrote about "Medicine as a Profession for Women," she focused on the beneficial interaction between "the science of the medical profession and the every-day life of women" as wives, mothers, and homemakers.[3] The career that Elizabeth suggested for young Florence was nursing because, as she explained to Sam in 1874, "I think it very important to instruct young women in those arts which come directly into play in life."[4]

The Blackwell sisters considered the rearing of all of their children, including Sam and Antoinette's daughters and Alice Stone Blackwell, as a joint responsibility. The sharing occurred through extensive correspondence, through the clan's summers together at Martha's Vineyard, and through long visits by each child to various aunts and uncles.[5] For example, in 1867, at the age of ten, Alice lived with "Aunt Elizabeth" while her parents campaigned for a woman suffrage referendum in Kansas. In 1869 Alice lived with Sam and Antoinette for several months, probably while her parents were absorbed in moving to Boston and establishing the *Woman's Journal.*

Antoinette's daughters also visited various Blackwell households, primarily Lucy and Henry's in Boston and Elizabeth's in England. In 1865 Antoinette had considered these visits emergency measures brought on by immediate necessity. By the 1870s she seems to have accepted them as a normal part of the family's life. In 1871-72 eleven-year-old Edith spent an entire year with her grandparents in upstate New York; Sam reported to Elizabeth, "Edie [is] apparently happy at her Grandfather's, going to a fair school there, and growing fleshy."[6] The next year Edith went to Boston to live with Lucy and Henry "for as long as convenient."[7] At the same time, Elizabeth Blackwell persuaded Antoinette and Sam to send Floy to live with her in England, although her travel expenses would drain their tight financial resources. Florence made a second trip to England two years later.

Elizabeth's goal was apparently to correct what she believed were years of faulty education, for which she blamed Antoinette. Her immediate goal was to improve Florence's physical health, which Elizabeth described as "simply wretched." "If I could keep her five years," Elizabeth wrote to Antoinette in 1873, "I think I could teach her to walk—not spasmodic walking, but a steady hearty enjoyment of her locomotive powers."[8] One wonders whether Florence really was in such poor health; in 1875 Antoinette referred to her five daughters as examples of girls who "enjoy a vigor of constitution above the average."[9] Antoinette did not necessarily accept the Blackwell sisters' self-imposed responsibility for—and meddling in—her own relationship with her daughters.

Elizabeth's deeper interest, however, was in Florence's moral development. She wrote to a friend, "'Tis funny how our household becomes a gentle reformatory for unmanageable nieces! We never punish, but we live them into right ways."[10] "Right ways," for the all-female Blackwell household, meant less attention to young men and other adolescent fantasies, and a disciplined regime of exercise and reading. The daily regime Elizabeth set up for Florence was supposed to discourage day-dreaming. Elizabeth wrote to Sam that she allowed Florence to read novels ("but I watch them") and to take long walks along the pier ("if I can get her a suitable companion").

Elizabeth told Antoinette, "Florence is very docile—ready to follow any suggestions and I think will be both reasonable and affectionate as soon as her soul begins to awake from the lethargy of physical debility."[11] Docility seems a strange commendation, coming from a woman like Elizabeth Blackwell who had been anything but docile as she fought for education and recognition as a physician.

After six months Elizabeth reported some progress:

> I think this living in a large household of adults is enlarging her experience, teaching her discretion and strengthening her judgments. It is a slow process, this gradual mental development and formation of character; but I have been pleased lately with little indications of sound judgment, that have pleased me.[12]

Antoinette, remembering that at Florence's age she had been earning money teaching school and preparing for college, may have wondered whether Florence would have benefited from an environment more challenging than the quiet English seaside. If so, she did not question whether a regime of carefully structured activities was likely to foster initiative, creativity, self-reliance—the very qualities that Antoinette had gleaned from her own farm childhood, and Elizabeth and Emily Blackwell from theirs, enabling them to blaze new paths.

In fact, the qualities Elizabeth tried to instill in Florence—affection, discretion, docility, good judgment—were consistent with popular prescriptions for female character and behavior. For example, Orestes A. Brownson wrote:

> Woman was created to be a wife and a mother; that is her destiny. To that destiny all her instincts point, and for it

nature has specially qualified her. Her proper sphere is home, and her proper function is the care of the household, to manage a family, to take care of the children, and attend to their early training. For this she is endowed with pai ence, endurance, passive courage, quick sensibilities, a sy mpathetic nature, and great executive and administrative abilities. She was born to be a queen in her own household, and to make home cheerful, bright and happy...

> She has all the qualities that fit her to be help-meet of man, to be the mother of his children, to be their nurse, their early instructress, their guardian, their life-long friend; to be his companion, his comforter, his ministering angel in sickness; but as an independent existence, free to follow her own fancies and vague longings, for her own ambition and natural love of power, without masculine direction or control, she is out of her element, and a social anomaly, sometimes a hideous monster.[13]

The only significant difference between Brownson's values and those of the Blackwell sisters was his belief that women should define themselves primarily in relation to men—sentiments with which the Blackwells vehemently disagreed.

When Florence returned from England, she was as restless as ever. She showed little interest in anything but several dashing young men. Antoinette attributed her daughter's dissatisfaction to an extended adolescence. She wrote to Lucy Stone in 1878:

> Florence will be 22 in Nov. Still the child is younger than many girls at 18. None of my children, though large in size, develop early. It is the nature of the Browns, who were made to live long and to develop slowly; but they do become grown up after a while. If Florence were either settled that she was not to marry, or if she was happily married, she would begin to unfold naturally in new directions. She has mother-wit enough; but it is, as you suggest, that her mind is elsewhere; and to increase the evil, her surroundings have led her to the belief that too much wisdom does not generally contribute to the kind of future which she most desires.[14]

It is not clear whether the "surroundings" included Antoinette's own household. She wrote extensively that women could successfully combine intellectual wisdom and family responsibility. She may have felt, however, that her writing and her example were not strong enough to counteract the messages Florence received from outside her home. For example, one author warned:

> Men do not care for brains in excess in women.... It is sympathy, not antagonism—it is companionship, not rivalry, still less supremacy, that they like in women.... The brains most useful to women, and most befitting their work in life, are those which show themselves in common-sense, in good judgment, and that kind of patient courage which enables them to bear small crosses and great trials alike with dignity and good temper.... As the true domain of woman is the home, and her way of ordering her domestic life the best test of her faculties, mere intellectual culture does not help in this; and, in fact, is often a hindrance rather than a help.[15]

Perhaps responding to Florence's lack of interest in serious studying, Antoinette does not seem to have envisioned her daughter having a career. At twenty-two Antoinette herself had completed five years of teaching school and two years of college, and was preparing with determination and enthusiasm to enter Oberlin's Theological Department. She made no attempt, however, to push or even encourage Florence to do anything as daring. Instead, she accepted the goals Florence set for herself. Antoinette wrote to Lucy Stone:

> I believe she is right in thinking that she is best adapted to a home of her own; and that she could learn to be a good wife, mother and housekeeper, with a good deal of energy to spare for wider outside interests.[16]

Antoinette had no desire, however, to spend her own time teaching Florence how to be a good housekeeper. She still considered housework at best a necessary but unpleasant chore. Lucy Stone, on the other hand, was an excellent and creative housekeeper. When Florence found her parents' Somerville home too boring, Antoinette agreed to let her go live in Boston with Lucy and Henry and their daughter Alice, only a few months younger than Floy, a student at Boston University. Antoinette rationalized the visits as a way of helping Lucy:

I think if you need someone to do the little caretaking
things... she will do for you as well as she can.

* * * * *

You see Lucy we do not hesitate to send you child after
child on extemporized visits. I hope you will give them so
many little things to do while they stay with you that they
will at least save you as much trouble as they make.[17]

Antoinette also hoped that at Lucy's house Florence would
learn "to do all kinds of work thoroughly well." She wrote to
Lucy about Florence in April 1878:

> Whatever her future, household skills in all directions will
> do her good and be to her a real and lasting service. So you
> have our full approbation in "putting her through" the
> whole routine as effectively as you can.[18]

Once in Boston, however, Florence tried to break out of the
domestic mold the family assumed was set. Probably with her
cousin Alice's encouragement, she decided she wanted to learn
public speaking. Surprisingly, Antoinette, instead of rejoicing
that Florence had finally found something interesting to do—
something, in fact, quite like her own career—complained to
Lucy about Florence's tendency of "going on with the elocu-
tion [lessons] instead of taking hold of housework."[18]

A year later Florence again stayed in Boston for some
months, and this time she complained that she was overbur-
dened with housework. She wrote to her adopted cousin, Kitty
Barry:

> You perceive that I am still at Aunt Lucy's; how much
> longer I shall stay is still very uncertain. Yesterday her
> hired girl left and I am at present doing the work with
> Aunt L's help and some from Alice when she can.
>
> But I do not know how long I can stand it.... The
> trouble is I go to church three evenings in the week and
> twice on Sunday and I do not know whether I can work all
> day and attend prayer-meetings all night.

Florence's interest in public speaking began to focus on
religion:

> Has Alice told you about my plans of studying theology. I
> have made up my mind to follow in Mother's footsteps

and preach if I can only I should of course do it in the
Methodist Church.... The only fear with me is have I
strength and grit enough to go through the hard work and
study necessary.

For the last two months I have had church and theology on the brain and have not been able to think of much
else.[20]

Antoinette might have been able to encourage her daughter in
the "strength and grit" necessary for theological study. If she
recognized her daughter's ambition, however, she did not
respond to it. With Florence in Boston, and Antoinette
absorbed in the day-to-day caring for a household and the
younger children, it is possible that mother and daughter did
not even discuss their common interests. Florence did become a
lay preacher; according to one of her cousins, she spoke "in a
manner so like Aunt Nettie's that Alice found it funny."[21] The
family continued to view Florence as aimless and idle, interested only in flirting.

Emily and Elizabeth Blackwell continued to be concerned
about Florence. Emily wrote to Elizabeth:

I would rather see both of them [their own adopted chil-
dren] dead, than have them grow up as some of our nieces
and a good many American girls do, feeble, lazy, self-
indulgent and common.... F. is absolutely idle and gre-
garious. She must pass her time in company and gossip, if
she can't have any but bad company, then bad it must be.[22]

The Blackwell sisters blamed Sam and Antoinette for Florence's behavior; Emily continued:

My dealings with her have left me with a feeling of indignation against her parents, for she might have been made
very different. She is not indocile, she has a great deal of
shrewd practical sense, but her standards, the atmosphere
mentally & morally through which she looks at things,
is *so deplorably common*, narrow & undeveloped....
[She is] being destroyed by her life at Somerville.[23]

The Blackwell sisters' consternation at Florence's upbringing and character came to a head during the summer of
1881. Antoinette and Sam and their younger daughters stayed
in New Jersey, but Florence, by then almost twenty-five, went

to Martha's Vineyard. Emily Blackwell volunteered to act as
guardian. She soon regretted it, however, when Florence fell in
love with Elliott Mayhew, a year-round Vineyard resident.
Emily wrote indignantly to Elizabeth in August:

> It had never entered my head that Fl. could get up any
> flirtation. It had never suggested itself to me that she
> would seriously think of one of the young farmers. But I
> found her in full tide, going with him every Sunday twice
> to church, and out with him every week-day he could find
> the leisure, meeting him morning and evening when he
> brought our milk, and in every other occasion she could
> possibly contrive.[24]

After recovering from her initial amazement, Emily confronted
Florence for a serious talk:

> I . . . found she had taken a great fancy to the young man,
> and was earnestly bent on attracting him, and marrying
> him if she continued to like him. . . . She entreated me not
> to break the matter off, represented to me that there was
> nothing before her if she could not marry, assured me that
> such a home as Mr. Mayhew could give her should seem to
> her infinitely more desireable than any other prospect she
> had, and said she believed he was more attractive to her
> already, than any man she had ever met.[25]

By most standards, Elliott Mayhew does not appear to have
been such an unsuitable husband for Florence. The Mayhew
family was one of the oldest on the island, and Elliott's father
owned considerable amounts of land near the Blackwells'
Quitsa homes. Elliott himself owned a general store, with a sign
over the door reading "E. Elliott Mayhew, dealer in almost
everything."[26] Emily had to admit, after making inquiries in
the neighborhood, that Elliott bore "a very good character, and
is a manly honest young fellow. . . . I thought at the bottom he
had more worth than Florence and more sense."[27]

Nevertheless, Emily insisted that "the whole association
was such that I was astounded by the idea."[28] The principal
objection to Elliott was what the Blackwell sisters considered
his lower-class status. Emily was concerned when she found
out that "his sister bears a very bad character, and his mother is
a very common rough but clever woman."[29] Alice Stone Blackwell observed, "It is a relic of silly aristocratic English notions

to see anything discreditable in keeping store."[30] But to the older Blackwells a storekeeper was definitely a lower-class person, assumed to be overly interested in sex, not to be trusted around an impressionable young woman like Florence. Emily told Elizabeth, "I was never more perplexed in my life than to decide what was the best course in the matter."[31]

Emily Blackwell was not alone in her concern. During the 1870s and 1880s, the behavior and character of young women—especially those in growing urban areas—were scrutinized much more carefully and publicly than they had been during Antoinette Blackwell's youth. Newspaper articles stressed the importance of sexual purity and avoiding marriages with "inappropriate" men. Etiquette columns in such popular magazines as the *Ladies' Home Journal* helped mothers, daughters, and guardians decide what was proper behavior:

> It is never lady-like to kiss a gentleman or to let him kiss you, unless you are engaged to marry him, or he is a near relative.
>
> * * * * * *
>
> Be very careful not to write to any man if he has written to you until you know his standing and character. Young women cannot be too particular in making acquaintances with men. Life-long sorrows have resulted from such proceedings.[32]

These warnings, together with the pressure on young women to adopt marriage and motherhood as their primary goals, must have confused many young women other than Florence Blackwell.

Emily was appalled to learn that Antoinette and Sam would not interfere at all in the blossoming courtship. They apparently trusted that Florence was old enough to make her own decisions. Antoinette's novel *The Island Neighbors*, written ten years earlier, had as part of its plot an uncanny foreshadowing of the conflict between Florence and her Blackwell aunts. In describing the disapproval of her heroine's guardians at her choice of a beau they considered lower class, Antoinette had commented, "What a world of ineffectual worry we elders are always falling into over the love affairs of the young people, for whom we choose to consider ourselves responsible."[33] Perhaps she also recalled her own courtship, when she and Sam had conspired to avoid the scrutiny of the close-knit Blackwell family. Now, faced with the same situation in her own family, Antoinette was content to allow her grown-up daughter to make her own decisions.

Unlike the Blackwell aunts, Antoinette did not consider it unfortunate that her daughter wanted to marry Elliott Mayhew. Her own marriage was so satisfying, after more than twenty years, that she would have no reason to discourage her daughters from following the same pattern. Nor did she share the Blackwells' concern about Elliott's background; Antoinette herself had grown up on a farm and she respected and liked the Vineyard's year-round residents.

Emily Blackwell finally decided that there was nothing she could do to change Florence's mind—or Antoinette's. She wrote to Elizabeth:

> [I realized] that it was perhaps the one chance of her settling into a respectable if common marriage. So I agreed not to send her home, and there followed ten days vexation trying to keep her within bounds, and to keep the children out of the atmosphere that she filled the house with.[34]

In October, Emily was able to report to Elizabeth:

> I was so glad to put Florence on the Somerville train, and feel that I had returned her safe to her parents, and was free of that bother. Never again will I take with me anywhere any of those girls now they are old enough to flirt.[35]

Florence and Elliott were married in 1882, despite Emily's and Elizabeth's objections. The couple settled happily in the old "Brown house," near Elliott's family and not far from the Blackwells' summer cottage. In a letter to Alice, Florence apologized for having so little time to write, in between housekeeping and "spooning":

> I believe in matrimony decidedly when one gets a saint like Elliott. He could not be kinder or more considerate, thinks I am about perfect, so of course I have to try to be, so as not to disappoint him.... You have not a ghost of an idea how thoroughly good he is all the way through ... and his ideas about women would delight Aunt Lucy.[36]

In fact, from Florence's description, Elliott Mayhew sounds similar in character to Sam Blackwell; Florence appears to have adopted as a model for marriage the closeness she saw between Sam and Antoinette.

Antoinette's second daughter, Edith, followed more closely the pattern set by her Blackwell relatives, and again Antoinette did not interfere. By 1876, when she was almost sixteen, Edith was studying at home, preparing for college. She seems to have assumed, with few qualms, that she would have some kind of professional career. That fall she wrote to Kitty Barry:

> You asked me if I should like to be a doctor. I really don't know whether I should or not, of course it wouldn't be very pleasant to have to get up at any hour of the night to see patients, but I suppose there always are unpleasant things in every business. I have no *special taste* in that direction, but I suppose I might as well study medicine as anything else.[37]

In part Edith's ambition stemmed from a talent for healing people and animals, which showed itself early in her life. Her younger sister later wrote about Edith:

> In childhood quick in an emergency,
> Binding with thong to stop successfully
> A horse's bleeding leg, while others stood
> Watching the young and skillful hands make good.[38]

Edith's decision to study medicine undoubtedly owed something to the example of Emily and Elizabeth Blackwell. Edith did not face a battle to establish, as a matter of principle, her rights to travel alone, to attend college, to study and practice medicine. Unlike her mother, Edith could choose from a number of colleges and universities. She would join the approximately 11,000 women who were attending college— one-third of all college students, albeit a small minority of the women of college age.[39] Edith chose Swarthmore College, a small coeducational Quaker college in the pretty countryside outside Philadelphia. She then enrolled in the Woman's Infirmary Medical School, founded by Elizabeth Blackwell in 1868 and ably administered by her sister Emily during the time Edith attended.

Yet her clear choice of work did not save Edith from emotional difficulties. Antoinette reported to Lucy in the spring of 1883:

Except when roused up, Edith is mentally depressed and
nervous. So, she must go on resting. She clings to
home.... Edith does not dislike the study of medicine. She
is in a morbid tired state.... It is all nerves and the dismay
of them.

...All the doctors in the world could not convince me
that there is not some real difficulty which keeps her
nervous, often depressed, and unable to use her mind.
What it is I don't know; and am sure a real interest will be
the right medicine. But it must take time.[40]

Lucy Stone suggested, as a tonic, that Antoinette have her
daughters share in the household chores, instead of relying on
hired servants. But Edith's emotional problems may well have
stemmed less from lack of housework than from the pressures
of her studies. Emily Blackwell and her associate, Mary Putnam Jacobi, one of the leading professors at the medical school,
held their students to extremely high academic standards.[41]
Edith's earlier education may not have prepared her for those
demands. She managed to overcome her lethargy, however, and
after graduating at the head of her class, she began to practice
medicine.

Antoinette's middle daughter, Grace, had more serious
emotional problems than Edith's. Even as a young girl, Grace
showed signs of the chronic depression and mental illness that
were to continue throughout her life. For a time Grace lived
with Lucy in Boston, attending a private girls' school. Although she could help out around the house, she had trouble
traveling alone or making decisions. Later, apparently during
her late teens, she in turn was sent to visit Elizabeth Blackwell
in England to study art and, the family hoped, to recover from
her depression. Grace quickly became bored and restless in the
small seaside town, and came home after less than a year
without any significant improvement.

If Antoinette and Sam noticed that Grace was suffering
from more than adolescent growing pains, they did not
acknowledge the problem. They continued to move her from
one household to another within the extended Blackwell family. Like Florence, Grace fell in love with a man from the
Vineyard; this time, both Antoinette and the other Blackwells
opposed the match, and the relationship was ended. The conse-
quent disappointment only aggravated Grace's mental
depression.[42]

In a sense, Antoinette Blackwell's daughters followed in her footsteps; the differences among them mirrored the ambiguities in her own vision of women's roles. Antoinette was as satisfied with Florence's settling into marriage—with a bit of preaching on the side—as with Edith's decision to study medicine. She was not overly concerned either with the demands of popular etiquette or with pushing all young women into a model based on professional work outside the home.

Alice Stone Blackwell

Chapter 13

UNITED METHODS

Throughout the 1880s, Antoinette Blackwell focused on work with various women's organizations. Following publication of *The Physical Basis of Immortality* in 1876, Blackwell did not complete another book for almost twenty years. She must have continued to read and write philosophical articles, at least to clarify her own thoughts. But her primary energy seems to have gone into public work more than in any period since her marriage. The official records of the organizations with which she worked document primarily her long-standing role as a speechmaker; she presented a paper at almost every meeting of the AAW throughout the 1880s. Her own letters and other documents, however, reveal an additional role as a facilitator, cultivating personal relationships within organizations and bringing people together for creative work.

In contrast to women like Susan B. Anthony, Elizabeth Cady Stanton, and Lucy Stone, who were putting virtually all their energy into the suffrage movement. Blackwell continued to participate in a number of organizations: suffrage associations (both national and local), the Association for the Advancement of Women, and the American Association for the Advancement of Science (AAAS).

The AAW gave Blackwell a forum for her ideas and a constituency to which her writing was directed. It is not clear what influence the AAW may have had on the larger society or even on the social reform movements of the 1890s. For Blackwell, however, the AAW's impact was less important than the friendships and encouragement she found there, a pleasant break from her often solitary study. The AAW held congresses each autumn in various cities. In addition, its officers met twice a year in private homes to plan activities. Blackwell hosted several of those meetings at her home. The other women active in the organization, Blackwell's intellectual peers, became warm friends.

Among Blackwell's close associates during these years were Abigail Williams May, Julia Ward Howe, and Maria Mitchell, all quite different from one another. Abby May was a

cousin of both liberal minister Samuel J. May and Louisa May
Alcott. She was an active Unitarian, a trustee of Booker T.
Washington's Tuskegee Institute, an active suffragist, and the
first woman member of the Boston School Committee and the
Massachusetts Board of Education. After her death in 1888,
Blackwell wrote about her:

> Abby May was one of the most effective workers... and
> was always a universal favorite. Miss May was one of the
> least self-seeking, most self-forgetful and most generally
> helpful of the co-workers during my sixty years of cooper-
> ation with many types of women. She was simplicity itself
> in dress, nearly always wearing a plain skirt of elegant
> material and something like a pretty loose jacket, both in
> the neatest harmony.... There were few of my co-workers
> to whom I was more sincerely and lovingly attached.[1]

Julia Ward Howe, a deeply religious well-to-do Boston
widow, impressed Blackwell with her power of concentration
and her fluency with languages. Blackwell later described their
travels together:

> After a meeting of the A.A.W. in Detroit... I spoke in one
> of the city churches and Mrs. Howe in one of the churches
> at Ann Arbor. Next day I joined Mrs. Howe at Ann Arbor
> ... and we spent the early part of the morning in examining
> the University.... After four or five days of almost inces-
> sant occupation it was a relief to enjoy the scenery from a
> [railroad] car-window. Turning toward Mrs. Howe, who
> sat in the opposite seat, reading, I was interested to rise and
> look over her shoulder. She was intently reading in a
> Greek text.[2]

Maria Mitchell was professor of astronomy at Vassar College. Mitchell respected Blackwell as an intellectual peer, and
called on her as a public speaker:

> Are you rich enough & good-natured enough to come to
> Po'Keepsie & give a lecture on any semi-scientific subject,
> & pay all your expenses except that of board while here? I
> *know* the question is audacious, but I am about to *run* a
> free course of Lectures on science, for *women*, in the hope
> of awakening some of the P. women. The city has never
> got over the effect of Rip Van Winkle's nap. I take upon
> myself the expense of advertising & the room which will be
> a small one. I will take good care of you.[3]

Blackwell cherished these associations; she later wrote about the AAW:

> Many most satisfactory life-long friendships were formed among the members.... This frequent meeting of co-workers has always been to me one of the chief rewards of a somewhat strenuous life.[4]

Among the AAW's leaders, Blackwell found recognition and acceptance as a public speaker, a writer, and a friend.

Blackwell's long years of work as an amateur scientist were also recognized at last by the predominantly male intellectual community. In 1881 she was elected to membership in the American Association for the Advancement of Science, established in 1848 to promote discussion of scientific topics. Like the AAW, it met annually in different cities throughout the United States. The AAAS provided one of the first forums for the discussion of Darwinism and of Gregor Mendel's new theories about the mechanism of genetic inheritance. Blackwell was one of a small minority of women in the association, but denied "that manhood has been guilty of any special inhospitality to the thought of womanhood." She attributed the overwhelmingly male membership to circumstances apparently beyond anyone's control:

> The Science Association was more than ready to receive women for membership and to admit their papers along lines of observation.... But the giants in the mansions up above have never found it easy to extend comfortable hospitality to the undistinguished, men or women, who seem to climb upward by the aid of their own personal beanstalks. This probably is well. In this regard the men who make science a specialty are in no wise different from other professional thinkers. In effect they all require a strong mark registered before it can be accepted. This in itself is enough to account for a comparative limitation of the achievements of woman along the line of independent discoveries or new interpretation of unsettled questions.[5]

As in the temperance movement thirty years earlier, Blackwell did not actively crusade for women's opportunities within the AAAS other than by her presence and participation.

Blackwell was considered sufficiently distinguished to deliver papers at some of the AAAS's annual meetings, although there is no evidence that her ideas about either science or metaphysics had any significant influence on the course of scientific thought. In her presentations, Blackwell extended the scientific theories she had presented in *The Sexes Throughout Nature*. In 1884, for example, she prepared a paper on "The Comparative Longevity of the Sexes," for both the AAW congress in Baltimore and the AAAS meeting in Philadelphia. She used statistical tables from all over the world to demonstrate the natural balance between the total number of men and women. According to her interpretation of the census data, the women who die of "female ailments" balance men killed in war or occupational accidents, and the predominance of women in old age is balanced by the greater number of male infants. Blackwell theorized that the energy required for women's reproductive function was available in later years as a reserve source of vitality. She concluded, rather defensively, that women are not "the weaker sex" either physically or psychically.[6]

During these years, Blackwell traveled extensively throughout the United States, primarily to attend conventions. The AAAS met in Montreal, Minneapolis, Philadelphia, Ann Arbor; the AAW in Chicago, Baltimore, Des Moines, Louisville. Train service was rapid and relatively comfortable, in comparison with Blackwell's earlier trips.

Despite her extensive traveling, however, Blackwell's perception of the world outside of her own circle of family and friends remained limited. She could see and appreciate superficial differences, but her imagination seldom penetrated to the real-life experience of people who were poor, nonwhite, or uneducated.

Blackwell's response to evidence of disparities between wealthy and poor was similarly limited to superficial individualistic commentaries. The 1880s were years of transition and turmoil in the country, the years when all the elements of the nation's economy for the next hundred years were set. Large factories provided middle-class families with appliances that changed the details of daily life: telephones, central heating, indoor plumbing, even a piano for the parlor. Food was also processed by large companies whose names quickly became household words: Pillsbury flour, Chase and Sanborn coffee, Borden's condensed milk, Swift meats, Wrigley's chewing gum. The Standard Oil Company consolidated oil drilling and refining operations throughout the country. Transcontinental railroads made the whole country a unified market for goods, although the erratic cycles of railroad construction threatened the stability and certainty that other businesses needed. Wealth and power became concentrated in cities and big corporations; debtors and farmers alike suffered from a continual decline in both wages and prices throughout the last three decades of the century. In 1886 the country was shaken by a blizzard, followed by five successive droughts that disrupted food production. Workers in many industries protested low wages, long hours, and unhealthy working conditions by going out on strike, and the newspapers fanned fears of a foreign-inspired anarchist revolution. In Chicago's Haymarket Square, police marched on a public union meeting, a bomb was thrown into the crowd, and a bloody riot ensued. Many intellectuals, their faith already shaken by Darwin's evolution theory, searched for new sources of morality and legitimacy. A few earnestly looked for methods of alleviating, or at least understanding, the social stresses that accompanied the new industrial order.[7]

Antoinette Blackwell was no more—or less—aware of the social tensions around her than many of her peers. Her report of a visit to the carefully landscaped, multimillion-dollar estate of George Washington Vanderbilt, heir to one of the nation's largest fortunes, near Asheville, North Carolina, focused on the estate's superficial appearance:

> I went one morning with a young woman who was acting as a missionary among the colored people, visiting several cottages, generally kept in a rather tidy manner. Most of the laborers in the neighborhood were employees of the Biltmore estate of Mr. Vanderbilt, receiving good wages and having steady work.... The grounds were very beautiful. And so it seems a rich man may do great good by what appears almost ostentatious self-indulgence. Indeed Mr. Vanderbilt has since done much social work for the improvement of the neighborhood.[8]

In 1855 a younger Antoinette Brown had ventured into the slums and prisons of New York City, ministering to individuals and attempting—unsuccessfully—to ferret out the roots of what she called "shadows of our social system." Nothing in the intervening years had deepened her understanding of the causes of poverty or the dynamics of the economic order. By the 1880s her daily experience was so far removed from slums, poor people, prisons, and other institutions that she no longer felt the agonizing need to understand and explain them, much less to act forcefully to change the world. She was a philosopher with little grasp of economic realities, not an activist like Jane Addams and Florence Kelley, founders of Chicago's Hull House, who saw, spoke out against, and worked to change the condition of working-class women.

The limitations in Blackwell's vision severely hampered her attempts to analyze social reality. Nowhere did this appear more forcefully than in her work as chairman of the AAW's Committee on Reforms and Statistics. Each year the committee sent a questionnaire to all the state vice-presidents, who investigated conditions in their local communities and sent back reports—the beginning of what would become sociological surveys. The questionnaires covered topics ranging from the length of punishment inflicted on men and women, to noninstitutional methods of caring for orphans, to the role of women as science teachers and researchers. As chairman of the committee, Blackwell was responsible for presenting a summary and interpretation of the results to the next AAW congress. Her reports reflect a curious mixture of proposals, colored by her lack of awareness of the large corporations that dominated the national economy. She assumed that most persons were both laborers and capitalists, as had been true in the small village of her childhood, the small towns she knew in New Jersey and Martha's Vineyard, and the hardware store Sam and Henry Blackwell had owned in Cincinnati.

Blackwell tried to integrate and harmonize the viewpoints of both workers and entrepreneurs. She suggested that all needy and ablebodied persons could find work if industrial production expanded, ignoring the fact that more goods were already being produced than consumers wanted to buy. She fully endorsed limiting work to eight hours per day, a rallying cry of the most radical labor organizers. She was puzzled by the difficulty of determining fair compensation for both the "direct labor of industrial production" and the "brain work" and capital investment necessary for managing a business. In 1886—the year of the Haymarket riot—Blackwell proposed that in conflicts between workers and employers, "a wise cooperation can master all difficulties," a conclusion based more on her cosmic vision than on any concrete evidence from industrial workers. She recommended impartial arbitration of labor disputes, with both strikes and lockouts as a last resort. She joined many other philanthropists in suggesting that some way be found for laborers to become shareholders in their enterprises, so that they would share the rewards and incentives for increased productivity and efficiency. Finally, she urged cooperation among women, both rich and poor, and the development of "large enterprises which are either wholly or in part under their own management."[9]

Two years later, Blackwell's summary of the state reports focused specifically on women workers. She condemned both "sex-graded-work" and "sex-graded-pay for the same kinds of work" as an "heir-loom from past heathendom." She lamented that women workers were barred from working anywhere except concentrated "in the awfully crowded down below which forms the basement to all grand structures." She suggested that "If women desire full money values for services, the direct way to gain it is to go into business for themselves."[10] Although that advice may have been appropriate for some professionally trained women, it can hardly have spoken to the needs of the thousands of poorly educated women working long hours to earn barely enough for food. After her family's experience during the 1870s trying to work on a free-lance basis, and her own unsuccessful attempts to earn money on a steady basis, it is curious that Blackwell retained a naive faith that ample opportunities were available for anyone with enough initiative. Blackwell did propose that "energetic, capable women combine to gain independent resources, and to help poorer, less competent women to find better paid openings."[11] However, there is no evidence that she did anything to implement that suggestion.

Blackwell also accepted widely held stereotypes concerning nonwhite people. In her early scientific writings, she assumed without question "that of the five or six typical races of men, each is as unique in mental as in physical traits." In 1869 she wrote about black Americans:

By his long suffering, his patience, docility, and teachability while in slavery—by his forbearance, magnanimity, and courage during our long war, and by his self-poise since he has become a freeman, he certainly has given high evidence of a wonderful susceptibility to some of the sublimest virtues. His hilarity, his love of music, his religious fervor, and his enjoyment of tropical warmth and harmony of color and outline, make it at least presumable

that he may yet lead in a civilization of gorgeous artistic
beauty, of social good fellowship, and generous fraternity,
such as the world has not known hitherto.[12]

Blackwell believed she was less prejudiced than many
people she met. After one AAW congress in Atlanta, Blackwell,
Julia Ward Howe, Ednah Dow Cheney, and several other
speakers visited schools and colleges, both black and white. At
Tuskegee Institute they were guests of Booker T. Washington,
the black educator who advocated vocational training appropriate to the rural South. The women gave several talks to "a
large and flourishing audience of colored students," and to a
"mothers' meeting" of elderly illiterate women. Blackwell, as
the one minister among the visitors, was invited to address the
theological students "concerning their work as students and
their work in [later] life." On the way home, Blackwell was
surprised to find that a male friend "fairly doubled up with
laughter ... staring in utter astonishment" when he heard that
they had been private guests of a black family.[13] She was able to
accept individual black persons as equals, but did not challenge the racial prejudice that pervaded the whole society.

Blackwell's view of blacks as inherently different from
whites but equally valuable was more generous than the views
of many other reformers and suffrage leaders, whose speeches
were peppered with references to "the ignorant foreign vote," and
the evils of enfranchising "4,500,000 ex-slaves, illiterate and
semi-barbarous."[14] Within the woman suffrage movement,
pressure from southern women encouraged woman suffrage
arguments framed to placate politicians committed to main-
taining white supremacy. In fact, it was Henry Blackwell—
earlier a committed abolitionist—who first argued, in 1867,
that women should be allowed to vote because the votes of
white women in the southern states would outweigh those of
Negro men and women. If Antoinette Blackwell disagreed, she
did so silently.

The high point of Blackwell's organizational work in this
period was the International Council of Women held in
Washington, D.C., in the spring of 1888. Officially the council
was planned as a commemoration of the fortieth anniversary of
the 1848 Woman's Rights Convention in Seneca Falls, which
Elizabeth Cady Stanton and Susan B. Anthony counted as the
birth date of the woman's rights movement. That mythology
provided a convenient rallying point, although it ignored the

continuity of feminist thought and action from Abigail Adams and Mercy Otis Warren through Mary Wollstonecraft, Lucretia Mott, Margaret Fuller, and the Grimké sisters to Elizabeth Cady Stanton herself. The council consisted of invited speakers from fifty-three organizations concerned with every aspect of women's organizational efforts. Missionary societies, literary clubs, labor leagues, temperance organizations, social purity crusades, professional associations, as well as local, state, and national suffrage organizations, were all represented. Eighty speakers gave papers in symposia on education, philanthropy, woman's legal disabilities, politics, religion, industrial work, and professions. For the first time in many years, the "collateral issues," which had been so important to Blackwell and the Association for the Advancement of Women, were brought together with the suffrage movement.

Blackwell played a minor role in the religious services that opened the council, assisting Rev. Anna Howard Shaw. She also gave a paper during the religious symposium entitled "What Religious Truths can be Established by Science and Philosophy." But the most important session for her was the "Conference of Pioneers," honoring those who had worked for woman's rights for many decades: Stanton, Frederick Douglass, Lucy Stone, Henry Blackwell, Antoinette Brown Blackwell. Many other workers from the early years wrote in their greetings: Ernestine Rose, John Greenleaf Whittier, Amelia Bloomer, Theodore Weld, Caroline Severance, Thomas Wentworth Higginson. Mary Grew, an elderly Philadelphia Quaker, introduced the session:

> It is meet, it is fitting that we come here and stand a while on this mount of retrospection and prospective vision, and recount all the steps of the way as far as we can recount them, and while we rejoice and take courage in thinking over the wonderful things which have been done in the name of justice, and are full of hope, full of faith, we do not forget that the work is not done.... Some of us very aged ones may not live to see the completion of this work; may not join in the jubilee which shall celebrate the emancipation of women.... We shall bequeath it to you, young friends; to you gathered here, with the fresh chrism of consecration on your brows; bequeath it to you with all its glorious opportunities, its solemn responsibilities, and with our parting word, "Be faithful unto death or victory."[15]

Over and over the listeners, many of them too young to remember, were reminded of women's struggles simply to speak from a public platform. Antoinette Blackwell told both of her fight at Oberlin to become a minister and of the "Half-Worlds" Temperance Convention when she was refused the right to speak. These and similar war stories helped younger women identify with the feminist movement's immediate past, and reminded all of them of the intense work that would be needed to achieve further gains. The 1888 council also demonstrated the respectability that the once-radical suffrage movement had gained. Among the scheduled events was a gala reception at the White House, hosted by President and Mrs. Grover Cleveland. The 1500 people who attended wore the yellow lapel ribbon that had become the badge of the suffrage organizations.

The suffrage movement itself was in the midst of internal changes, in part due to younger women coming into positions of leadership. The two national organizations, which had separated bitterly in 1869, had few remaining substantive differences. In both groups, debates over "extraneous" issues, such as divorce on grounds of drunkenness, had yielded to concentrated campaigns for suffrage. After twenty years of arduous work, neither organization could claim tangible victories. The federal amendment favored by Stanton and Anthony languished in congressional committee, while state after state voted down suffrage referendums and legislation. On the other hand, the idea of woman suffrage had become respectable. Both suffrage organizations were staffed by women who were at least a generation younger than Blackwell, Stone, Stanton, and Anthony—women who had come to maturity after the Civil War. These women had never risked public ridicule to travel alone to speak out on issues such as abolition; they had not been booed off platforms for daring to speak to mixed audiences. They tended to be respectable, professional, and middle class. Many of them had been too young to have witnessed the bitter events leading up to the split. The formal split persisted largely because of personal animosities among the leaders.[16]

Antoinette Blackwell had carefully avoided taking sides in the suffrage split. She had remained close to the leaders of both organizations and had avoided the internal issues in each. She explained to Lucy Stone:

> I hate the machinery of both the A[merican Woman Suffrage] Association & the Congress; but have concluded that

those who run societies must have their own way about that. I shall work with them "under protest," not public protest, only to you privately.[17]

Blackwell was bothered by the divisiveness and ill will in the suffrage movement. She remembered the "fraternal character" of the past:

In the early days of the suffrage movement there was a marvelous harmony and sympathy of feeling which impresses me more and more as the years go by and average life with its discordances makes itself more and more manifest. The home of every suffragist was a home for all suffragists. One good point made or one good deed done was earnestly rejoiced in by every other worker. There seemed to be no jealousies and very little self-seeking. We all stood together in a difficult and common cause.[18]

As a minister, Blackwell believed that animosities and personal grudges should be relinquished for the sake of the greater good of cooperation. She envisioned a pluralistic association of people and groups working toward common goals. In 1889 Blackwell wrote to Frances Willard, chair of the International Council of Women:

Of ladies with whom I am or have been closely associated in any kind of work...I believe there is not one who would object to United Methods, to sincere helpful cordial just cooperation—with the utmost freedom for differences of opinion (within moral limits) and with equally wide differences in objects and in practical ways of trying to secure them. I believe they all wish to feel assured that they can join hands to march abreast, with more dignity and power side by side.[19]

Blackwell's concern led her to seek advice from William Henry Channing, one of the ministers who had encouraged her to seek ordination. Channing replied from his home in London:

As to the "right policy for the future," on which you ask my advice.... Act towards these Sisters, as you will wish to have acted in the World of Perfect Truth. All the women engaged in our world-wide movement... should strive to uphold one another on the highest ground of Mutual Reverence, Honor, Trust. Pardon seventy times seven one

anothers littlenesses, frailties, follies, perversities.... Be
unswervingly patient, constant, steadily faithful.... Realize your highest *Ideal* of *Womanhood* by embodying it in
Character & Life. Rouse one another, by practical example, ever to forget the past & press onward! And whenever
you find one another going astray or misleading others,
reprove each other *lovingly, bravely, gently* and *hope-
fully*. Never despair of one another! Never draw back! ...
Never break old ties of friendship! Stand shoulder to
shoulder to win the triumph of right. Keep up both your
organizations if it best helps the common cause. But do
not criticise and condemn one another in so doing. Our
movement is too grand for rivalries and strife.... [20]

With this encouragement, Blackwell attempted to mediate
between Stanton and Anthony, still the acknowledged leaders
of the National Association, and Lucy Stone.

Of the three, Blackwell had fewest ties to Stanton, apparently because of differences in style and temperament. By the
1880s, however, either their differences had become less acute or
Blackwell's feelings had mellowed; she wrote about Stanton to
Stone, "I do so like a woman who can both know and speak her
own mind and stand on her own feet."[21] In December 1885
Stanton invited Blackwell to visit her:

> But you better plan when you have another day to spare to
> stay all night. I wish you could come & bring Lucy Stone
> that we might have one pleasant reunion before we pass to
> the next sphere of rest or action.[22]

Blackwell readily agreed, and invited Stone to come down to
New Jersey "to have it seem like the old days.... I should like it
to be we four together, with all the remembrances not desirable
buried; and judgment left where it belongs."[23] But both she and
Stanton underestimated the amount of bitterness that Lucy
Stone still harbored. Stone's response was a vehement no:

> As to meeting with Mrs. Stanton it is out of the question
> with me. She sent a letter to Mr. Shattuck ... in which she
> said I was "the biggest liar and hypocrite she had ever
> seen"—After that, you will see that I cannot with any
> self-respect meet her with a pretence of good fellowship.
> When Susan came here to get her share of the Eddy fund, I
> invited her to come and spend the day with us.... Instead,
> she sent a hateful note that made me feel the last plank

between us had broken—I am too busy with the work that remains to take time to mend broken cisterns.[24]

Lucy Stone might consider mending broken relationships among suffrage workers as a diversion, an unnecessary luxury, which had to be set aside in the unflinching push to victory. Antoinette Blackwell, in contrast, considered personal relationships and the harmony within the movement more important than achieving any specific political goal. Although her efforts to bring Stone, Anthony, and Stanton together were not successful, Blackwell undoubtedly talked with each one of them in an attempt to diminish their resentments. She also met with Lucy Stone's daughter—her own favorite niece, Alice Stone Blackwell—who did not share her mother's antipathies.

Despite Stone's rebuff, negotiations between the two organizations progressed. Alice Stone Blackwell represented the American Association in the merger talks. In 1890 the two organizations formally merged into the National American Woman Suffrage Association (NAWSA). There was one more conflict over who should become president of the joint organization. Antoinette Blackwell agreed with Lucy Stone that Susan B. Anthony should not take the position immediately:

I believe a good deal in Susan. She has the strength to work and should work; but under the circumstances she has no *right* to ask to be 1st Union President, and I shall tell her so and why. Of course she will be President soon; and probably ought to be. As a spinster she has given all her time![25]

When the formal reunification took place, Elizabeth Cady Stanton was made nominal president for two years, after which Anthony took over until 1900. The new organization's energy, however, came from the younger women like Carrie Chapman Catt, the spunky daughter of Iowa farmers; doctor and minister Anna Howard Shaw; and Stanton's daughter, Harriot Stanton Blatch.

Antoinette Brown Blackwell with grandchild, ca. 1901

sh *Chapter 14* re

MINISTER EMERITUS

By the mid 1890s Antoinette Blackwell could pause and look back over her full life. She was nearly seventy years old, an age when many women of her day considered their usefulness past. On a statistical basis she could expect to live another nine or ten years;[1] because her parents had both lived much longer than the average, she might be more fortunate.

In her later years Blackwell saw herself as a minister, although she had not had her own parish for four decades. One friend wrote about her:

> Her neighbors always interested her—she was absorbed in people and in their lives. They always came to her with their troubles, financial, matrimonial, and the bringing up of children. Everybody leaned on her. Hers was the true vocation of the clergyman.[2]

She preached sermons whenever the opportunity arose, sometimes abstract metaphysics, sometimes what one listener called "plain, sustaining spiritual advice."[3]

There were many female ministers among Blackwell's peers, women she met through the AAW and other organizations. The 1880 census listed 165 women ministers with parish jobs, of whom thirty-three were Unitarians or Universalists. Many of these women were active in suffrage and reform organizations, including Phebe Hanaford, Augusta Chapin, and Anna Howard Shaw. In addition, numerous women, of whom Mary Baker Eddy became the most famous, left traditional Christian denominations and founded a variety of unorthodox spiritual groups. Others, like Julia Ward Howe, simply preached whenever they could without any official recognition. Blackwell's oldest daughter, Florence Mayhew, was a lay preacher at the Chilmark (Massachusetts) Methodist Church. Howe initiated a regular gathering of women ministers—official or not—which began to refer to itself as a "Women's Church." Blackwell apparently had no part in this group, despite her friendship and admiration for Howe.

Some of the women demanded that Christian doctrine and tradition be reinterpreted in ways that would restore women to their rightful position. Matilda Joslyn Gage told the International Council of Women in 1888 that a fresh class of clergy was needed for both men and women:

> The religious teachers of the present day need to be brave and liberal persons, possessing knowledge of science, history, and the laws of evolution. They need to be persons—they need to be women—who shall dare break away from all the false traditions of the middle ages, fearless in preaching the truth as to the absolute and permanent equality of the feminine with the masculine, not alone in all material, but in all spiritual things.[4]

Blackwell herself, despite her position as the first woman recognized as an ordained minister, did not serve as a leader in this new ferment.

In the early 1890s Elizabeth Cady Stanton, unable to travel to conventions or on lecture tours because of her poor health, decided to compile commentaries on the Biblical passages relating to women's roles. She tried to enlist the help of the increasing number of women who were trained in Hebrew, Greek, and the discipline of Biblical scholarship. She also asked many leading feminists, including Antoinette Blackwell, to respond to two questions:

1. Have the teachings of the Bible advanced or retarded the emancipation of women?
2. Have they dignified or degraded the Mothers of the Race?[5]

Stanton's interest in religious questions was secondary to her political goals. She wrote to Blackwell:

> I have been trying...to do this for two reasons. First, because as long as the religion of the country teaches women's subjection her status is necessarily degraded in the state....2nd There is no way in which we could get wide spread agitation on the whole question of woman's true position as in opening a vigorous attack on the church.[6]

Blackwell decided not to get involved with the project, except to offer Stanton the notes she had made at Oberlin during her orthodox years. She told Stanton simply, "I am glad you are taking up the Bible side of the Woman Question in a thorough way."[7] Blackwell wrote a brief letter, which was included with others in the published volume, concluding:

> If the suggestions and teachings of the various books of the Bible, concerning women, are compared with the times in which severally they were probably written, in general they are certainly in advance of most contemporary opinion.[8]

That apology for religious tradition was a far cry from the vigorous analysis of Biblical texts that Antoinette Brown had written as a young woman.

Stanton interpreted the conservatism of Blackwell and other women as a fear of public scandal.[9] But Blackwell's attitude seems to have stemmed from roots other than a fear of disrepute. She preferred not to link religious beliefs with political doctrine; for her, religious truths were an end in themselves, not a tool for attaining political goals. More importantly, Blackwell was not prepared to challenge traditional Christian beliefs and institutions. Her big step was breaking into that institutional framework as it existed, gaining recognition and legitimacy on the terms set by others. Later, after much internal struggle, she abandoned orthodox doctrine to the extent of becoming Unitarian. Unlike Stanton, however, Blackwell was not prepared to question the whole structure of Christian theology a second time. She had found a framework that felt comfortable for her, and saw no reason to set it aside for political gains.

Instead of joining Stanton, Blackwell continued her own philosophical inquiries. The intellectual atmosphere had changed considerably since Blackwell's earlier books in 1870s. Science as an intellectual discipline had become professional and elitist, allied with capital and industry and technology, divorced from morality and philosophy. Science itself was increasingly fragmented into discrete disciplines: chemistry, biology, physics and all its subdivisions such as mechanics, acoustics, electromagnetism, optics, radioactivity. Science was no longer a matter for popular lectures and amateur specimen collecting, and scientists insisted on insulating themselves from "marginal" fields of thought such as psychoanalysis.

In this environment Blackwell essentially swam upstream. She must have read extensively in professional scientific literature, determined to bridge the widening gap between scientists and the rest of humanity. But her goal, in 1890 as earlier, was a vision in which the details that science provided about the universe fit together into an integrated, balanced whole that explained the fundamental processes of life.

The Philosophy of Individuality, or The One and the Many, Blackwell's first book in almost twenty years, was published in 1893. The book contains separate chapters on motion, matter, light, radiation, and organic life. It is not a general science textbook, but rather a reinterpretation of scientific data according to the author's vision of the universe. She began by explaining her goal:

> With this growing diversity of theory, there is also a growing belief in a broadly underlying unity. The facts of Nature evidently must all be brought together in one comprehensive and co-operative interpretation.... The great desideratum is to find a principle which is inclusive of every detail of every process; of quite every phase of all phenomena. If there be such a principle, peculiarities, finding their place here, would in no sense impair the unity of the whole, but would accentuate it rather.[10]

A major portion of the book focuses on the relationship between matter and energy, body and mind. Unlike her peer, Christian Science founder Mary Baker Eddy, who postulated that mind and matter are irreconcilably opposed, Blackwell wrote that "mind and matter are but the two faces or sides of one relative existence." The book continues:

> Materialists and Idealists alike accept the fact that abiding changelessness underlies and somehow sustains all changes. It is the *substance* of all phenomena.... The world of the forever-changing must be in some way evolved from, and in some way upheld in antithesis to, the abiding reality. We must endeavor then to rationally comprehend, and be able intelligibly to state at least a possible, a distinctly thinkable method by means of which this superficial paradox can be merged into an entirely consistent, comprehensive whole.[11]

Blackwell included a discussion on the moral implications of her views, a topic suited to her role as a philosopher and preacher rather than a scientist. First she spoke in general terms:

> *Life in the organic sense* is made up of the definitely
> *coordinated processes* of associated individual lives....
> The organic life is the associated life of the firm, not that of
> any individual member of the firm. It indicates a unity in
> the specialized modes of co-operation which tends towards
> a common end—that of promoting the general interest of
> the firm as a whole.[12]

It is not clear from such passages whether she was thinking about
cell metabolism, atomic structure, or a committee meeting of
the Association for the Advancement of Women—or all of
them, as microcosms and macrocosms within the same plan.
Later in the book she wrote more specifically of the ethical
implications of the cooperative principle in human society:

> We discover the essential germs of Nature's basis of morals
> laid deeply in the first foundations of organization itself....
> Since the individual mind can gain its experience only by
> the help of others, its first and last desires must be for more
> and wider adapted co-operation; then as intelligence and
> moral sense become developed, its ever present problems
> are how best to help both others and one's self, doing
> injustice to none, but advancing all associated interests.[13]

Blackwell believed firmly that human beings are not by nature
autonomous atomistic individuals, and that the impulse
toward cooperation and mutuality is a deep and fundamental
part of us. Perhaps her own experience, knowing firsthand the
dependence of infants, her own reaching out for companionship and cooperative work, the deep unity she found in marriage, put her more in touch with this cooperative impulse than
were male writers whose model was the lone man struggling
against a hostile, impersonal universe.

The Philosophy of Individuality, like Blackwell's other
books, ends more like a sermon than like a scientific treatise,
reaffirming her underlying religious faith:

> Behind all process is the Infinite Mind which origi-
> nated all process indirectly, because He originated the
> ultimate units of being, endowing them with power to
> cooperate in accordance with their own persisting consti-
> tutions. The present Universe is the legitimate outcome.
> The future Universe will be the infinitely grander and
> better outcome.... The great practical Creative plan will
> work out its own final justification....

Has any been taught a worship of fear and trembling,
let him begin to worship only in trust, in hope, in rejoicing, in spontaneous adoration. We are not captives to a
mighty conqueror who requires our homage, who is flattered by our humility, and delighted by our meekest self-
seeking petitions which but magnify his supreme authority.
All this may have belonged to a benighted and congruous
past. But our God is the sender of rains upon the evil and
on the good! He is not afar off. If we look within or
without He is here; He is everywhere. If we would worship
Him we can worship only in spirit and in truth.[14]

With these closing words Blackwell answered both the atheistic
spirit of the 1890s and the concept of an angry vengeful God
that she had repudiated in the 1850s.

The Philosophy of Individuality does not leave the reader
with a clear sense of the integrated world view its author
wanted so desperately to explain. A contemporary reviewer
wrote about it:

This is a work of considerable learning and evident originality.... One criticism as to the form, however, is important: the book is enormously too diffuse.

The author's fluency is remarkable, but she does not
always speak to the point. She often gives the impression
of adding sentence to sentence and paragraph to paragraph with scarcely the faintest show of logical consecu-
tiveness in the argument. This is partly due, perhaps, to
a well conceived plan—the central doctrine is to be
viewed from different points, the advance is to be neither
in a straight line nor circular, but spiral. We think the
method in the present case mistaken. The reiterations are
wearisome, the haze in which the subject is left at every
turn is in the highest degree perplexing. It is to be feared
that owing to these defects of form the book is likely to
receive less attention than the novelty and interest of its
speculations deserve.[15]

Blackwell felt frustrated by the difficulty of articulating clearly
her vision of an integrated universe. Her all-inclusive approach
made linear analysis difficult. Her education, by the 1890s,
would have been noticeably that of an amateur, albeit a persist-
ent amateur. She may also have been hampered by her relative
isolation from other intellectuals who might have helped her
clarify her thinking. What is striking is her determination to try
once more to explain.

Blackwell also continued to attend conventions called by various organizations. In 1893 she was invited to present a paper at the upcoming Parliament of Religions in Chicago. She hesitated, afraid she might be too old or too conservative to appeal to younger women. Rev. Augusta Chapin hastened to reassure her:

> Allow me to say that I think you are mistaken in suppos-
> ing that the "young people generally" regard you as a
> "fossil." On the contrary, I believe it is understood that
> you are up with the times in scholarship and life, and that
> no one of all is capable of presenting an abler paper.[16]

Like many organizations—the Purity Alliance, the Association for the Advancement of Women, and the now-united National American Woman Suffrage Association—the parliament met during the Columbian Exposition. The Exposition itself was a spectacular electrically-lit tribute to American industrial wealth. More than 300,000 telephones now linked cities throughout the country, as did the always expanding railroads. Especially in the cities, many people enjoyed an abundance of new appliances and consumer goods. By the time the Exposition opened in May 1893, however, the country was in the grip of a severe depression, worse than that of 1873. By December, more than 600 banks had failed, along with one-sixth of the nation's railroads and a number of other major industrial corporations. Hundreds of thousands of people lost their jobs, and thousands more went out on strike.

The Blackwell family did not suffer serious losses, however, and Antoinette's writings did not reflect the dark shadow attached to her own prosperity. In Chicago, she focused on the activities planned by and for women. Unlike the 1876 Centennial, the Exposition included an official World's Fair Board of Lady Managers, a Woman's Building in which many organizations met, and official exhibit space for the suffrage movement.[17] Blackwell reported to Lucy Stone:

> On the whole I like the freedom of the place. One has no
> social duties; and yet a good deal of busy stirring social
> experience. It is a curious study of human nature....
>   The Parliament of Religions was a grand demonstra-
> tion in favor of toleration and an underlying unity for all.
> It was like a new Pentacost. I have no time to attempt to
> describe it; but you have many exchanges and will read all
> you care to see.—I had another meeting in the Woman's

Building...and then the Women Ministers meeting and other things keep me extremely occupied. A.A.W. holds its anniversary 21st birthday on Aug. 4th.[18]

For Blackwell the only shadow over the Chicago trip was a personal one. Lucy Stone, her beloved Lucy, was seriously ill. She had long been bothered by migraine headaches and obesity. In 1893 she began to have digestive problems, which were finally diagnosed as stomach cancer. Blackwell's letter from Chicago continued:

> I cannot tell you how sorry I am to hear that you are not getting better as I thought when I left home. Probably you must wait to find what Nature can do for you, but she is a wonderful physician. I hope, I do hope, that she can even make you, through all this, younger and stronger than ever. If there was any thing I could do to make you better or more comfortable, be sure I am more than ready to do it.... Alice must keep us posted as to how you are. There are so many things I would like to talk over with you.... Oh dear, I hope you are only comfortably sick and are still full of hope and good cheer. Everything grows brighter! Most lovingly, your old friend & sister.[19]

But Lucy Stone's illness was not the kind that could be cured by time. She died on October 23, 1893, at age 75. Her last words to her daughter Alice were, "Make the world better."[20]

It is difficult to assess the effect of Stone's death on Blackwell. Lucy Stone was her first intimate friend outside her immediate family, and despite geographical distance and the daily cares of their families and work, their friendship had endured for almost fifty years. Blackwell must have felt the loss deeply. By 1893, however, she firmly believed in immortality and her hope for a future reunion may have blunted her grief.

Lucy Stone's death marked the first loss among Blackwell's close friends. Many of the women—and men—with whom she had worked since the 1850s were still alive and active. She commented to Elizabeth Cady Stanton:

> It is grand that all of our lifetime workers refuse to grow old. They make splendid illustrations of the good results which come from the steady use of brains—especially of "pluck" and Will.[21]

Instead of beginning work at twenty and "retiring" at an arbitrary sixty-five, many of the active reformers in the nineteenth century began their most creative work in their thirties or even later, and expected to go on working as long as their strength lasted. But inevitably the years took their toll. Each suffrage convention included memorials to "pioneers" who had died during the previous year: Ernestine L. Rose, John Greenleaf Whittier, Abby Hopper Gibbons, Elizabeth Peabody, Matilda Joslyn Gage.

Although Susan B. Anthony was still active as president of the merged National American Woman Suffrage Association, she also looked back across her half century of public work. She was writing the fourth volume of the massive *History of Woman Suffrage*, and conferring with Ida Husted Harper, who was writing Anthony's biography. Anthony, in a retrospective mood, asked Blackwell for any letters she might have saved over the fifty years of their friendship. Blackwell agreed to send them. Unlike Anthony, however, she was not yet ready to review her own life:

> I plunge again into work, as we all do after a breathing spell & as I hope we may till we reach the 90 decade at least.
>   I begin to feel that what I do must be done quickly, and so work almost harder than ever—half undecided what it is best to take up first. . . . Life is too short for all we would like to do but we will keep busy till the end.[22]

Blackwell did take time away from her desk to travel. She especially enjoyed traveling with Sam; she later told her niece, Alice Stone Blackwell:

> It was always a comfort for us to get away together—all the holidays were better for us even without the children. We were more to [illegible] when they were not around us.[23]

In 1895 they went to England, the first time Antoinette had been abroad:

> The most delightful part of that outing was the looking up of the places which Mr. Blackwell had enjoyed as a little English boy, less than nine years old. . . . We hunted up every place which he remembered with interest—the church where his father and mother were married, the walks which the children took with their governess, the

homes where they spent their summers, sometimes in
rural green and blossomy neighborhoods, sometimes by
the seaside.

In a large part of our outing we were with friends,
either visiting in the vicinity of friends' homes, or as in
France, joining with acquaintances in travel; but in Wales
Mr. Blackwell and I were quite alone. We took furnished
lodgings, getting our meals sent in nicely cooked and
simply wandered out by ourselves, in the wilds and along
the footpaths, resting, chatting, and admiring. As we were
to make our way directly to Liverpool and then home, we
gathered ivy and other wild things which we did succeed
in bringing back and planting in our country home.[24]

The trip must have brought back memories of other moments
in their life together, such as their leisurely drive across New
York state in the fall of 1865, thirty years before.

They returned to a new home on West 64th Street, New
York City, just off Central Park, with three of their daughters.
Edith returned from teaching physiology in North Carolina
and set up a private medical practice in one room of the house.
Grace, in her mid thirties, remained depressed and did not take
on the challenging kind of work her sisters had chosen. She
was, nevertheless, a delightful companion who could identify
bird calls and wildflowers and tell wonderful stories.[25] Agnes,
who had learned to paint primarily from her aunt Marian
Blackwell, was studying art at Cooper Union in lower Manhat-
tan after teaching for a year in Texas. She was also keeping
company with Samuel "Tom" Jones, a young teller at New
York's Chemical Bank. They were married in 1897, surrounded
by the entire Blackwell clan from both sides of the Atlantic.
Ethel Blackwell, the youngest daughter, was studying medicine at Johns Hopkins University in Baltimore. Sam returned
to his full-time job at the Mexican and Central & South American Telegraph Company, where he had been for fifteen years;
that job plus some successful investments gave the family considerable financial security in these later years.

Antoinette returned to her books and essays; she continued
to rework her scientific and philosophical theories. In 1897, for
example, she submitted an essay on "The Seat of Consciousness" to *Popular Science Monthly*; it was rejected as being too
intricate for the journal's general audience.[26]

Both Sam and Antoinette were in good health as they
celebrated their seventy-fifth birthdays—Sam in 1898,

Antoinette in 1900. They spent the summer of 1900 at Martha's Vineyard, as usual, with the entire Brown-Blackwell clan. Henry Blackwell and Alice lived in one house on the beach. Antoinette's older brother William Brown probably was not still alive, but his son and grandchildren had a house near the Blackwell enclave. Emily Blackwell's adopted daughter Anna, called "Nan," had married Elon Huntington and had several small children. Antoinette's oldest daughter, Florence, had one adopted son, Walter. Agnes and Tom Jones had a two-year-old girl and a new baby. Alice Stone Blackwell, hardly one to be overly sentimental, wrote to her cousin Kitty Barry after watching Sam and Antoinette walking hand in hand along the beach, "Such a pair of lovers I never saw."[27]

In the fall of 1900 Sam and Antoinette, along with their daughter Agnes and her family, moved to a house in East Orange, New Jersey. Sam continued to work in New York. He looked toward the future, writing to his brother Henry in 1900, "The faith, hope and charity imbedded in the nature of man is Heaven's greatest gift and truest prophecy—our one assurance that 'the future will transcend the past, an endless betterment designed to last.'"[28] Antoinette apparently wished he would retire. She wrote to Elizabeth Blackwell in the spring of 1901:

> Sam seems now to really think about leaving business and will perhaps do so during the present year; he has not quite decided or definitely fixed a time; but I have determined, so far as influence goes, that it shall not go into the next year, and for Grace's sake we may even spend next winter in California.[29]

But the trip to California never happened. During that summer Sam had two major operations. Antoinette took care of him herself; she wrote to Alice early in August, "He is the very personification of patience; never murmurs or complains, and accepts everything graciously."[30] Instead of recovering as Antoinette had expected, Sam suffered a series of strokes and died late in October.

The entire Blackwell family was shocked by Sam's death. He was the first one of the Blackwell siblings to succomb to age. Elizabeth Blackwell wrote to Henry, "I can hardly realize that my next in age, my childhood's companion, the devoted father, the upright exemplary man, is gone from among us."[31] Of all of the Blackwell siblings, Sam had the shortest list of worldly

achievements. But the Blackwell family deeply appreciated
him, regarding him as more or less a saint. Antoinette later
recalled:

> Lucy Stone once said he was the most consistent man in
> applying [the] Golden Rule she ever knew.... Someone
> once asked her if she ever knew anyone who always did as
> he w[oul]d be done by, & she named him. I never heard &
> no child ever heard him speak a cross word. He kept his
> temper perfectly.... Uncle Sam never made an enemy. I
> never knew him to have an enemy in his life. He was so
> kind & looked after every body's interests.[32]

It must have been difficult for Antoinette to say good-bye to the
man who had been her friend, lover, and spiritual companion
for more than forty-five years. Antoinette's chief consolation
was her firm belief in a life beyond death; she told Alice Stone
Blackwell a few years later, "I feel now that when I go forward I
shall go right to him."[33]

Antoinette Blackwell reached out to comfort others. When
Elizabeth Cady Stanton died suddenly in her New York home
in October 1902, Harriot Stanton Blatch asked Blackwell to
speak at the private memorial service. It was fitting for Blackwell to deliver the eulogy for a woman whose friendship had
endured for so many years, through numerous disagreements,
and who shared with her an underlying respect and a vision of
female dignity.

Her long life with Sam had strengthened Antoinette's
devotion to the concept of marriage. After his death, she wrote
at least one article on marriage and divorce:

> The family is the basis of civilization. It is the unit of
> social relations, though it has no right to become the fetter
> to any upright individuality.... The most fundamental of
> all human relations must be the most carefully safeguarded....
> Divorce must be a serious, well-considered thing in
> principle and in the application to every case, if marriage
> is not to become a contract so trivial that it will find no
> need of legal supervision. If marriage means a life union,
> its dissolution must mean the cutting as of a knife that
> cleaves almost to the vitals.... To me [the marriage
> vow] is the most binding of all human pledges, unless
> it be the obligation of parenthood, which it inherently
> involves.[34]

Although she was not as adamantly opposed to divorce as she had been in the 1850s, Blackwell never joined Stanton and other feminists in their call for easier divorce laws.

Blackwell was pleased that her daughters' marriages promised to meet this high ideal. Florence and Elliot Mayhew were comfortably settled in Chilmark, as were Agnes and Tom Jones in New Jersey. Late in 1901, Ethel Blackwell married Alfred Robinson in a small family ceremony. Ethel gave up practicing medicine in order to raise a family. By December 1902 Antoinette reported to Elizabeth Blackwell, "All of the sons-in-law are good men, and the marriages are more than usually satisfactory."[35]

During the first few years after Sam's death, Antoinette arranged the family's finances for the future. She was most concerned about Grace, who had suffered a nervous breakdown after her father's death. Antoinette set aside $7000 from Sam's estate to provide an income for Grace, and arranged for her to live with a housekeeper on Martha's Vineyard. Antoinette also sold the New York City house and gave each of her daughters $1000 from the proceeds. Antoinette herself had enough income from their accumulated earnings to allow her to live comfortably for her remaining years.

Blackwell gradually cut back on her extensive traveling to conventions and speaking engagements. The Association for the Advancement of Women, her favorite organization, suffered particularly from the aging of many of its leaders. After the mid 1890s, the meetings that were held were taken up with nostalgia; Alice Stone Blackwell described one "informal reunion" at Julia Ward Howe's house in 1901:

> The meeting was mostly given to telling reminiscences; we did not transact business; & we had a very nice luncheon.... When I came away they were just voting that the A.A.W. should continue its existence.[36]

Unlike the suffrage association, the AAW did not attract younger women. By 1900, college-educated women were increasingly professional, drawn to more specialized organizations instead of the eclectic all-inclusive AAW. Antoinette Blackwell explained in 1909:

> The A.A.W. has been comparatively inactive in recent years. Other societies had so far influenced the public in

favor of women on the platform that we were no longer
needed as intermediates, since people had become interested in special reforms like suffrage, peace, and social
welfare. The society was always educational in its functions. It accomplished a large and important educational
work.[37]

Ednah Dow Cheney wrote to Blackwell:

> The spirit of the A.A.W. is working in us all, and if we find
> new Expression for it, by new tongues and pens I shall be
> very thankful, but I shall not persist in clinging to the old
> bottles if the new wine has shattered them.[38]

By 1901, however, Cheney confessed, "I fear we must accept the
inevitable and lay A.A.W. gently to sleep."[39]

Blackwell continued to write for publication. She composed poetry throughout her life; in fact, the entire family
entertained each other by writing jingles and verses about
ordinary events, ranging from a description of their dressmaker
to a spontaneous rhyme to awaken guests. Now Blackwell
attempted to use verse to express her philosophical beliefs. In a
series of poems, published in 1902 as *Sea Drift*, she used the
ocean as a series of metaphors expressing her ideas. She looked
to the ocean for comfort, for courage, for health, for inspiration. It represented endless energy:

> Thy rhythmic tides, they slumber not nor sleep,
> Like God's own love—with blessed rise and fall,
> The slow, time-beating pulse of cosmic life—
> They breathe a great world music all their own,
> And move staid Earth to thrill in sympathy,
> Low murmuring melodies in soft response,
> Athrob! Athrob! in ceaseless ebb and flow,
> Systole, dyastole, of breathing sea;
> And thy full beating pulse is kin to man's,
> The heart throbs of a common joyous life.[40]

The ocean also illustrated, she felt, an integration of opposites:

> The restless tides that never sleep,
> Are anchored safe in moveless deep.
>
> Some balm is grown for every ill,
> And each low vale adores its hill.

Rest, fulcrum proves to all unrest,
And motion springs from moveless breast.

Content is core of discontent,
From crooked bow straight arrows sent.

Post haste can snatch a quick relay,
Calm night repair the fretted day.

Sleep, mainstring is to waking life,
And peace is pivotal in strife.

So brawling tides that cannot sleep,
Are anchored firm in voiceless deep.[41]

That reconciliation was what Blackwell hoped for in the
human realm. The poems reflect her profound faith in the
progress of the universe—not a narrow political progress, but
the cosmic triumph of good over evil:

To all who live where shadows fall
Light's clear handwriting on the wall
        Shines fitfully;
But day will surely triumph yet,
And over all her beacon set,
        For land and sea.[42]

The final poem, entitled "The Outlook," is almost a sermon or
a benediction:

Aglow with Life's enfolding sun,
Interpreted by one sustaining law,
All paradox unfolds without a flaw;
        The seen and unseen worlds are one.

The harmonies of truth give dole,
Insight is clearer than the keenest sight,
Its vision deeper than the debts of light—
        Attuned to Nature's whole.

Conviction crowns the sanguine hope,
Reveals intelligence, the living One;
Mankind its threads, in vivid life outspun;
        None need in lingering shadows grope.[43]

Sea Drift was favorably received; one unidentified reviewer
wrote:

> Dr. Blackwell has written many things, good ones, and
> one notes with pleasure the high quality of her verse.
> Women of "causes" seldom get credit for much else, but
> Dr. Blackwell is a genuine poet as well as a reformer.[44]

While it may have appealed to a broader audience than her
prose metaphysical works, the book contributed little to either
philosophy or literature.

Early in 1903, Antoinette went on a cruise to Italy and the
Middle East. Her family worried that her health might fail on
such a long trip; before she left Antoinette told Elizabeth Blackwell, "If I should slip into the next life quite unexpectedly I
would about as soon go down bodily to feed the fishes as be
cremated."[45] Blackwell easily struck up friendships among her
traveling companions; she wrote to reassure her family that
"none of you need worry at my being alone and friendless if I
should be ill which I have not the least intention of doing."[46]

Antoinette was disappointed by the Middle East itself,
especially Palestine:

> Palestine, for all its many charms, its great variety of
> scenery, its rich associations, brought only a chill of disil-
> lusion. The little town of Bethlehem with its tawdriness
> and almost impossible streets... seemed more to inspire
> regret than reverence.... So many of the places supposed
> to be associated with Jesus and the crucifixion have been
> desecrated by the memento-mongers that the sense of rev-
> erence is to a great extent dispelled.[47]

She was intrigued, however, with the contrast between ancient
ways and modern ones:

> The sail up the Nile was unexpectedly charming and
> restful. To see before one in refreshing contrast, Old Egypt
> and the Egypt of today—the cemeteries where both men
> and animals had been interred as sacred relics, the old, old
> methods of using the waters of the Nile by drawing it by
> bucket-and-pole, in evidence through miles and miles of
> country as we sailed downward, offset by the modern
> English method of holding back the water by great dams
> until it was needed to fertilize the land, the old towns and
> the new with their electric car advertising, forsooth! Singer
> Sewing machines manufactured in my own American
> city!, the long rows of white veiled and white clothed
> women with their gleaming eyes, and in other places the

women with bare faces, hideous rings and other symbols
in noses, lips and foreheads—all these things broadened
one's sense of the actual varieties of life on our one little
planet.[48]

When Antoinette returned home, she went to live with
Agnes and Tom Jones in Elizabeth, New Jersey. Agnes wrote to
Elizabeth Blackwell and Kitty Barry in the fall of 1903:

It is pleasant having Mamma with us. She seems very well
and has not had any sign of a cold so far this winter.[49]

Antoinette took on a new role as "Grandma" to Agnes's two
growing children.

Living with Agnes, Antoinette Blackwell was able to realize another of her dreams: a parish of her own, but without the
doctrinal restrictions she had rejected so many years before. In
1903, she helped organize a Unitarian Society in Elizabeth. At
first the group met in a small hall at the top of a dingy, narrow
flight of stairs, with Blackwell conducting services. They soon
realized that their attendance would improve if they had their
own church. Blackwell donated a portion of the plot on which
her house was located, and a small church building was soon
erected. A new minister, Arthur H. Grant, was brought in. In
recognition of Blackwell's role in nurturing and assisting the
new church, he asked her to accept the title of "Minister Emeri-
tus." She preached there once a month as long as she was
physically able. The church in Elizabeth brought Blackwell
full circle: from her first youthful vision of being a minister,
through the traumatic experience in South Butler, followed by
the long years when she preached only sporadically as a guest
in other ministers' pulpits, and finally to preaching regularly
in a pulpit of her own choosing.

Blackwell thought of herself as a minister more than a
scientist or a reformer, and wished to be known as one. Within
feminist circles, she was renowned primarily as "the pioneer
who first opened the door of the American pulpit, having borne
her cross, if cross it were, and wearing her crown now."[50] The
steady work Blackwell had done over six decades, including her
scientific writings and her relatively radical proposals for redis-
tributing work between men and women, was lost between the
dramatic image of a young preacher defying centuries of religious tradition and the cordial serenity of a white-haired sage.

Alice Stone Blackwell and Antoinette Brown Blackwell riding in woman suffrage parade, ca, 1910

sɔ *Chapter 15* ɒℇ

THE OPEN DOOR

Antoinette Blackwell approached her eightieth birthday full of plans for the future, as shown by her spirited letters to Alice Stone Blackwell:

> I don't know when we shall go to the V[ineyard], suppose Jerry [Look] will plant the garden, as he agreed to last fall.... I have a dozen or more trees and shrubs to be planted, some from Rochester, some from Mr. Foster— roots in earth waiting. Then the cistern is now dug and the earth in a heap or heaps to be distributed.
>
> One is overwhelmed enough by claims in many directions too vital to be refused.... I have been too busy for comfort lately. The old barn is down and nearly reserected in a smaller estate; but the debree is still scattered here; and much work must be done in the "claring up" and getting the field in shape. I preached yesterday, and should attend our Club today and the State Unitarian Alliance tomorrow.[1]

For her birthday—May 20, 1905—she eschewed the elaborate and sentimental commemorations that were commonly put on among members of women's organizations. She told Alice that any celebration would be "only a family affair. The clubs etc. know nothing about it."[2] With characteristic modesty, she declined Alice's request for something to print in the *Woman's Journal*:

> As for giving "a fellow an item" that is not my way, but this time I do not object just to let our folks see that I am *alive*.[3]

But Alice, the self-appointed chronicler of the Blackwell family, took it upon herself to write a brief biography of Antoinette for the *Woman's Journal*:

> Mrs. Blackwell was very beautiful in her youth, and is now a strikingly handsome old lady. Her well-poised, calm and cheerful temperament keeps her as happy at 80 as at 18. In the winter she makes her home with a married

daughter at El Mora, New Jersey, and in summer her children and grandchildren gather under her wing in her seaside cottage at Chilmark, Martha's Vineyard.

She still contributes valuable articles to the press, is often invited to preach, and is in great demand at the gatherings of the New York and New Jersey club women, by whom she is much beloved. She is a conspicuous contradiction of the old notion that a professional woman must be an unamiable character and a failure in the relations of wife, mother, neighbor and friend.[4]

The article invited greetings from many people who had known Antoinette Blackwell at some time in the past and then lost track of her. Blackwell herself was flattered and a bit surprised by the response:

Your article, I was on the point of saying your obituary, was detailed to an extent I never supposed my history would be till I had gone to kingdom come. It certainly was full enough and extremely well put. You have brought down on my head a pile of congratulations by that and the first little notice it will take me a week to answer.

They come from one I knew as a small girl at the time of my ordination; from people whose names and being I had wholly forgotten; from friends made on the Orient trip; from Unitarian Alliances, Club women, etc.[5]

The letters she received show what Blackwell meant to many women, not only those close to her, but even those whom she knew only slightly, who had been deeply impressed by her. One such woman wrote her:

It has been a great regret to me, dear Mrs. Blackwell, that I have seen so little of you since the great pleasure came to me of knowing you personally. For many years, all through my girlhood and early womanhood, your course in life was to me that of the ideal woman, and in later and riper years my judgment has approved the testimony of my youth. A wife and a mother, fulfilling lovingly and faithfully all the duties of those holy offices and yet giving time to instruct and lead in intellectual and spiritual thought, such a woman is indeed fit to be enshrined in the hearts of all who perceive the deeper meanings of life, and strive, even in a humble way, to live them.

> I know your modest nature, and how you shrink from fulsome flattery, but I believe you will accept the honest words of an honest woman spoken as from one sister to another sister.[6]

That spring, Blackwell decided to go out to Portland, Oregon, for the convention of the National American Woman Suffrage Association. She reassured Alice that she was well and strong enough for the long trip:

> Now for my great piece of news, to me at least. I am planning to go to Oregon; . . . either start from New York, or if you and your honored and venerable father do not object go in to Boston and go on with the Bostonians. Of course, I go mostly for the journey and the wonderful scenery; but mean to take part in the meetings also—cold shoulders or otherwise, and I do not think they will turn very cold in June. . . . I am to speak in the Unitarian Church in Plainfield on May 7th, I spoke in Elizabeth church on April 16th and suppose I shall preach here again on May 21st. . . . I tell you this to try to prove my strength for the long journey. I really am very well.[7]

The festivities began on June 23 with a large reception in Chicago that Blackwell must have attended. Late that night a special train full of delegates left for Portland. It stopped along the way—in Omaha, Nebraska, and Cheyenne, Wyoming, for example—for suffrage rallies whose speakers included Antoinette Blackwell, Henry Blackwell, Alice Stone Blackwell, Anna Howard Shaw, Carrie Chapman Catt, and Susan B. Anthony.

The NAWSA Convention was held in Festival Hall on the grounds of the Lewis and Clark Exposition. The suffrage movement itself was in the doldrums; it had been ten years since any new states had been added to the woman suffrage column. The convention's atmosphere was nevertheless quite festive. The business sessions were interspersed with numerous teas and dinner parties at hotels and in the homes of Portland's elite—activities that Harriot Stanton Blatch termed "tinkle and teacups" when she returned the next year from England, where suffragists were hunger striking in London's jails.[8]

The high point of the convention was a reception for Susan B. Anthony, with a band playing "Auld Lang Syne" and hundreds of admirers waiting to shake her hand. Anthony was the "commander in chief" who had given her life to the suffrage cause, but who was now so frail that everyone felt she would not live to see it triumph. Her accomplishment was of a tangible sort, spearheading a visible political movement. "To be successful," she is quoted as saying in 1854, "a person must attempt only one reform, and I shall always fight to keep woman's rights free from every other issue."[9] Her life was so singleminded that her name became virtually synonymous with the suffrage movement.

Blackwell's contribution and presence at the convention was more modest. She preached to an overflowing congregation at the Sunday evening worship service. She also addressed the convention on the evolution in woman's work. Carrie Chapman Catt, one of NAWSA's young leaders, introduced Blackwell, commenting, "The combination of her sweet personality and her invincible soul has won friends for woman suffrage wherever she has gone."[10] Within the suffrage movement, Blackwell was praised for what she was, not, as with Anthony, what she had accomplished. Blackwell's speech was retrospective and noncontroversial:

> My grandmother taught me to spin, but the men have relieved womankind from that task and as they have taken so many industrial burdens off our hands it is our duty to relieve them of some of their burdens of State.[11]

From Portland, Blackwell and some of her peers—women and a few men, all past seventy, who had been working together for half a century—took a sightseeing steamer to Alaska and back before returning to the East.

When Blackwell returned from Oregon, she moved to an apartment in New York, on West 115th Street, with her doctor-daughter Edith. As they were packing, they sorted through all of the papers Sam and Antoinette had accumulated. Antoinette wrote to Alice Stone Blackwell:

> We are neither dead nor sleeping but slaves to the occasion. To pack up one's small belongings would be a trifling matter; but to go through 66 years of accumulated papers . . . and to make some partial clearance of correspondence of two people who habitually saved nearly

everything is a serious and long drawn out task by no means agreeable in itself. Then to have one's heart torn over and over and all the time with remembrances is hard.[12]

The sorting process must have encouraged Blackwell to review and evaluate her life; she wrote to Alice in December 1905:

> Do you know that I sometimes feel that my work in life has been directed into so many different channels, all of them more or less connected, and yet apparently so wide apart, that not only much of it is lost to most of my various coworkers, but I also am so far out of their usual field of sympathies and efforts that my place in their best affections never has been and never can be in a very warm niche. So much the more reason for praising your love and amply returning it!
>
> Not that I in the least regret any one of my several lines of effort. If life were to begin over again, even with my present experience, I should keep on very much along the old lines, and in not very far from the same proportions of interest and endeavor, only . . . I should try to find time for rather more sociability. As it is, & as the end cannot be so very far off, I must work while my day lasts.[13]

It would be several years, however, before she was ready to consider a full autobiography.

Early in February 1906, Blackwell went to Baltimore for the annual NAWSA Convention. She was more concerned with lending the weight of her presence to the cause than with the details of the business sessions. A younger suffragist described Blackwell's response to such conventions:

> Mrs. Blackwell and I were once returning by slow train from a Suffrage convention of a dullness only believable to the initiated and of appalling length. It had been an exhausting occasion. . . . I remember asking her how she could be so fresh and rested at the end of a wearisome day? "Learn, my dear," she said, "while you are young, at all these meeting when nothing is happening to concern you, to withdraw."[14]

Susan B. Anthony, sick and frail but still fighting, dominated the convention; her final words to her followers were,

"Don't stop now."[15] On Anthony's eighty-sixth birthday, a large delegation went to Washington—but without Anthony. Blackwell and seven other women testified before the U.S. Senate Committee on Woman Suffrage on behalf of the federal suffrage amendment, known as the Anthony Amendment. President Theodore Roosevelt sent her a birthday tribute; Anthony is said to have retorted, "When will men learn that what we ask is not praise but justice?"[16]

A month later Susan B. Anthony was dead. Quaker Emily Howland wrote to Blackwell:

> It is hard to realize the world without her. I think that she had the attributes of the great leader. She was magnetic, sympathetic, and possessed untiring energy and enthusiasm. She leaves all women the better, as with larger opportunities they must be, because she has lived.[17]

For Blackwell the loss must have been personal as well; for more than fifty years, Anthony had been her friend—prodding, teasing, arguing with her.

Soon Antoinette was faced with death at home. In June 1906 the whole Blackwell clan went as usual to Martha's Vineyard. But the normally idyllic seaside was scarred by tragedy. One of the grandchildren came down with typhoid fever, introduced into the household by the family cook. Antoinette's daughter Edith, the family doctor, cared for the child until he recovered, but caught the dread disease herself and died. She was only forty-six years old. Antoinette Blackwell's heart must have been heavy as she buried her daughter in the cemetery in Chilmark. In a poem a few years later, she spoke of "grim Death...claiming the tender, the rare."[18] Blackwell's unshakable belief in a life after the death of the body enabled her to integrate the event, however painfully, into her life and faith.

That fall, rather than trying to live alone, Antoinette moved once again into the home of her daughter Agnes, in Elizabeth, New Jersey. She had her own small bungalow to work in during the day, which gave her much-needed independence. Blackwell continued to write and to participate in her community. In 1907 she reported to Alice Stone Blackwell:

> Well, what with being housekeeper, getting settled in the new home, trying to keep up engagements and

expected participations in various public and semi-public directions, having Grippe and not entirely over its hoarseness etc. head and hands were full enough.

But with all that, for reasons, it seemed best to write a brief summary of some of my—may I say *philosophical* investigations. Well I wrote 25 pages of a paper, and sent it off on Christmas morning to the "The Open Court." Very possibly they may not take it. Then I shall probably revise, perhaps enlarge somewhat, and publish as a leaflet to scatter here and there. That class of subjects remain, as ever, my central interest in the thought and effort [of the] outside world.

The Xmas held at the larger house and arranged by Agnes in a charming manner in all of its details was given by us jointly. Including the four maids and the babies there were 21 to feed....

We have had a number of Committee meetings on Church affairs and one or two Club gatherings with a light tea...with more to come.

...I am to speak each 4th Sunday of each month.[19]

In June 1908 Henry Churchill King, president of Oberlin College, wrote to invite Blackwell to commencement ceremonies later that month to receive an honorary Doctor of Divinity degree. It would be the seventy-fifth anniversary of Oberlin's founding, more than sixty years since young Antoinette Brown had begun her studies there. Oberlin had been the field for her first struggle against the prevailing views of "woman's place," but Blackwell put thoughts of that struggle behind her. One friend described Blackwell's reaction:

> She spent no time in reflecting how little Oberlin had done to speed her on her way into the ministry. Not a word did she say about the change in the views of Oberlin, nor that the recognition came late. She simply smiled and devoted her attention to obtaining the proper kind of doctor's gown.[20]

Wearing the prescribed academic garb, Antoinette Brown Blackwell stood on the platform at commencement—a unified ceremony, not the separate "ladies" ceremony she had been through in 1847. Oberlin too put behind itself any anxious thoughts about the struggle within its walls over a woman's preaching, instead taking credit for its own pioneering. In

introducing Blackwell to President King, Dr. Charles Wager
told the audience:

> It is appropriate for the institution that was the first to
> provide for the higher education of women to honor, at its
> seventy-fifth anniversary, a woman who has eminently
> justified that daring innovation, a woman who was one of
> the first two in America to complete a course in Divinity,
> who as preacher, as pastor, as writer, as the champion of
> more than one good cause, has in the past conferred honor
> upon her Alma Mater, and who today confers upon it no
> less honor by an old age as lovely as it is venerable.[21]

That afternoon a reception was held in her honor.

During her visit at Oberlin, Blackwell spoke at a reunion
of the Ladies' Literary Society, which she and Lucy Stone had
founded more than sixty years earlier. It was too late for Stone
to appreciate that Oberlin, so stubborn at the time, had finally
seen the light; too late for James Tefft, who had stood by
Blackwell in those difficult early years; too late for Sam Blackwell to see his beloved wife honored and revered. But for
Antoinette Blackwell, and for later generations of Oberlin students, it was a fitting tribute from the college that had made her
journey possible despite its own limitations. When she returned home she took the time to write an article on "New
Departures in Education" for the *Oberlin Alumni Magazine*,
urging the college to instruct students less in abstract theory
and more in practical social justice.[22]

Blackwell began to reminisce about her many experiences.
Sarah Gilson, a young suffragist, felt that "the story of her long
struggle for freedom should be put in permanent form," and
convinced Blackwell to relate her experiences in a series of
interviews during the winter of 1909.[23] The resulting "Memoirs"
contain a wealth of human anecdotes, but very little political
analysis. Gilson commented about Blackwell, "She was never
resentful. . . . I have never known another human being with so
little bitterness of spirit."[24] Even when she described events in
which she had been actively discriminated against, Blackwell
excused her opponents' behavior by reiterating her belief in
gradual progress. She also de-emphasized her own assertiveness, the active energy and persistence she had so often demonstrated in the face of opposition or indifference.

That year brought an additional opportunity for reflecting on her life. In the fall of 1909, Henry Blackwell died suddenly after a slight chill. While Henry himself does not seem to have been a central figure in Antoinette's life, he was closely linked to the two people who had meant the most to her, Sam and Lucy. But his death also touched her in another way, reminding her of her own mortality. She wrote to Alice Stone Blackwell:

> It touches me deeply, partly perhaps because Henry & I were born in the same month & I have long questioned which of us would stay here the longest. But I am still vigorous, not very likely to greatly overdo, & almost pledged to add nearly ten years still to complete my father's almost 94.[25]

Elizabeth and Emily Blackwell, Sam's last surviving sisters, died in England the next year.

By the fall of 1911 Blackwell began to feel she needed a real vacation, perhaps some traveling. She wrote to Emily Howland, Quaker feminist and teacher, who was close to Antoinette's age:

> I must have a long rest from much mental work, am strong and well but rather overtaxed with this last book. I do not need or want waiting on, can still walk a mile and do much outside work, and expect to for the next two months.[26]

She wanted to go to California on a sightseeing trip, but discovered that all the places she most wanted to see were "either quite inaccessible or so snowy as to be nearly tabooed." Instead, she reported to Howland in January 1912:

> One of my daughters and I have taken a stateroom on the Hamburg line for Feb. 24th to Panama and the West Indies islands, including two stops in Venezuela.... We are to be gone just one month from New York, stop at the ports from 6 hours to two or three days. So there will be rest between land excursions.[27]

The cruise impressed upon Blackwell the limitations of her own aging body. Her hearing had begun to fade, making it difficult for her to attend suffrage meetings. Her eyesight also began to deteriorate. She may have been reluctant to acknowledge the changes, especially to her immediate family. She did write to her contemporary, Howland:

> You know already that I am safe at home after a successful journey. I must tell you a good deal about it....
> Now I must confess to you something... in confidence. My hearing keeps much the same, possibly increases a very little in deafness; but my eyes both have cataracts, one worse than the other. In good light I see apparently as well as ever, enjoy scenery as well, read about as well in the day time; but not by artificial light. When I come into a rather dark station or any shaded room from a bright light, for a few minutes I am almost blind. That soons ends however. But it makes a difference in independent traveling. It also compels companionship on my childrens account. I cannot worry them.[28]

As Blackwell's eyes clouded over, her daughter Agnes took on an increasing role as secretary and correspondent, enabling Blackwell to continue the writing that was so important to her.

Other than that, Blackwell was in remarkably good health. She was occasionally bothered by digestive problems, but refused to follow her doctor's advice and take a bit of wine with her meals; she would smile and nod when he gave her the prescription, but adhered firmly to her temperance principles.[29] She worried that she might not be able to finish the many tasks still ahead of her; she wrote to Alice in March 1911, "Even my eyes are getting fractious, and who can tell how long the mind can hold its steady grip."[30]

Even as she approached her ninetieth birthday, Blackwell thought of herself as active, always looking forward eagerly to the next project. Sarah Gilson described an incident that impressed her:

> At a twenty-fifth anniversary dinner of the New York League of Unitarian Women at Hotel Astor in 1912, Mrs. Blackwell and Robert Collyer, two octogenarians, with the light shining on their white hair and their beautiful strong old faces, sat side by side at the speakers' table. It was one of Dr. Collyer's last public appearances and he was at his best. He finished his address by saying "Here we

are, two old pilgrims sitting in the sunshine waiting for
the angel to come," and bending from his great height, he
kissed her on the forehead. Next morning we found that
she had not heard exactly what he said [because of her
deafness] and when we told her, her head went up spirit-
edly, "Very well," she said, "he may *sit* if he wants to,
waiting for the angels, but I'm not waiting, I have too
much to do."[31]

Among Blackwell's projects were her gardens, one on the
grounds around her study-bungalow in New Jersey and one at
Martha's Vineyard. Gilson wrote:

> Every morning after breakfast—I last saw her do this when
> she was ninety years old—Mrs. Blackwell would start out
> equipped for the garden with sunbonnet and gloves carry-
> ing her hoe and for two or three hours she always worked
> vigorously.[32]

During the summer her chief project was planting hardy scrub
pines and fruit trees on the sandy slopes near her Chilmark
home, overlooking Menemsha Pond, with some assistance
from a local gardener named Jerry Look. She reported to Alice
Stone Blackwell in April 1911, "Have ordered 100 Oaks for
M.V. Must make hay while the sun shines!"[33] Many of the
islanders, fishermen rather than farmers, doubted that trees
would grow in the teeth of sea and wind; but Blackwell's peach,
apple, spruce, and elm trees flourished, and remain standing in
what became known as "the Arboretum."

Blackwell's other major project during these years was a
final revision of her earlier books on the nature of the universe.
She urgently needed to get her ideas on paper one last time, to
integrate all of her experiences. The writing itself went slowly
and tired her. She wrote to Alice Stone Blackwell:

> Can you believe it I am still working over "that everlasting
> book." I think enough has been said and directly wake up
> at night and some point insists some thing more should be
> said about it or a brand new one gets the floor.
>
> They are all a set of loyal allies and I have to yield.
>
> Then I work under serious difficulties in these days
> getting slower and slower in doing things. Well I shall be
> 88 two months from to day.[34]

She hoped the new book would be "a climax to the others and... much easier to read."[35] By 1913 she realized the subject demanded not one book but two, which meant more rewriting. Finally she felt satisfied:

> I am... really getting towards the close of topics to be treated of, though there will be corrections and additions to make. But if I could get the main part typewritten it could go to publishers to be refused or considered rejected....
>
> If [it is] not [accepted] all right. At last I have really told my last full thought on those great subjects and can soon go to work on the bungalow and its grounds.[36]

Finally two books came out: *The Making of the Universe* in 1914 and *The Social Side of Mind and Action* in 1915, the culmination of more than sixty years of solid intellectual work.

The Making of the Universe restated Blackwell's views on the relationship between the Creator and the world. She knew she was speaking to a disillusioned audience, and, as a minister as well as a scientist or philosopher, sought to respond:

> For some time past public opinion has been becoming more and more unsettled, afloat, without an efficient rudder. Old foundations are shaken. Props which once upheld structures that formerly seemed more stable than the mountains which do get washed away by the rains and the fall of rocks rolled down by gravity; and some of the most beloved old mental constructions are tottering and now seem threatening to fall....
>
> Good-works and helping the more helpless to help themselves, is useful and practical; but it does not face the more and more imperative question of, where are we drifting? Is there any truth so broad, so firmly grounded that we can rest upon it, do our own work and follow our destinies in confidence and hope, even if real and full assurance?[37]

As in her previous works, Blackwell insisted that the true nature of the universe could be ascertained by studying the details of Creation:

> On my theory, Creation is a working thought-scheme, is applied correlation. The entire method, marvelous and

complex as it is in its productive correlations, is as simple as an alphabet after one has learned it, and learned how to apply it to some small extent.[38]

She traced once again the correlations and interdependencies she found in the natural world, which to her were evidence of a Creator at work.

Blackwell seems never to have shared the disillusionment of her contemporaries—muckraking journalists, Populists, Socialists, and others—who no longer viewed the American version of material progress as an unmitigated blessing. She assumed that human effort, including technological development, was making a positive contribution to the universe:

> Thus a little cambric steel needle was made an individual needle by the correlations between the needle's eye, its slim body and its sharp point. It is a completed structure of its kind; but by itself it can do no work....
>
> The little household needle by a proper modification can be put into a modern sewing machine with treadle, wheel and numbers of other interrelated, delicate adjustments. Instead of one little hand-push of the needle at every stitch, two perhaps tired eyes focussed upon every stitch, the main part of the work is now done automatically. An easy almost automatic first push—becoming more and more automatic by habit—moves on step by step till the work many fold in quantity of work measured by the time taken, and many fold also less nerve and muscle wear and mental strain.
>
> This illustrates one type of relationship and its gains in real values.[39]

For Blackwell, the interrelatedness of the universe, including the human world of machines and social organizations, revealed God:

> The Absolute is the architect, plan and method are His. He is supervisor, sustainer, helper, inspirer, giver of everything, and doing His own vast work but not the builder—except of the countless primary units....
>
> Instead of doing all the work of the universe himself, God has made work the gateway to all progress for his children. He has given them of his own Being and of the properties of his own being, duration and force.[40]

Ultimately, however, Blackwell's theories remained just that—
her own theories—resting not on scientific evidence or logical
argument but on her personal faith, the same faith in "Providence" that had sustained her through the difficult months at
Oberlin, her children's deaths, and numerous other crises. She
ended with an affirmation of faith:

> The worship of Infinite Goodness and Wisdom must be
> gratitude deeper than words, appreciation which can
> forget itself in sweet and solemn appreciation of all, that
> has been bestowed upon all. The faintest perception of
> this is inspiring. The sympathy of others and sympathy for
> others is the best possible compensation for all of life's ills.[41]

Blackwell's final book, *The Social Side of Mind and
Action*, was completed and published in 1915, after the beginning of the Great War in Europe. It is more a sermon, a moral
exhortation, than a description of the universe. Blackwell
started by restating the problem as she saw it, which was how to
find truth and moral guidance in an unsettled world:

> The repeatedly told story of the unsettled condition of
> modern days,—of the mental, moral, and now inconceiv-
> ably physical world-wide upheaval,—need not in this con-
> nection be repeated. The old authoritative foundations of
> moral and religious guidance and assurance,—foundations
> that for so long seemed more stable than the earth itself,—
> have either crumbled to powder, or broken into fragments.
>   Those who, like people on floating ice, still cling to
> the broken parts with eyes more or less closed, clasp the
> only refuge that seems left to them. They dimly know that
> the waters are moving, are drifting them onward; but till
> they can see clearly whither they are bound their only
> safety seems to lie in still clinging ever more closely to the
> old-time, unquestioned, strong support....
>   In this essay it is not intended to either endorse or
> criticise, but, as far as possible, to build up assured convic-
> tions based upon self-evident foundations, which each
> reader can perceive and test satisfactorily.[42]

As in her previous books, Blackwell asserted that truth
could be found reflected in nature:

> If Divine Wisdom has not directly told us what is
> right and true, are we all afloat and without a rudder?

> Assuredly not! God has embodied in His universe the
> entire system of universal truth.... Nature and beauty
> then are truth's message to humanity.[43]

Although Herbert Spencer no longer dominated American
thought, Blackwell retained the faith and outlook she had
developed under his influence in the 1870s.

In this book Blackwell focused on the social and moral
implications of the interdependence that was revealed by the
natural world. She believed that because any change produced
compensatory changes to keep the universe in balance, there was
no escape from the consequences of one's actions:

> Whether our man-made laws are good or bad, Nature's
> laws,—its rewards or penalties,—all work in perfect
> accord with each other. Conduct and its effects are merely
> cause and its outgrowing results....
> When we act in harmony with any physical law we
> are benefited. Whenever we disobey a physical law we
> suffer the penalty, which is in exact proportion to the
> imperative law.... If one jump from a house or a preci-
> pice, the law of gravitation is not broken; the one that
> jumps is broken or crushed.[44]

Because of their interrelatedness, Blackwell urged, human
beings have a moral obligation to help and sustain one
another. Failure to do so—selfishness, oppressiveness, "rugged
individualism"—constituted sin, a word Blackwell had scarcely
used since the early 1850s, but which now appeared with full
vigor:

> The effort to find some way out of personal responsi-
> bility for personal sin was a sore temptation. It is now
> proving itself to be a failure, a moral impossibility; but
> with it has gone the brooding horror of reprobation and
> human suffering.
> All humanity now stands upon the one broad plat-
> form of personal and social conduct. On the one side of all
> activities are motives and deeds. On the other side their
> natural, unfailing, innately correlated consequences.
> Nothing arbitrary is found, no injustice, cruelty nor ill
> will, nothing but the fairness dreamed of in the whole
> complex of Divine provision!
> What we know of life,—as it is and as it has been,—
> makes it certain that there must still be long and deep

repentance, with its beginnings of a better life, and still
plenty of need for social service, for forgiveness,—not guilt
blotted out.[45]

In these phrases Blackwell seems to move away from the liberal
Unitarian beliefs of her adult life, back to the cries of evangelists in her childhood. The closing sentences of this final book
resonate with the sentiments, if not the phraseology, of her
childhood mentor, Charles Grandison Finney:

> If we can get a conception of God sufficiently compre-
> hensive to enable us to believe in His ever-existent good-
> ness and wisdom,—that will give us rest and peace.
> If we can admit that the internal correlation of equal
> but opposite forces of Infinite Being would produce finite
> beings, created mutually dependent in all copartnerships
> constitutionally enforced in order to increase both per-
> sonal and social values,—that will give us courage and
> hope.
> If we can recognize the innate necessity of ever-
> lasting, conscious existence for all humanity,—that will
> give us undoubting faith in God, in ourselves, and in our
> opportunities, both individual and social. All life will
> then be glorified. Sin itself will slowly but surely die.[46]

Blackwell knew these two books were her last substantial
efforts; she wrote to Alice Stone Blackwell in the spring of 1915:

> Now I must rest but there will be proof to read and I
> write for suffrage now and then so as not to be self condemned.
> All well as usual. Children all doing finely in school.
> Agnes overworked and also trying to correct my uncopied
> writing for me. I can write in strong light but can read it
> only with double glass with extreme difficulty especially if
> corrections are to be made and one has only two hands. But
> on the whole I am remarkably well cheerful and hopeful
> and believe my books will get recognized after a while as
> more than mere speculation. Besides one must make hay
> stacks at sunset when the next day threatens.[47]

The reference to "sunset" reflects a change in her outlook from
her cheerier references a few years before to "making hay while
the sun shines," a growing realization that the end was nearing.

In May 1915 Blackwell celebrated her ninetieth birthday,
amidst warm greetings from friends and associates throughout

the country: a congratulatory telegram from Carrie Chapman Catt, president of the National American Woman Suffrage Association; another from the Unitarian Laymens League; a poem from a Chilmark neighbor; and a letter from the Legislature League of New York reelecting her honorary vice-president.

That summer Blackwell preached her final sermons at the Unitarian Church in Elizabeth and in Chilmark. The *Boston Globe*, reporting on the latter event, called her "in many respects the most remarkable woman in the country."[48] In a final act as a pastor, she donated her bungalow-study to All Souls Church, the Unitarian church that she had helped form and which had become a thriving congregation, for use as a parsonage. The trustees wrote to thank her "for this new proof of generosity toward All Souls Church and the great interest you have always taken in the welfare of this organization."[49]

Despite her apparent retirement and her physical disabilities, Blackwell remained interested in public events, especially in the revitalized feminist movement. She wrote in 1914:

> As a woman whose husband scorned the idea of an obedient wife and did loyal service, in teaching human equality of rights and privileges, I will never give my adherence to an exclusively male-made and a male-administered government in family, in church or in state. I, who lived and saw the evils of that awful dispensation, and early protested with heart and voice and still protest.
>
> Women's future part in civil, religious, society and domestic world-making remains to unfold itself.[50]

By 1915 there was reason to be optimistic. Woman suffrage had become a reality in six states before 1911, and everywhere was a respectable political cause.

Beginning in 1911, Harriot Stanton Blatch's Equality League (later known as the Women's Political Union) and the newly organized Women Suffrage Party sponsored festive parades in New York City each spring. Antoinette Brown Blackwell, as one of the revered pioneers of the suffrage movement, rode in a special automobile in the parades, accompanied by one of her daughters, by Alice Stone Blackwell, or by her granddaughter, Ethel Blackwell Jones. Blackwell accepted her role with some exasperation; before one of the parades she wrote to Alice from Martha's Vineyard:

Who is the *chief* manager of the Suffrage Parade. A lot
of things from N.Y. come to me, so many I but half attend
to them, and am rather mixed about the different Suffrage
Branches as to the March where all act. If you can at once
send me the chief promoter here it will help me. I shall
probably leave here early on Thursday, dawdling around
till night, then take Fall River boat. The whole thing is so
tiresome I half regret planning to go to N.Y. Such is life.[51]

First a few hundred, then several thousand, then tens of
thousands of women dressed in white and gold marched in
formation up Fifth Avenue. A participant later described one of
the parades:

There were women who had no one at home with whom to
leave the baby, and who pushed the baby carriage all the
way. There were lovely young girls and women in fashionable clothes, others in well-worn garments. Mothers
brought their young daughters, and daughters took care of
old mothers. There were groups of women architects,
typists, explorers, aviators, physicians, lawyers, nurses,
painters, writers, editors, actresses, chauffeurs, real estate
and insurance agents, decorators, teachers, farmers, mil-
liners, dressmakers, librarians, even pilots, and the trade
union girls...hat makers, shirtwaist makers and glove
makers, laundry workers, all marching in military order to
the music of many brass bands, Scotch pipers or women
trumpeters. Multitudes of fluttering flags and pennants.
Slogans in big letters, some of them gently satirical. "This
comes of Teaching Girls to Read," one assured the
onlookers, and another, "No Nation Can Rise Higher
Than Its Women."[52]

The parades were hardly the center of the suffrage movement.
Under the able leadership of Carrie Chapman Catt, NAWSA
and local groups conducted an intense political campaign for
both federal and state suffrage amendments. It was the kind of
organizing that Blackwell had always avoided; now, at ninety,
she watched from the sidelines.

In 1915, despite massive campaigning organized by Catt,
woman suffrage referendums were narrowly defeated in New
Jersey, New York, Massachusetts, and Pennsylvania. It was
widely assumed that the liquor industry, fearing that if women
could vote they would immediately vote in prohibition, was financ-
ing the intense antisuffrage propaganda. Some prosuffrage

workers turned to more militant tatics. Quaker Alice Paul and members of her Woman's Party picketed the White House day after day, at times chaining themselves to the iron fence; like their counterparts in England, they were sent to prison and went on hunger strikes to draw attention to their cause. The more respectable suffrage workers expressed dismay at these extreme tactics; the demonstrations did succeed, however, in keeping the suffrage issue highly visible.

There were modest victories; in the fall of 1916, Jeannette Rankin of Wyoming was elected to the House of Representatives, the first woman to serve in Congress. In 1917 four more states—including Rhode Island, the first one on the East Coast—granted women the vote.

In 1917, in what one feminist called "a shot heard round the world," New York male voters accepted woman suffrage. It was the turning point, both symbolically and practically: New York's forty-two congressmen would provide substantial assistance when the federal amendment was taken up again. Blackwell, who must have felt a tremendous sense of personal fulfillment, penned a poem for the *Woman Citizen*, successor to the *Woman's Journal*:

> New York, my native State, to thee I sing
> Wisely thou heard'st time's bell of Freedom ring.
> In war and woe free, full clear tones are heard,
> And men in many lands are deeply stirred.
> Now may our waiting States all wisely hear
> And Nation re-instate this Fateful year.[53]

Within a year the House of Representatives finally passed the Federal Woman Suffrage Amendment, still known as the Anthony Amendment, which would be ratified just in time for the 1920 presidential elections.

For most of the nation, woman suffrage was a minor issue compared to the war raging in Europe. It was a brutal war, waged with poison gas, bombs, shell attacks. Blackwell shared the hope of many that it would be a war to end all wars:

> The so-called feminine traits are becoming the most admired characteristics of poets, artists, religious and literary teachers and authors, musicians, Nature students and all of the more refined interests and occupations. Has even war possibly received its death blow? Is the present

needless greedy, widely devastating turmoil but little more
than the last struggles of a discredited method of settling
national difficulties?[54]

Woodrow Wilson was reelected in 1916 on a pledge to keep the
United States out of the war. In April 1917, however, the United
States was drawn into the fray. Blackwell herself was not
caught up in the new war fervor, both because of her age and by
philosophical temperament. Emily Howland, a pacifist, wrote
to Blackwell:

> I have thought of you very often in these topsy turvey
> days on which we have fallen, sometimes with the feeling
> that I would write you, more often with the wish that I
> could have a talk with you on these strange days that we
> have lived to see. I felt that your calm philosophic mind
> must brace your optimism so surely, that you were borne
> above the chaos of miseries and horrors that seemed to
> submerge the world, and saw that the end would be order
> and peace and more justice for all than the world had ever
> known. I try to hold this faith but I confess I see little in the
> present making in that direction.[55]

By that time, Antoinette Blackwell appeared for the most
part to be wrapped up in her own world, a world of memories
and visions. In 1918 Alice Stone Blackwell wrote about her in
an article for the *Christian Register*:

> She is now setting a fine example of courage and
> cheerfulness under the disabilities of deafness and the loss
> of sight through cataract—a heavy deprivation to one so
> fond of reading. But she says it has been good for her: it has
> compelled her to sit quiet and "take account of stock"
> spiritually. No one seeing the brightness of her blue eyes
> and the gay and intelligent smile twinkling over her still
> beautiful face, would imagine that she was almost blind.
> Few who have to sit in the dark can look back through
> memories so remarkable and so varied.[56]

The world in which Blackwell now sat quietly taking her
spiritual stock had changed profoundly in the century spanned
by her life. The ocean was slowly creeping up the beach near
the Blackwells' Vineyard house, swallowing up the old corn-
field and the road to Gay Head. Blackwell's children were

themselves growing old, and even the grandchildren were growing up. Ethel Jones, an artist like her mother Agnes, was off to Vassar College; Blackwell must have wondered what *her* life would be like. On the surface, young women had much more freedom, wearing short skirts or even pants for bicycling and hiking—how Lucy Stone would have enjoyed *that*, after all the fuss over bloomers!—and going out with boys without a chaperone along. But the deeper problems of women to which Blackwell had devoted so much thought—the interaction of family responsibilities and careers, the need to prove women's capabilities for intellectual and professional work—remained unresolved, still to be confronted by women following in Blackwell's footsteps.

Her last years were softened by the continual caring of her family and friends. Never was she left alone. Her daughters, especially Agnes, and Alice Stone Blackwell, who seemed almost like a daughter, cared for her physically and provided a base of emotional support. Their affection shows through in the letters that passed among the family even about routine details. Alice wrote from Chilmark to New Jersey:

> We are anxious to know whether you got home safely—Florence, Ethel & I, & probably Grace too, though I have not had a chance to hear her say it, as I have the others. Please take Agnes firmly by the scruff of the neck, & hold her until she writes Florence a postcard to say whether you got home in good condition or whether the journey brought on a renewal of the bowel trouble. Of course Agnes is overwhelmingly busy, but she must be coaxed or coerced into taking time to write a post card.... I hope you found the bungalow in good condition, & the garden doing as well as could be expected under the circumstances.... Your aff. niece, Alice, who wants to know how you are.[57]

Alice and Agnes helped Antoinette with correspondence as her eyesight faded, enabling her to keep in touch with the few remaining friends who had been her coworkers for so many years. Rev. Phebe A. Hanaford wrote:

Dear Sister in the Gospel Ministry,

> I have been intending to write you a long letter, but the days go by and I accomplish little with my pen. Yet I

ought not to complain of having a lame arm, when that is
so little compared with the trouble you have with your
eyes. If I were near you, I would gladly read to you and
often write for you, and I have had proof, as you know,
that dear Lucy Stone's splendid daughter could and does
write sometimes for you. Of course I am glad the ballot is
given at last to New York women, and I wonder that
Massachusetts delays....

You and Lucy Stone were faithful to the Cause of
Woman, and have a right to rejoice in the success of all
laborers for human rights....

I do not expect a reply, but I shall keep on loving you,
and remain ever your grateful friend.[58]

Emily Howland shared with Blackwell her surprise and pleasure at finally being a voting citizen:

It still seems unreal and when a candidate asks me to
favor his nomination at the primary he does not appear to
realize the novelty of the situation as much as I do. He
cannot know what the change must be to rise from subjec-
tion to freedom and the law-making power, for one who
had so long awaited this time.[59]

Although Blackwell did not consider suffrage one of her
central concerns, younger suffragists considered her one of
their foremothers. In the spring of 1920, with passage of the
federal amendment in sight, the secretary of the National
American Woman Suffrage Association wrote to Blackwell:

I am pleased ... to say that the expression from all was
that of veneration for those of you who in the early days
helped to arouse an indifferent people to the merits of this
great Cause, and to whom we are indebted for the victory
which we are now enjoying.[60]

November 2, 1920, was a chilly gray day, threatening rain.
Like women all over the country, Antoinette Brown Blackwell
for the first time had the opportunity to vote for the next
president of the United States. She went with one of her daughters to the El Mora School near her Elizabeth home. The
significance of the occasion almost seemed more important
than her choice of candidates. Blackwell's daughter Agnes
favored the Democratic nominee, Ohio governor James M.

Cox, whose main attraction was his support of the League of Nations. Cox's Republican opponent, heavily favored by the newspapers, was Warren G. Harding. Probably no one in the Blackwell family even considered voting for the third party candidate, Socialist Eugene V. Debs. According to her daughter's account, when they discussed the matter at home Blackwell would say only, "Yes, my dear, I will vote as I think best when the time comes." The account continues:

> They drove over to Elizabeth by automobile picking up a camp stool at a neighbor's so that Mrs. Blackwell might rest if the line of voters was long, but when she appeared, about noon, the line made way for her. The signing of her own name was quite an occasion, as she could not see, and the officials were most kind. The daughter and a clerk went into the booth with her and when the clerk asked for instructions, she said in a voice which could be heard by all, "I wish to vote the Republican ticket, all things considered, at the present time. It seems to me the wisest plan." Her decision was greeted with applause by the waiting lines of voters.[61]

Blackwell never explained her reasons. It is possible that for anyone who had come of age during the abolition movement, the Republican Party retained a certain edge as the party of Abraham Lincoln and emancipation. In addition, while Harding was a senator, he had consistently supported both woman suffrage and Prohibition. When the votes were tallied, they revealed the same pattern as in the states where women had been voting for years: women, like men, voted for different parties and candidates, not as a unified bloc that could push through prohibition or any other reform. The vote was not, as Elizabeth Cady Stanton and Susan B. Anthony had hoped, an effective means of achieving other rights for women.[62]

Through that spring and summer of 1921, Antoinette Blackwell slipped more and more into her own internal world, preparing for the final journey that now must have seemed so close. She did not fear death itself; she had written to Alice some years before:

> But after all it is only to me slipping through a door which opens to receive a new guest.... May I some day if possible slip away in some or after some quick call still in the midst of activities & unlessened interests.[63]

She looked forward to what she firmly believed would be a reunion with Sam and all her other loved ones.

In the fall of 1921, Agnes wrote to her English cousin Kitty Barry, "Mother is as usual, very placid and content but very fragile. She gets up for a few minutes or an hour every day."[64] Blackwell remained at home, cared for by her family. Late in November 1921, in her ninety-seventh year, she died in her sleep. Her body was cremated, and the ashes taken to her beloved Vineyard home. The manner of her death fulfilled as closely as possible her living wish.

NOTES

ABB: Antoinette Brown Blackwell
ASB: Alice Stone Blackwell
ECS: Elizabeth Cady Stanton
Gilson ms.: In 1909, when she was in her eighties, Blackwell told the
            story of her life to Sarah Gilson, a younger suffragist
            who apparently intended to publish her biography.
            These *Memoirs*, totaling over 300 typed pages, are the
            most complete account of Blackwell's life and a rich
            source of anecdotal detail. By that time, however, Black-
            well's memories of her early years were selective, nostal-
            gic, and rambling. In addition, it is likely that Sarah
            Gilson exercised considerable editorial discretion over
            the manuscript. She also included texts of some of
            Blackwell's letters and speeches, as well as her own
            biographical comments. The manuscript is located in
            the Blackwell Collection in the Schlesinger Library.
HWS: *The History of Woman Suffrage* was published in six
            volumes. Volumes I, II, and III were edited by Elizabeth
            Cady Stanton, Susan B. Anthony, and Mathilda Joslyn
            Gage. The first two volumes were published in Roches-
            ter, New York in 1881; Volume III in 1886. Volume IV,
            edited by Susan B. Anthony and Ida Husted Harper,
            was published in Rochester in 1902. Volumes V and VI
            were edited by Ida Husted Harper and published in
            New York in 1922.
LC: Library of Congress, Manuscript Division
LS: Lucy Stone
NYPL: New York Public Library
OC: Oberlin College Library
SBA: Susan B. Anthony
SCB: Samuel Charles Blackwell
SL: Schlesinger Library, Radcliffe College. The Blackwell
            papers are cataloged as A-77, A-145, and A/B632/a3.

All quotations are reprinted with original spelling and punctuation,
except for additions and clarifications placed in brackets.

৯ Chapter 1 ন্ৰ

There are no extant and cataloged letters for the period prior to 1846, probably because young Antoinette Brown did not know anyone outside of her home community. Specific information about Antoinette and her immediate family in her early years comes almost entirely from much later autobiographical accounts by Antoinette and her oldest brother, William.

1. William Brown memoirs, p. 10, Blackwell, SL.

2. Gilson ms., p. 47

3. Ibid.

4. Ibid., p. 16.

5. See generally Karl Polanyi, *The Great Transformation* (Boston: Beacon Press, 1944).

6. Gilson ms., p. 16.

7. Ibid., p. 38; William Brown memoirs, p. 4, Blackwell, SL.

8. The Brown house, pictured on page 2, is still (1982) standing at 1099 Pinnacle Road, Henrietta, a short distance from the New York Thruway. It is a private residence. The fields across the road have been developed into a residential subdivision; one street is named "Blackwell Lane."

9. Gilson ms., p. 29

10. Ibid., p. 46.

11. See generally Charles C. Cole, *Social Ideas of the Northern Evangelists 1826-1860* (New York: Octagon Books, 1966); Whitney R. Cross, *The Burned-Over District* (1950; New York: Octagon Books, 1981); Alice Felt Tyler, *Freedom's Ferment: Phases of American Social History to 1860* (Minneapolis: University of Minnesota Press, 1944).

12. *Dictionary of American Biography*, s.v. "Charles Grandison Finney"; Cross, *Burned-Over District*, pp. 154-68; Richard C. Wolf, "Charles Grandison Finney: Mr. Oberlin, 1835-1875," *Oberlin Alumni Magazine*, Vol. 71, No. 5 (Sept.-Oct. 1975), pp. 2-5.

13. Joshua 24:15; William Brown memoirs, p. 8, Blackwell, SL.

14. William Brown memoirs, p. 6, Blackwell, SL.

15. Gilson ms., p. 24.

16. William Brown memoirs, p. 6, Blackwell, SL.

17. Gilson ms., p. 33.

18. Ibid., p. 32.

19. Ibid., p. 36.
20. Ibid.
21. Ibid., p. 31.
22. Ibid., p. 30.
23. Ibid., p. 38.
24. Ibid., p. 45.
25. Ibid., p. 43.
26. Ibid.
27. Ibid., p. 42.
28. Ibid., p. 43. For a description of female seminaries, see Thomas Woody, *A History of Women's Education in the United States* (New York: Science Press, 1929), Vol. 1, pp. 305-457; Eleanor Flexner, *Century of Struggle: The Woman's Rights Movement in the United States*, Chapter 2, "Early Steps Toward Equal Education," rev. ed. (Cambridge, Mass.: Harvard University Press, Belknap Press, 1975).
29. Gilson ms., p. 44.
30. Ibid., p. 52.
31. Ibid., p. 45.
32. Ibid.
33. Ibid., p. 32.
34. Arthur C. Calhoun, *A Social History of the American Family* (Cleveland: Arthur H. Clark, 1918), Vol. 2, p. 89.
35. Nancy F. Cott, "The Conversion of Young Women in the Second Great Awakening" (Paper delivered at the second Berkshire Conference on the History of Women, Cambridge, Mass., October 26, 1974; transcript, SL); Nancy F. Cott, *The Bonds of Womanhood: "Woman's Sphere" in New England, 1780-1835*, Chapter 3, "Religion" (New Haven: Yale University Press, 1977).
36. For text of the Pastoral Letter, see Flexner, *Century of Struggle*, p. 46; Gilson ms., pp. 77-78.
37. William Brown memoirs, p. 10, Blackwell, SL.
38. Gilson ms., p. 52.
39. Anonymous applicant to Oberlin College, quoted in Robert S. Fletcher, *History of Oberlin College* (Oberlin: Oberlin College, 1943), Vol. 2, p. 514.
40. *Catalog of Oberlin Collegiate Institute*, March 1834, OC.
41. Gilson ms., pp. 17-18; see also C. S. Lewis, *The World's Last Night* (New York: Harcourt Brace Jovanovich, 1960), p. 107.
42. *Black's Medical Dictionary*, s.v. "Tuberculosis."

43. Gilson ms., p. 50.
44. William Brown memoirs, p. 15, Blackwell, SL.
45. Gilson ms., p. 48.
46. See Lutz K. Berkner, "Recent Research on the History of the Family in Western Europe," *Journal of Marriage & Family*, Vol. 35, No. 3 (Aug. 1973), p. 398.

๖ *Chapter 2* ๙

Unless otherwise noted, the Oberlin materials are available at the Oberlin College Library.

1. Gilson ms., p. 54.
2. Robert S. Fletcher, *History of Oberlin College* (Oberlin: Oberlin College, 1943), Vol. 2, p. 600.
3. Gilson ms., p. 54.
4. Geoffrey Blodgett, "Finney's Oberlin," *Oberlin Alumni Magazine*, Vol. 72, No. 2 (March-April 1976), p. 3; Charles Nordhoff, *Communistic Societies of the United States: From Personal Visit and Observation* (New York: Harper & Brothers, 1875); Mark Holloway, *Heavens on Earth: Utopian Communities in America 1680-1880* (New York: Dover, 1966).
5. *First Annual Report of the Oberlin Collegiate Institute*, November 1834.
6. Gilson ms., p. 66.
7. Ibid.
8. Blodgett, "Finney's Oberlin," p. 9. See also Ellen Henle and Marlene Merrill, "Antebellum Black Coeds at Oberlin College," *Women's Studies Newsletter* (Spring 1979), reprinted *Oberlin Alumni Magazine*, Vol. 75, No. 4 (Jan-Feb. 1980), pp. 18-21.
9. Jill K. Conway suggests that the Oberlin experiment virtually required that women be admitted as students so that they would be available to do cooking and laundry. Jill K. Conway, "Coeducation and Women's Studies: Two Approaches to the Question of Woman's Place in the Contemporary University," *Dedalus, American Higher Education Toward an Uncertain Future*, Vol. 1 (Fall 1974), p. 242; idem, "Perspectives on the History of Women's Education in the United States," *History of Education Quarterly* (Spring 1975), pp. 1-11.

10. Gilson ms., p. 55

11. Fletcher, *History of Oberlin College*, Vol. 2, p. 684.

12. Ibid., Vol. 1, p. 377.

13. Fletcher, "Distaff and Gavel: Women's Organizations in Early Oberlin," *Oberlin Alumni Magazine*, Vol. 36, No. 6 (April 1940), p. 19.

14. William L. O'Neill, *Everyone Was Brave* (Chicago: Quadrangle Books, 1969), pp. 4-5, suggests that the woman's rights movement grew in part out of increasing restrictions on women in the 1830s and 1840s.

15. Gilson ms., pp. 53-54.

16. Ibid., p. 55.

17. LS speech at Oberlin College, July 1883, *Cleveland Leader*, July 5, 1883, Blackwell, LC.

18. I Timothy 2:11.

19. Among the male members of the class of 1847, eight were to become ministers, three teachers, and one lawyer. *Triennial Catalogue of Oberlin College: 1857* (Oberlin: J.M. Fitch, 1858).

20. *First Annual Report of the Oberlin Collegiate Institute*, November 1834.

21. James H. Fairchild, "Woman's Rights and Duties," *Oberlin Quarterly Review*, Vol. 4, No. 3 (July 1849), pp. 248-49, 237 (pages misnumbered in copy at OC; should be 338-39, 327).

22. Ibid., p. 356.

23. Ronald W. Hogeland, "Coeducation of the Sexes at Oberlin," *Journal of Social History*, Vol. 6, No. 2 (Winter 1972-73) pp. 160-76; Fletcher, *History of Oberlin College*, Vol. 2, p. 675.

24. Richard C. Wolf, "Charles Grandison Finney: Mr. Oberlin, 1835-1875," *Oberlin Alumni Magazine*, Vol. 71, No. 5 (Sept.-Oct. 1975), p. 10.

25. LS to parents, August 16, 1846, reprinted in ASB, *Lucy Stone: Pioneer Woman Suffragist* (Boston: Little, Brown, 1930), p. 71 and Fletcher, *History of Oberlin College*, Vol. 1, p. 292.

26. Gilson ms., p. 58.

27. Frances J. Hosford, *Father Shipherd's Magna Carta* (Boston: Marshall Jones, 1937), pp. 25-27.

28. Gilson ms., pp. 65-66; Fletcher, *History of Oberlin College*, Vol. 2, p. 770; ABB to LS, September 22, 1848, Blackwell, SL.

29. Manuscript book, "Minutes of the Young Ladies Association of Oberlin Collegiate Institute for the Promotion of Literature and Religion," 1846-1851.

30. ABB to LS, October 5, 1846, Blackwell, LC.

31. Gilson ms., p. 69.

32. ABB to LS [Rochester, Michigan, Winter 1847], in Gilson ms. p. 117.

33. ABB to LS [Rochester, Michigan, Winter 1847], in Gilson ms., p. 119.

34. Gilson ms., p. 71.

35. Notes taken by ASB of a conversation with ABB, [1905-10], Blackwell, LC.

36. The identification of lesbian behavior presents a ticklish problem for historians. On the one hand, women in Victorian America often used sentimental language to describe relationships with each other. See Carroll Smith-Rosenberg, "The Female World of Love and Ritual," *Signs*, Vol. 1, No. 1 (Fall 1975). On the other, one should not assume that lesbian relationships did *not* exist; these letters suggest an erotic interpretation. Andrew Sinclair, *The Emancipation of the American Woman* (New York: Harper & Row, 1965), p. 155, says simply, "At Oberlin, Antoinette Brown fell in love with Lucy Stone, with all the passion and sentimental license possible between women of the time." My best guess is that Brown and Stone's relationship did, for a brief period in 1847, include a sexual dimension, which would account for both the emotional intensity of their friendship and the heightened disappointment that followed. John Blackwell has suggested (conversation with author, August 25, 1982) that for Antoinette Brown, Lucy Stone served as a confidante who enabled Antoinette to discover herself, in the course of revealing herself to someone with whom she felt entirely free and secure. *See e.g.*, Erik H. Erikson, *Life History and the Historical Moment* (New York: W.W. Norton, 1975), pp. 56-57.

37. ABB to LS, Henrietta, March 28, 1848, Blackwell, SL, also in Gilson ms., p. 120.

38. ABB to LS [Rochester, Michigan, Winter 1847], Gilson ms. p. 118.

39. LS to ABB, August 21 [1848?], Blackwell, LC.

40. ABB to LS, June 2, 1850, Blackwell, LC.

41. Gilson ms., pp. 64-65.

42. ABB to LS, Henrietta, July 19, 1847, Blackwell, SL, and Gilson ms., p. 120.

♫ *Chapter 3* ℞

1. Gilson ms., p. 76.
2. Joel 2:28.
3. Faculty meeting minutes from 1846 through the 1850s were destroyed in the 1901 fire in the old chapel. Robert S. Fletcher, *History of Oberlin College* (Oberlin: Oberlin College, 1943), Vol. 2, p. 935.
4. James H. Fairchild, "Woman's Rights and Duties," *Oberlin Quarterly Review*, Vol. 4, No. 3 (July 1849), pp. 251-52 (pages misnumbered in copy at OC; should be 341-42).
5. Ibid., p. 357.
6. Gilson ms., p. 72-73.
7. Ibid., p. 70.
8. *Catalogue of the Officers and Students in Oberlin Collegiate Institute, 1847-48*, p. 23; OC; similar listings in catalogues for 1848-49 and 1849-50.
9. ABB to LS, n.d. Gilson ms., p. 127.
10. *First Annual Report of the Oberlin Collegiate Institute*, November 1834, OC.
11. ABB to LS, [June] 1848, Blackwell, SL.
12. Gilson ms., p. 113.
13. ABB to LS, [June] 1848, Blackwell, SL, and Gilson ms., p. 129.
14. ABB to LS, [June] 1848, Blackwell, SL, and Gilson ms., p. 130.
15. ABB to LS, [June] 1848, Blackwell, SL, and Gilson ms., p. 130-31.
16. Gilson ms., p. 82.
17. Ibid., p. 114-15.
18. ABB to LS, [June] 1848, Blackwell, SL, and Gilson ms., p. 132.
19. I Cor. 14:34; I Tim. 2:11-12.
20. ABB to LS, Henrietta, March 28, 1848, Blackwell, SL, and Gilson ms., p. 123.
21. Antoinette L. Brown, "Exegesis of I Corinthians, XIV, 34, 35; and II Timothy, 11, 12," *Oberlin Quarterly Review* (July 1849), quoted in Gilson ms., pp. 104, 110.
22. ABB to LS, n.d., Gilson ms., pp. 126-27.
23. ABB to LS, [June] 1848, Blackwell, SL, and Gilson ms., p. 129.
24. ABB to LS, September 22, 1848, Blackwell, SL.
25. ABB to LS, [June] 1848, Blackwell, SL.

26. ABB to LS, Henrietta, June 28, 1848, Blackwell, SL.
27. ABB to LS, [June] 1848, Blackwell, SL.
28. LS to ABB, August 21 [1848], Blackwell, LC.
29. ABB to LS, February 25, 1849, Blackwell, LC.
30. LS to ABB, [late 1849], Blackwell, LC.
31. ABB to LS, Henrietta, December 28, 1849, Blackwell, SL.
32. Ibid.
33. Ibid.
34. Ibid.
35. ABB to LS, Henrietta stone mansion, "almost 1850," Blackwell, LC.
36. ABB to Horace Greeley, January 8, 1855, Greeley Papers, NYPL.
37. ABB to LS, Oberlin, [1850], Blackwell, SL.
38. LS to ABB, West Brookfield, June 9, 1850, Blackwell, LC.
39. ABB to LS, Oberlin, [Summer 1850], Blackwell, SL.
40. Ibid.
41. *Catalogue of the Officers and Students in Oberlin Collegiate Institute, 1847-48*, p. 36, OC.
42. ABB to Olympia Brown, January 10, 1881, Olympia Brown papers, SL.
43. Fletcher, *History of Oberlin College*, Vol. 1, p. 220.
44. ABB to LS, 1848, Blackwell, LC.
45. Gilson ms., p. 116.
46. ABB to LS, Oberlin, [1850], Blackwell, SL, and Gilson ms. pp. 123-24.
47. ABB to LS, Oberlin, n.d., Blackwell, SL.
48. Ibid.
49. Gilson ms., p. 115.
50. ABB to LS, Oberlin, August 13, 1850, Blackwell, SL.

ꙙ Chapter 4 ꙗ

1. Gilson ms., p. 140.
2. LS to ABB, June 9, 1850, Blackwell, LC.
3. ABB to LS, [Spring-Summer 1850], Blackwell, SL; ABB to LS, August 13, 1850, Blackwell, SL.
4. Gilson ms., p. 143-44.
5. Ibid., p. 143.
6. Holmes to ABB, March 9, 1851, Blackwell, SL.
7. Gilson ms., pp. 144-45.

8. ABB to LS, December 19, 1850, Blackwell, LC.

9. For general descriptions of the lyceum circuit, see Alice Felt Tyler, *Freedom's Ferment* (Minneapolis: University of Minnesota Press, 1944); Elinor Rice Hays, *Morning Star: A Biography of Lucy Stone* (1961; New York: Octagon Press, 1978); and Elizabeth Cady Stanton, *Eighty Years and More* (London: T. Fisher Unwin, 1898); in addition to Antoinette Brown's recollections.

10. Gilson ms., p. 146.

11. ABB to C. H. Plummer, December 15, 1854, Alma Lutz Collection, SL.

12. Gilson ms., p. 153.

13. The influence of Margaret Fuller on an entire generation of reformers needs further exploration. It is suggested by Katharine Anthony, *Margaret Fuller* (New York: Harcourt, Brace & Howe, 1920), p. 96, as well as by the overlap in personnel between her "disciples" and the clergymen who subsequently came out in favor of woman's rights (and in opposition to many of their peers).

14. Gilson ms., p. 149. None of the texts of these early speeches is available in cataloged sources.

15. Ibid., p. 187.

16. Ibid., pp. 153-54.

17. Unidentified newspaper clipping, Blackwell, SL. Contrast with the view of a modern historian, who described Antoinette Brown as "a quiet emotional girl, who was to fail as a public lecturer from want of self-confidence...a dull lecturer." Andrew Sinclair, *The Emancipation of the American Woman* (New York: Harper & Row, 1965).

18. DeRuyter (Wisc.) *Banner of the Times,* October 11, 1853, Blackwell, LC.

19. *National Anti-Slavery Standard,* December 17, 1853, Gilson ms., pp. 351-52, and Woman's Rights Collection, SL; *Banner of the Times,* ibid.; *New York Tribune,* September 2, 1853.

20. Gilson ms., p. 156.

21. ABB to SBA, January 14, 1852, Blackwell, SL.

22. ABB to LS, March 23, 1852, Gilson ms., p. 148, and Blackwell, LC.

23. ABB to LS, May 15, 1852, Blackwell, SL; copy in different handwriting (Alice Stone Blackwell?), Blackwell, LC.

24. For general descriptions of the pre-Civil War reform movements, see Tyler, *Freedom's Ferment;* and Charles C.

Cole, *The Social Ideas of the Northern Evangelists, 1826-1860*
(New York: Octagon Books, 1966).

25. Gilson ms., p. 145.

26. ABB to LS, December 19, 1850, Blackwell, LC.

27. Report of Annual Meeting of the New York State
Women's Temperance Society, Rochester, N.Y., 1853; HWS
Vol. I, pp. 508-09; and NAWSA Archives, LC.

28. Quoted in Mildred Adams, *The Right to be People* (Philadelphia and New York: Lippincott, 1967), p. 34.

29. *New York Tribune,* September 2, 1853.

30. Gilson ms., p. 162.

31. Speech at the 1853 Convention of the Women's State
[New York] Temperance Association, HWS, Vol. 1, p. 495.

32. The best overview of the pre-Civil War woman's rights
movement is Eleanor Flexner, *Century of Struggle: The
Woman's Rights Movement in the United States,* Chapter 6,
"From Seneca Falls to the Civil War" (Cambridge, Mass.:
Harvard University Press, Belknap Press, 1975). See also Alice
S. Rossi, "Social Roots of the Woman's Movement," *The Feminist Papers* (New York: Columbia University Press, 1973).
Speeches and discussions at woman's rights conventions from
1850 through 1859 were published annually and are available
in a bound volume, *Proceedings of Woman's Rights Conventions* (NYPL). Edited proceedings of some of the conventions
also appear in Volume 1 of HWS.

33. Gilson ms., p. 246; *Proceedings of Woman's Rights Conventions, Third National Convention,* New York, September 8,
1852, p. 20.

34. ABB to LS, [Fall 1852], Gilson ms., p. 142.

35. Discussions of the bloomer controversy can be found in
Flexner, *Century of Struggle,* pp. 83-84; Aileen S. Kraditor, ed.,
Up From the Pedestal (Chicago: Quadrangle Books, 1968), pp.
122-36; ASB, *Lucy Stone: Pioneer Woman Suffragist* (Boston:
Little, Brown, 1930), pp. 106-12.

36. Elizabeth Cady Stanton, *Eighty Years and More* (London: T. Fisher Unwin, 1898), p. 201.

37. LS to ABB, November 24, 1852, Blackwell, LC.

38. Interview with Antoinette Brown Blackwell's granddaughter, Ethel Jones Whidden, Chilmark, Massachusetts,
October 1974.

39. Gilson ms., p. 159.

40. Notes taken by Alice Stone Blackwell of a conversation
with ABB, [1905-10], Blackwell, LC.

41. Gilson ms., p. 160.

42. ABB to LS, February 18, 1854, Gilson ms., p. 174-75.

43. ECS to SBA, February 19, 1854, Stanton Collection, LC.

44. ABB to LS, August 4, 1852, Gilson ms., pp. 136-37.

45. Ibid., p. 137.

ঌ *Chapter 5* ৎ

1. ABB to LS, Henrietta, August 7, 1851, Blackwell, LC.

2. ABB to LS, August 4, 1852, Blackwell, SL, and Gilson ms., pp. 135-36.

3. Notes taken by Alice Stone Blackwell of conversation with ABB, [1905-10], Blackwell, LC; see also Gilson ms., p. 165.

4. ABB to Smith, August 16, 1853, Gerrit Smith Collection, George Arents Research Library, Syracuse University, Syracuse, N.Y.

5. Gilson ms., p. 168.

6. ABB to LS, March 29, 1853, Blackwell, LC.

7. ABB to LS, August 16, 1853, Blackwell, LC, and Gilson ms., p. 173.

8. ABB to LS, South Butler, February 18, 1854, Gilson ms., p. 174.

9. Diary of SCB, November 8, 1853, copy in other handwriting (Alice Stone Blackwell?), Blackwell, LC.

10. Notes taken by Alice Stone Blackwell of conversation with ABB, [1905-10], Blackwell, LC.

11. ABB to Smith, August 23, 1853, Gerrit Smith Collection.

12. ABB to Smith, August 16, 1853, Gerrit Smith Collection.

13. Gilson ms., p. 165; see also *Dictionary of American Biography,* s.v. "Gerrit Smith."

14. ABB to Smith, August 23, 1853, Gerrit Smith Collection.

15. Notes taken by Alice Stone Blackwell of conversation with ABB, [1905-10], Blackwell, LC; see also Gilson ms., p. 165.

16. Luther Lee to ABB, August 22, 1853, Blackwell, SL.

17. The basic chronology of the Half World's Temperance Convention is from the *New York Tribune,* September 1-15, 1853, which includes proceedings of the two temperance conventions, Antoinette Brown's sermon, and the woman's rights convention. Unless otherwise noted, all quotations in this section are from the *Tribune*'s account.

18. ABB speech at the Fourth National Woman's Rights Convention, Cleveland, Ohio, October 1853, Gilson ms., p. 273, and HWS, Vol. I, p. 159.

19. ABB speech, printed in Gilson ms., pp. 262–64 and HWS, Vol. I, pp. 553–54.

20. Gilson ms., p. 170.

21. Poem by Gerrit Smith, September 15, 1853, Blackwell, SL, and Gilson ms., p. 171.

22. Gal. 3:28; "Woman's Right to Preach the Gospel," reprinted in Donald W. Dayton, ed., *Five Sermons and a Tract by Luther Lee* (Chicago: Holrad House, 1975), pp. 80, 99.

23. *New York Tribune*, September 19, 1853.

24. Gilson ms., p. 166.

25. Harriot K. Hunt, *Glances and Glimpses* (Boston: John P. Jewett, 1856), p. 304.

26. Biographical sketch of ABB by Ethel Blackwell Robinson, n.d., Woman's Rights Collection, SL.

27. Luther Lee to ABB, April 30, 1855, Blackwell, SL.

28. See, for example, a pamphlet entitled "A Tribute to Olympia Brown," given by the Theological School, Canton, N.Y., May 31, 1963, Olympia Brown Collection, SL: "Olympia Brown was indeed the first woman to achieve fully recognized ministerial standing from a denomination." See also clippings from the *Christian Leader*, 1944, Woman's Rights Collection, SL.

29. Gilson ms., p. 170.

30. HWS, Vol. I, p. 124.

31. Ibid., pp. 141-42.

32. ABB to ECS, Andover, Mass., December 28, 1854, Blackwell, LC.

33. ABB to Smith, October 13, 1853, Gerrit Smith Collection.

34. Notes taken by Alice Stone Blackwell of conversation with ABB, [1905-10], Blackwell, LC.

35. Announcement in *New York Tribune*, December 19, 1853.

36. ABB to SBA, February 22, 1854, Blackwell, SL.

37. Gilson ms., pp. 170-71.

38. Ibid., p. 179.

39. Ibid. Later in her life Blackwell attributed the South Butler crisis to "scientific difficulties" arising from reading Darwin and Spencer (Gilson ms., p. 178; letter to Olympia Brown, January 10, 1881, Olympia Brown Collection, SL). It is my conclusion that this was chronologically impossible. In 1853 Charles Darwin had barely begun work on the theoretical basis of *Origin of Species*, which would not be published until 1859. The few friends who saw his earlier drafts did not even

recognize its theological implications. Herbert Spencer's first book, *Social Statics* (1851), and an essay entitled "The Development Hypothesis" (1852), had been published in London and sketched the outlines of what would come to be known as Darwinism. Spencer's work received little notice in the United States, however, until after 1856, when it was publicized by popular lecturer Edward Livingston Youmans. Not until 1872, close to twenty years after Brown's theological crisis, did Youmans found *Popular Science Monthly* in order to promote Spencer's later books. See *Dictionary of American Biography*, s.v. "Edward Livingston Youmans"; *Readers Encyclopedia of American Literature*, s.v "Popular Science Monthly"; Ruth Moore, *Evolution* (New York: Time-Life Books, 1962), pp. 40-41; A. Hunter Dupree, *Asa Gray* (Cambridge, Mass.: Harvard University Press, 1959), pp. 237-52. Everett Mendelsohn, Professor of History of Science, Harvard University, personal interview with author.

40. Gilson ms., p. 181.

41. Ibid., pp. 180-81.

42. Gilson ms., p. 180.

43. Ibid., p. 181.

44. Ibid., p. 180.

45. ABB to Smith, January 18, 1855, Gerrit Smith Collection.

46. Gilson ms., pp. 179, 181.

47. William Henry Channing to ABB, February 2, 1854, Blackwell, SL.

48. *Black's Medical Dictionary*, s.v. "Brain Fever": "Brain fever is a popular name for several conditions. One is the state of prostration following some severe mental strain, which is not very serious and passes off in the course of a few weeks of rest."

49. ABB to Horace Greeley, January 8, 1855, Greeley Collection, NYPL.

ᕷ Chapter 6 ᕤ

1. ABB to LS, Henrietta, August 16, 1854, Blackwell, SL and Gilson ms., p. 182.

2. ABB to Horace Greeley, September 6, 1854, Greeley Collection, NYPL.

3. Gilson ms., p. 182.

4. ABB to LS, Henrietta, August 16, 1854, Blackwell, SL and Gilson ms., p. 183; ABB to LS, Henrietta, August 14, 1854, Blackwell, SL.

5. ABB to Greeley, November 20, 1854, Greeley Collection, NYPL.

6. ABB to Gerrit Smith, February 8, 1855, Gerrit Smith Collection, George Arents Research Library, Syracuse University, Syracuse, N.Y.

7. ABB to Greeley, January 8, 1855, Greeley Collection, NYPL.

8. ABB to Greeley, January 21, 1855, Greeley Collection, NYPL.

9. ABB to Smith, February 8, 1855, Gerrit Smith Collection.

10. Gilson ms., p. 185.

11. Ibid.

12. The settlement house movement, led by women such as Jane Addams and Lillian Wald, did not arise until the end of the century, some twenty-five years after Brown's work in New York. William L. O'Neill, *Everyone Was Brave* (Chicago: Quadrangle Books, 1969), p. ix. suggests: "In retrospect, perhaps the best course for feminists would have been to join the Socialist Party, which alone promised to change the American social order enough so that women could exercise in practice those rights they were increasingly accorded in principle."

13. Gilson ms., p. 188.

14. ABB to SCB, n.d., Blackwell, SL.

15. *New York Tribune*, May 3, 1855.

16. *New York Tribune*, May 7, 1855.

17. Gilson ms., p. 179. (Note: the numbering of pages is faulty; nos. 179-88 are repeated. This is the second set.) For background material on the Blackwell family, see Elinor Rice Hays, *Those Extraordinary Blackwells* (New York: Harcourt, Brace and World, 1967).

18. HWS, Vol. I, p. 89. Speeches at woman's rights conventions indicate that battering of wives—often assumed to be caused by the husband's drinking—was a common occurrence and was one of the central concerns of the conventions. See, e.g., speech by Emily Collins, HWS, Vol. I, p. 89.

19. LS to ABB, July 11, 1855, Blackwell, LC.

20. ABB to LS, March 29, 1853, Blackwell, LC.

21. Albany, N.Y., February 14-15, 1854, HWS, Vol. I, p. 593.

22. Tenth National Woman's Rights Convention, Cooper Institute, N.Y., May 10-11, 1860, HWS, Vol. I, p. 728.

23. Gilson ms., p. 180 (second set).

24. ABB to LS, Henrietta Stone Mansion, "almost 1850," Blackwell, LC.

25. ABB to LS, September 22 [1848?], Blackwell, SL. For a discussion of a group of women who self-consciously chose to remain single, see Judy Colucci Breault, "The Unholy Tribe: Love, Deviance and Reform in Pre-Bellum America" (Paper presented at the 2nd Berkshire Conference, Radcliffe College, October 27, 1974).

26. LS to ABB, June 9, 1850, Blackwell, LC.

27. ABB to SBA, November 5, 1854, Blackwell, SL.

28. ABB to ECS, Andover, Mass., December 28, 1854, Blackwell, LC.

29. LS to ABB, March 29, 1855, Blackwell, LC.

30. ABB to SCB, May 10, 1855, Blackwell, SL.

31. ABB to SCB, May 27, 1855, Blackwell, SL.

32. SCB to ABB, n.d., Blackwell, SL.

33. ABB to LS, "Almost 1850," Blackwell, LC.

34. ABB to SBA, January 23, 1856, Blackwell, SL.

35. ABB to SCB, December 30, 1855, Blackwell, SL.

36. Gilson ms., pp. 180–81 (second set).

37. ABB to SCB, December 30, 1855, Blackwell, SL.

38. ABB to SCB, December 14, 1855, Blackwell, SL.

39. ABB to SCB, December 30, 1855, Blackwell, SL.

40. ABB to SCB, December 14, 1855, Blackwell, SL. The book, tentatively titled *Shadows of Our Social System*, was apparently never published. In the Gilson manuscript, p. 188, ABB indicated that reading Thackeray's *Vanity Fair* "darkened the face of everything and...helped to determine me not to finish writing a book depicting life of the slums."

41. Gilson ms., p. 191.

42. ABB to SCB, December 14, 1855, Blackwell, SL.

43. Ibid.

44. Ibid., reprinted in Gilson ms., p. 188.

45. Ibid.

46. ABB to SBA, January 23, 1856, Blackwell, SL.

47. SBA to ABB, [1850s], Blackwell, SL.

48. LS to ABB, January 20, 1856, Blackwell, LC.

49. Ellen Blackwell to SCB, January 15, 1856, Blackwell, SL.

50. Ellen Blackwell to ABB, February 6, 1856, Blackwell, SL.

51. ABB to SCB, December 30, 1855, Blackwell, SL.

52. Gilson ms., p. 180.

53. ABB to SCB, December 22, 1855, Blackwell, SL and Gilson ms., p. 187 (second set).

54. Gilson ms., p. 181 (second set).

৯ৡ *Chapter 7* ৡৡ

1. ABB to SBA, February 14, 1856, Blackwell, LC.
2. Gilson ms., p. 191.
3. ABB to SBA, March 12, 1856, Blackwell, SL.
4. Ibid., and Gilson ms., p. 222.
5. Gilson ms., p. 191.
6. ABB to LS, Henrietta, "Almost 1850," Blackwell, LC.
7. LS to ABB, n.d., Gilson ms., p. 222.
8. Gilson ms., p. 192.
9. Notes taken by Alice Stone Blackwell of a conversation with ABB, [1905-10], Blackwell, LC.
10. Greeley to ABB, April 17, 1856, and July 17, 1856, Gilson ms., pp. 290, 293. There are several letters from Horace Greeley to Antoinette Brown (Blackwell) in the Blackwell Papers, SL, which may include these, but all are virtually illegible.
11. Gilson ms., pp. 192-93.
12. Ibid., p. 195.
13. ABB to SBA, September 28, 1857, Blackwell, SL.
14. Information about a variety of birth control methods, ranging from herbal spermicides to condoms, was apparently fairly widespread among feminists and women medical practitioners, although there were strong moral disagreements about whether women should utilize them rather than relying on abstinence. Antoinette Blackwell probably had access to both information and devices that were sufficiently effective to enable her to space their children one to three years apart, as her mother's children had been. See Linda Gordon, *Woman's Body, Woman's Right: A Social History of Birth Control in America* (New York: Viking Press, 1976), pp. 40-49, 60-70.
15. ABB to SBA, April 23, 1858, Blackwell, SL.
16. SBA to ABB, April 22, 1858, and May 2, 1858, Blackwell, SL. Sarah Slavin Schramm, in *Plow Women Rather than Reapers: An Intellectual History of Feminism in the United States* (Metuchen, N.J.: Scarecrow Press, 1979), pp. 295-96, discusses the model, derived from Plato's *Republic*, which permits women to be rulers, but only if they give up their sexuality and parenting.
17. SBA to ECS, June 5, 1856 [1858?] in Theodore Stanton and Harriot Stanton Blatch, eds., *Elizabeth Cady Stanton as Revealed in Her Letters, Diary and Reminiscences* (New York: Harper and Brothers, 1922), Vol. II, p. 65.
18. ECS to ABB, n.d., Gilson ms., p. 233.

19. Gilson ms., p. 198.
20. Ibid., p. 194.
21. ABB to SBA, April 23, 1858, Blackwell, SL.
22. SBA to ABB, [1858], Blackwell, SL.
23. ABB to LS, August 3, 1858, Blackwell, LC.
24. ABB to LS, August 29, 1859, Blackwell, LC.
25. Gilson ms., p. 196.
26. SBA to ABB, September 4, 1858, Blackwell, SL.
27. ABB to SBA, September 29, 1858, Blackwell, SL. The manuscript letter is dated 1848, in Antoinette Blackwell's handwriting, but the subject matter, including references to "little Florence," indicates that the letter was actually written in 1858.
28. Ibid.
29. Gilson ms., p. 211.
30. ABB to LS, July 22, 1859, Blackwell, LC.
31. ABB to LS, April 14, 1859, Blackwell, LC.
32. Gilson ms., p. 197.
33. LS to ABB, February 20, 1859, Blackwell, LC.
34. LS to ABB, June 9, 1850, Blackwell, LC.
35. SBA to ABB, April 8, 1859, Blackwell, SL.
36. ABB to LS, April 14, 1859, Blackwell, LC.
37. ABB to LS, [1859], Blackwell, LC.
38. ABB to LS, July 22, 1859, Blackwell, LC.
39. ABB to SCB, Toronto, [1859?], Blackwell, SL.
40. ABB to LS, August 29, 1859, Blackwell, LC.
41. ABB to SBA, October 25, 1859, Gilson ms., pp. 228-29.
42. Ibid., p. 228.
43. Laura Kerr's fictional biography of Blackwell, *Lady in the Pulpit* (New York: Soman's Press, 1951), ends with a scene extrapolated from the letter quoted in note 41, and depicts Blackwell vowing never again to leave her child at home while she carries out her public work—a reflection more of the times in which Kerr was writing than of Blackwell's own views. Andrew Sinclair similarly concluded in *The Emancipation of the American Woman* (New York: Harper and Row, 1965), "She failed in New York. She was a dull lecturer. . . . She had six children and found refuge in domesticity" (p. 157). He mentions Blackwell's later life only once (p. 201), in connection with the 1896 suffrage convention. Blackwell herself told Alice Stone Blackwell that "People have thought I was a failure, up like a rocket and down like stick—was a trial to me—they didn't realize that my writing was in [the] same line." (Notes taken by

ASB, n.d., LC. Blackwell was apparently quoting Thomas Paine: "As he rose like a rocket, he fell like a stick." *Bartlett's Familiar Quotations* (11th ed., 1942), p. 271, s.v. "Thomas Paine.")

ꙍ Chapter 8 ꙅ

1. ABB to SBA, April 30, 1861, Blackwell, SL.
2. Gilson ms., pp. 198-99.
3. Ibid., p. 199.
4. Ibid.
5. ECS to ABB, n.d., Gilson ms., p. 234.
6. Mary Ritter Beard, ed., *America Through Women's Eyes* (New York: Macmillan, 1934), p. 194.
7. Speech New York, May 14, 1863, reprinted in Gilson ms., pp. 203, 206.
8. Gilson ms., p. 209.
9. Ibid., p. 210.
10. Gilson ms., p. 214. See Gale Huntington, *An Introduction to Martha's Vineyard* (Oak Bluffs, Mass.: Martha's Vineyard Printing, 1969); Henry Beetle Hough, *Martha's Vineyard: Summer Resort, 1835-1935* (Rutland, Vt.: Tuttle Publishing, 1936).
11. Gilson ms., p. 217.
12. Notes taken by Alice Stone Blackwell of a conversation with ABB, [1905-10], Blackwell, LC.
13. I have not attempted to give a complete or evenhanded account of the suffrage split. For a general overview, see Eleanor Flexner, *Century of Struggle: The Woman's Rights Movement in the United States*, Chapter 10, "The Emergence of a Suffrage Movement," rev. ed. (Cambridge, Mass.: Harvard University Press, Belknap Press, 1975). Ellen DuBois, *Feminism and Suffrage* (Ithaca: Cornell University Press, 1978), gives an account heavily favoring the Stanton-Anthony group. For primary sources, HWS Vol. II, contains some, but it was collected and edited almost entirely by leaders of the National Woman Suffrage Association and is not an unbiased account. The *New York Tribune*, May 13-19, 1869, and November 4-26, 1869, is a rich source, including texts of many speeches, letters from participants, and pungent editorial comments by nonsuffragist Horace Greeley.

14. ECS to Thomas Wentworth Higginson, May 22, 1868, ECS Papers, Theodore Stanton Collection, Mabel Smith Douglass Library, Rutgers University, New Brunswick, New Jersey.
15. ECS to ABB, April 22, 1869, Blackwell, SL.
16. *New York Tribune,* May 19, 1869.
17. ABB to Mary Louise Booth, May 17, 1869, Alma Lutz Collection, SL.
18. Margaret Hope Bacon, *Valiant Friend: The Life of Lucretia Mott* (New York: Walker and Co., 1980), p. 128.

৯৮ Chapter 9 ৫৭

1. Gilson ms., p. 213.
2. ABB to LS, Henrietta, "Almost 1850," Blackwell, LC.
3. ABB, *The Physical Basis of Immortality* (New York: G. P. Putnam's Sons, 1876), p. 297.
4. Gilson ms., p. 211.
5. ABB, *Studies in General Science* (New York: G. P. Putnam's Sons, 1869), p. v.
6. See Virginia Woolf, *A Room of One's Own* (New York: Harcourt, Brace and World, 1929), p. 81.
7. For background on Darwin and Spencer and the great debate, I have relied on *Encyclopedia Brittanica* (1976); A. Hunter Dupree, *Asa Gray* (Cambridge, Mass.: Harvard University Press, 1959 and 1968).
8. See D. H. Meyer, "American Intellectuals and the Victorian Crisis of Faith," in Daniel Walker Howe, ed., *Victorian America* (Philadelphia: University of Pennsylvania Press, 1976), pp. 59-77.
9. ABB, *Studies in General Science,* pp. 15, 19.
10. Ibid., pp. 230-31.
11. Ibid., pp. 248, 249, 251-52.
12. *The Man Versus the State* (1884); see *Encyclopedia Americana,* s.v. "Herbert Spencer" (International Edition, 1981).
13. ABB, *Studies in General Science,* p. 332.
14. Ibid., pp. 332-33.
15. Ibid., pp. 354, 356.
16. Gilson ms., p. 212.
17. Ibid., (unidentified).

18. *Revolution,* Vol III, No. 15 (April 15, 1869), p. 236.

19. ABB to Gerrit Smith, March 27, 1869, Gerrit Smith Collection, George Arents Research Library, Syracuse University, Syracuse, N.Y.

20. ABB, *Studies in General Science,* p. vii; cf. Woolf, *A Room of One's Own,* pp. 71-78.

21. ABB to Gerrit Smith, March 27, 1869, Gerrit Smith Collection. (The reference to "four children" is because the youngest, Ethel, was not born until later that year.)

22. Words of Captain Giles in ABB, *The Island Neighbors* (New York: Harper and Brothers, 1871), p. 95. I have assumed that the character's insights represent the author's—not always true, but in this case a fair assumption.

23. Notes taken by Alice Stone Blackwell of a conversation with ABB, [1905-10], Blackwell, LC, p. 6.

24. ABB to Gerrit Smith, March 27, 1869, Gerrit Smith Collection.

25. Biographical sketch of ABB by her daughter, Ethel Blackwell Robinson, Woman's Rights Collection, SL.

26. Quoted in *Reader's Encyclopedia,* s.v. "Novels." The phrase may be apocryphal, but is widely attributed. For a more interesting and sympathetic analysis, see Ann D. Wood, "The 'Scribbling Women' and Fanny Fern: Why Women Wrote," *American Quarterly,* Vol. XXIII, No. 1 (March 1971), pp. 3-24.

27. ABB to Mary Louise Booth, December 24, 1870, Alma Lutz Collection, SL.

28. "Women Writers," Handwritten ms. notebook, Somerville, N.J., n.d., Blackwell, SL. I have not found any indication that this draft was ever published.

29. ABB to Mary Louise Booth, December 24, 1870, and November 11, 1872, Alma Lutz Collection, SL.

30. ABB to Mary Louise Booth, August 2, 1871, Alma Lutz Collection, SL.

31. ABB, *Island Neighbors,* p. v.

32. Ibid., p. 11.

33. Ibid., p. 49.

34. ABB to Mary Louise Booth, August 2, 1871, Alma Lutz Collection, SL.

35. Ibid.

36. ABB to Mary Louise Booth, November 23, 1871, Blackwell, SL.

37. ABB to Mary Louise Booth, August 25, 1871, Alma Lutz Collection, SL.

♫ *Chapter 10* ♫

1. ABB to Phebe A. Hanaford, March 25, 1869, Olympia Brown Collection, SL.

2. ABB to O. Brown, Millburn, December 9, n.d., Olympia Brown Collection, SL.

3. Gilson ms., p. 211.

4. Ibid., pp. 212-13.

5. ABB to LS, Henrietta, "Almost 1850," Blackwell, LC.

6. Gilson ms., p. 191.

7. Elizabeth Cady Stanton, *Eighty Years and More* (London: T. Fisher Unwin, 1898), p. 136.

8. SBA to ABB, September 4, 1858, Blackwell, SL.

9. ABB, *Studies in General Science* (New York: G. P. Putnam and Sons, 1869), p. 333.

10. "The Relation of Woman's Work in the Household to the Work Outside," *Papers and Letters Presented at the First Woman's Congress of the Association for the Advancement of Women, ... New York, October, 1873* (New York: Mrs. William Ballard, 1874), p. 180; repr. *Woman's Journal*, November 8, 1873.

11. Linda Gordon, *Woman's Body, Woman's Right: A Social History of Birth Control in America* (New York: Viking Press, 1976), at p. 114, says there were none, apparently not noticing Blackwell.

12. ABB to Mary Louise Booth, August 2, 1871, Alma Lutz Collection, SL.

13. Gilson ms., pp. 213-14.

14. ABB to ASB, January 31, 1872, Blackwell, SL.

15. Gilson ms., p. 213.

16. Charlotte Perkins Gilman, *The Home, Its Work and Influence* (New York: McClure, Phillips, 1903), p. 105; Elizabeth Mickle Bacon, "The Growth of Household Conveniences in the United States from 1865 to 1900" (Ph. D. thesis, Radcliffe College, 1942). Discussions of "the servant problem" abound in any issue of the *New York Tribune* and women's magazines.

17. ABB to M. L. Booth, July 18, 1876, Alma Lutz Collection, SL.

18. "The Relation of Woman's Work in the Household to the Work Outside," p. 178.

19. Ibid., pp. 178, 180.

20. "Work in Relation to the Home," *Woman's Journal*, May 2, 1874.

21. "How to Combine Intellectual Culture with Household Management and Family Duty," *Papers presented at the Second Congress of the Association for the Advancement of Women, Chicago, October 15-17, 1874* (Chicago: Fergus Printing, 1875); repr. *Woman's Journal,* November 7, 1874.

22. Ibid.

23. ABB to ASB, January 31, 1872, Blackwell, SL.

24. "How to Combine Intellectual Culture with Household Management and Family Duty."

25. Edward Hammond Clarke, *Sex in Education, or, a Fair Chance for Girls* (Boston: James P. Osgood, 1873), pp. 12, 14, 127. The best general description of this mini-conflict is Janice Law Trecker, "Sex, Science and Education," *American Quarterly,* Vol. 26 (October 1974), pp. 352ff.

26. Clarke, *Sex in Education,* pp. 137, 120.

27. Julia Ward Howe, ed., *Sex in Education* (Boston: Roberts Brothers, 1874; repr. New York: Arno Press, 1972), p. 115.

28. E. [liza] B. [isbee] Duffey, *No Sex in Education, or, An Equal Chance for Both Girls and Boys* (Philadelphia: J. M. Stoddart, 1874), p. 117.

29. ABB, "Sex and Work," *Woman's Journal,* March 14, 1874, repr. *The Sexes Throughout Nature* (New York: G. P. Putnam's Sons, 1875; repr. Westport, Ct.: Hyperion Press, 1976), pp. 164-65. Excerpts from *Sexes* are also reprinted in Alice S. Rossi, ed., *The Feminist Papers: From Adams to deBeauvoir* (New York: Columbia University Press, 1973), pp. 356-77.

30. ABB, "Sex and Work," *Woman's Journal,* March 14, 1874, repr. *Sexes,* pp. 160-61.

31. ABB, "Heredity," *Papers Read before the Association for the Advancement of Women at its Eleventh Annual Congress, held at Chicago, Illinois, October, 1883* (Buffalo: Press of Peter Paul and Bro., 1884), p. 14.

32. ABB, *Sexes,* p. 229.

33. Ibid., p. 163.

34. Ibid., pp. 228, 229, 224.

35. Ibid., pp. 151, 131.

36. Ibid., p. 17.

37. ABB, "The Wisest Way," *Woman's Journal,* August 19, 1876.

38. ABB, *Sexes,* p. 11.

39. Ibid., pp. 20-21.

40. Ibid., pp. 134-35.

41. Ibid., p. 22.

42. *Popular Science Monthly*, Vol. 7, July, 1875, pp. 370-71.

43. ABB, *Sexes*, p. 183.

44. Ibid., p. 201.

45. Everett Mendelsohn, "A Human Reconstruction of Science," *Boston University Journal*, Vol. 21, No. 2 (Spring 1973), pp. 42-52.

46. "Comparative Mental Power of the Sexes Physiologically Considered," *Papers read before the Fourth Annual Congress of the Association for the Advancement of Women, Philadelphia, October 4-6, 1876*, SL.

47. Gilson ms., p. 213.

৯৸ *Chapter 11* ৫

1. "The Relation of Woman's Work in the Household to the Work Outside," *Papers and Letters Presented at the First Woman's Congress of the Association for the Advancement of Women,... New York, October, 1873* (New York: Mrs. William Ballard, 1874), p. 183; repr. *Woman's Journal*, November 8, 1873.

2. See, e.g., David M. Potter, "The Quest for the National Character," in John Higham, ed., *The Reconstruction of American History* (New York: Harper and Row, 1962), pp. 197-203.

3. "Marriage and Work," *Papers read at the Third Annual Congress of the Association for the Advancement of Women, Syracuse, October 13-15, 1875*, (Chicago: Fergus Printing, 1876), pp. 27-35.

4. ABB to "Bostonians," May 21, 1874, Blackwell, SL.

5. "History and Results of the Past Congresses," *Papers read before the Association for the Advancement of Woman at its Tenth Annual Congress, held at Portland, Maine, October, 1882*, p. 39. For an overview of the AAW, see Karen Blair, *The Club Woman as Feminist: True Womanhood Redefined, 1868 to 1914* (New York: Holmes and Meier, 1980).

6. "History... of the Past Congresses," p. 39.

7. ABB, "The Wisest Way," *Woman's Journal*, August 19, 1876.

8. ABB to LS, Somerville, September 13, 1875, Blackwell, LC.

9. "Where is the work of women equal, where superior, where inferior to that of men?" *Papers read before the Association for the Advancement of Women, 16th Women's Congress, Detroit, Mich., November, 1888* (Fall River, Mass.: J. H. Franklin, 1889), p. 86.

10. ABB, *The Physical Basis of Immortality* (New York: G. P. Putnam's Sons, 1876), pp. 9–11.

11. Ibid., pp. 6, 13.

12. Ibid., p. 321.

13. Ibid., pp. 16-17.

14. *Burlington [Iowa] Hawk Eye*, May 1877, clipping in Blackwell, SL.

15. *Boston Transcript*, n.d., clipping in Blackwell, SL.

16. *Albany Journal*, n.d., clipping in Blackwell, SL.

17. ABB to O. Brown, Millburn, December 9, [1861-62?], Olympia Brown Collection, SL.

18. ABB to R. R. Shippen, Somerville, N.J., December 29, 1878, Blackwell, SL. This document appears to have been a rough draft, but I have assumed it was recopied and sent.

19. Ibid.

20. Gilson ms., pp. 10-11.

21. The Theological Department did not confer any degrees until 1875. (*Alumni Register* of Oberlin College, November 1, 1960.) Later catalogues used "Sem." to indicate completion of the three-year theological course. E.g., *General Catalogue of 1908*, s.v. "Thomas Holmes."

22. ABB to LS [August 9, 1879?], Blackwell, LC.

23. ABB to SBA, September 29, 1858, Blackwell, SL (original misdated "1848"). (See Chapter 7, n. 27).

24. Phebe A. Hanaford, "Woman in the Church and Pulpit," *Papers and Letters presented at the First Woman's Congress of the Association for the Advancement of Women, New York, October, 1873*, p. 104.

25. *Papers read at the Third Annual Congress of the Association for the Advancement of Women, Syracuse, October 13-15, 1875*, p. 54.

26. *Historical Statistics of the United States* (1970), D 26-28.

27. "Address of the President," *Papers read at the Third Annual Congress of the Association for the Advancement of Women, Syracuse, October 13-15, 1875*, pp. 4-5.

28. Notes taken by ASB of conversation with ABB [1905-1910], Blackwell, LC; Dagmar J. Noll, Old Brooklyn Meeting House Restoration Committee, to author, November 13, 1976.

29. *Proceedings of the Eighth Meeting of the National Conference of the American Unitarian Association, Saratoga, N.Y., September 17-20, 1878,* p. 122.

30. ABB to LS, December 9, 1879, Blackwell, LC.

31. Ibid.

32. Notes taken by Alice Stone Blackwell of a conversation with ABB, [1905-10], Blackwell, LC.

33. Barbara M. Cross, *The Educated Woman in America* (New York: Teachers College Press, 1965), p. 30.

34. ABB to LS, September 27, 1878, Blackwell, SL.

35. "A Collegiate Education for Woman, and the Necessity of a Woman-Professor in the Mixed College," *Papers and Letters Presented at the First Woman's Congress of the Association for the Advancement of Women,...New York, October, 1873,* p. 62; repr. *Woman's Journal,* November 8, 1873.

36. Gilson ms., p. 140.

37. Ibid., p. 213.

38. ABB to LS, October 18, 1880, Blackwell, SL.

ꑃ Chapter 12 ꑂ

1. Notes taken by Alice Stone Blackwell of conversation with ABB, [1905-1910], Blackwell, LC.

2. Elizabeth Blackwell, *Counsel to Parents on the Moral Education of Their Children* (New York: Brentano's Literary Emporium, 1879).

3. Elizabeth Blackwell and Emily Blackwell, *Medicine as a Profession for Women* (New York: New York Infirmary for Women, 1860), repr. Alice S. Rossi, ed., *The Feminist Papers* (New York: Columbia University Press, 1973), p. 350.

4. Elizabeth Blackwell to SCB, September 21, 1874, Blackwell, LC.

5. For a general picture of the mechanisms for shared child-rearing within the Blackwell family, compare Elinor Rice Hays, *Those Extraordinary Blackwells* (New York: Harcourt, Brace and World, 1967) with Alice S. Rossi, "The Blackwell Clan," in *The Feminist Papers,* pp. 323-46.

6. SCB to Elizabeth Blackwell, November 6, 1871, Blackwell, LC.

7. ABB to LS, February 17, 1873, Blackwell, SL.

8. Elizabeth Blackwell to ABB, 1873, Blackwell, LC.

9. ABB, *The Sexes Throughout Nature* (New York: G. P. Putnam's Sons, 1875; repr. Westport, Ct.: Hyperion Press, 1976), p. 166.

10. Quoted in Hays, *Those Extraordinary Blackwells,* p. 160.

11. Elizabeth Blackwell to SCB, January 14, 1876, Blackwell, LC; to ABB, June 5, 1875, Blackwell, LC.

12. Elizabeth Blackwell to SCB, January 14, 1876, Blackwell, LC.

13. Orestes A. Brownson, "The Woman Question" (1869, 1873), reprinted in Aileen S. Kraditor, ed., *Up From the Pedestal* (Chicago: Quadrangle Books, 1968), p. 193.

14. ABB to LS, April 10, 1878, Blackwell, SL.

15. E. Lynn Linton, *The Girl of the Period* (London: Richard Bently and Son, 1883), Vol. I, p. 131.

16. ABB to LS, Somerville, April 10, 1878, Blackwell, SL.

17. ABB to LS, October 25, 1877, July 5, 1880, Blackwell, LC.

18. ABB to LS, April 10, 1878, Blackwell, LC.

19. ABB to LS, May 25, 1878, Blackwell, LC.

20. Florence Brown Blackwell to Kitty Barry, Boston, September 29, 1879, Blackwell, SL.

21. Hays, *Those Extraordinary Blackwells,* p. 205.

22. Emily Blackwell to Elizabeth Blackwell, August 13, 1881, Blackwell, SL.

23. Ibid.

24. Ibid.

25. Ibid.

26. Gale Huntington, *An Introduction to Martha's Vineyard* (Edgartown, Mass.: Dukes County Historical Society, 1969), p. 83; Ethel Jones Whidden, conversation with author, Chilmark, Mass., October 1974.

27. Emily Blackwell to Elizabeth Blackwell, August 13, 1881, Blackwell, SL.

28. Ibid.

29. Ibid.

30. ASB to Kitty Barry, August 27, 1882, Blackwell, SL.

31. Emily Blackwell to Elizabeth Blackwell, August 13, 1881, Blackwell, SL.

32. "Hints Upon Etiquette and Good Manners," *Ladies' Home Journal,* July, 1888, p. 17.

33. ABB, *The Island Neighbors* (New York: Harper and Brothers, 1871), p. 76.

34. Emily Blackwell to Elizabeth Blackwell, August 13, 1881, Blackwell, SL.

35. Emily Blackwell to Elizabeth Blackwell, October 2, 1881, Blackwell, SL.

36. Florence Blackwell Mayhew to ASB, quoted by ASB in her letter to Kitty Barry, July 23, 1882, Blackwell, SL.

37. Edith Brown Blackwell to Kitty Barry, October 8, 1876, Blackwell, LC.

38. Agnes Blackwell Jones, "Comforter," *Poems*, ed. Ethel Jones Whidden (New York: New York Journal of Commerce, 1941), p. 20.

39. Mabel Newcomer, *A Century of Higher Education for American Women* (New York: Harper and Brothers, 1959), pp. 46, 19.

40. ABB to LS, April 13, 1883; May 24, 1883; September 6, 1883, Blackwell, SL.

41. Edward T. James, Janet Wilson James, and Paul S. Boyer, eds., *Notable American Women, 1607-1950*, s.v. "Emily Blackwell."

42. This love affair was not mentioned in any printed sources. My information came from Gale Huntington, son of Emily Blackwell's adopted daughter, personal interview, Chilmark, Mass., October 1974.

﹌ *Chapter 13* ﹌

1. Gilson ms., p. 316.

2. Ibid., p. 317.

3. Mitchell to ABB, n.d., Blackwell, SL.

4. Gilson ms., p. 320.

5. Ibid., p. 323.

6. ABB, "The Comparative Longevity of the Sexes," *Proceedings of the American Association for the Advancement of Science* (Philadelphia, 1884), p. 515, and *Papers read before the Association for the Advancement of Women, Twelfth Annual Congress, held at Baltimore, Md., October, 1884* (Buffalo: Peter, Paul and Bro., 1885), pp. 41-55.

7. For general background, Ray Ginger, *Age of Excess: The United States from 1877 to 1914* (New York, 1975), focuses on economics; Daniel Walker Howe, ed., *Victorian America*

Philadelphia: University of Pennsylvania Press, 1976), on cultural and intellectual aspects.

8. Gilson ms., pp. 319-20.

9. ABB, "Woman's Industrial Position," *Papers read before the Association for the Advancement of Women, 14th Women's Congress, Louisville, Ky., October, 1886* (Atlantic Highlands, N.J.: Leonard and Lingle, 1887), p. 66.

10. "Where is the work of women equal, where superior, where inferior to that of men?" *Papers read before the Association for the Advancement of Women, 16th Women's Congress, Detroit, Mich., November, 1888* (Fall River, Mass.: J. H. Franklin, 1889), pp. 81-87.

11. Ibid., p. 86.

12. ABB, *Studies in General Science* (New York: G. P. Putnam's Sons, 1869), p. 330.

13. Gilson ms., pp. 318-19.

14. Carrie Chapman Catt, "Danger to Our Government" (1894), and Belle Kearney, "The South and Woman Suffrage" (1803), quoted in Aileen S. Kraditor, ed., *Up From the Pedestal* (Chicago: Quadrangle Books, 1968), pp. 261, 263. See also Aileen S. Kraditor, *The Ideas of the Woman Suffrage Movement, 1890-1920*, Chapter 7, "The 'Southern Question,'" (Garden City, N.Y.: Doubleday, 1971).

15. *Report of the International Council of Women, Assembled by the National Woman Suffrage Association, Washington, D.C., March 25 to April 1, 1888* (Washington, D.C.: Rufus H. Darby, 1888), p. 346.

16. For a general discussion of the reunification process, see Eleanor Flexner, *Century of Struggle: The Woman's Rights Movement in the United States*, Chapter 16, "The Unification of the Suffrage Movement," rev. ed. (Cambridge, Mass.: Harvard University Press, 1975).

17. ABB to LS, September 13, 1875, Blackwell, LC.

18. Gilson ms., p. 277.

19. ABB to Frances Willard, February 14, 1889, Blackwell, SL.

20. William Henry Channing to ABB, April 5, 1883, Blackwell, SL.

21. ABB to LS, August, 1889, Blackwell, SL.

22. ECS to ABB, December 29, 1885, Blackwell, SL.

23. ABB to LS, January 6, 1886, Blackwell, SL.

24. LS to ABB, January 10, 1886, Blackwell, LC.

25. ABB to LS, February 10, 1888, Blackwell, SL.

৯৮ *Chapter 14* ৭৮

1. *Historical Statistics of the United States* (Washington, D.C., 1975), p. 56.

2. Sarah Gilson, in Gilson ms., p. 6.

3. Ibid., p. 12.

4. *Report of the International Council of Women, Assembled by the National Woman Suffrage Association, Washington, D.C., March 25 to April 1, 1888* (Washington, D.C.: Rufus H. Darby, 1888), p. 407.

5. Elizabeth Cady Stanton, *The Woman's Bible* (New York: European Publishing, 1895, repr. Seattle: Coalition Task Force on Women and Religion, 1974), Appendix p. 185.

6. ECS to ABB, April 27, n.d., Blackwell, SL.

7. ABB to ECS, Somerville, Aug. 10, 1886, ECS Papers, Theodore Stanton Collection, Mabel Smith Douglass Library, Rutgers University, New Brunswick, New Jersey.

8. ECS, *The Woman's Bible*, Appendix, pp. 185-86.

9. Ibid., p. 9.

10. ABB, *The Philosophy of Individuality, or the One and the Many* (New York: G. P. Putnam's Sons, 1893), pp. 3-4.

11. Ibid., p. 26-27.

12. Ibid., p. 276.

13. Ibid., p. 351.

14. Ibid., pp. 504, 512.

15. Unidentified clipping, Blackwell, SL.

16. Chapin to ABB, July 5, 1893, Blackwell, SL.

17. HWS, Vol. IV, pp. 232-33.

18. ABB to LS, September 28, 1893, Blackwell, SL.

19. Ibid.

20. Elinor Rice Hays, *Those Extraordinary Blackwells* (New York: Harcourt, Brace and World, 1967), p. 268.

21. ABB to ECS, November 10, 1885, Blackwell, SL.

22. ABB to SBA, November 27, 1896, April 14, 1897, May 23, 1898, Blackwell, SL.

23. Notes taken by Alice Stone Blackwell of conversation with ABB, [1905-10], Blackwell, LC.

24. Gilson ms., p. 327.

25. Ethel Blackwell Jones Whidden, conversation with author, Chilmark, Mass., October 1974.

26. W. J. Youmans to ABB, June 24, 1897, Blackwell, SL.

27. ASB to Kitty Barry, July 12, 1900, Blackwell, LC.

28. Quoted in Hays, *Those Extraordinary Blackwells,* p. 298.

29. ABB to Elizabeth Blackwell and Kitty Barry, June 12, 1901, Blackwell, LC.

30. ABB to ASB, August 2, [1901], Blackwell, LC.

31. November 8, 1901, quoted in Hays, *Those Extraordinary Blackwells,* p. 298.

32. Notes taken by ASB of conversation with ABB, [1905-10], Blackwell, LC.

33. Ibid.

34. ABB, "How Shall We Solve the Divorce Problem," *New York American,* November 15, 1902.

35. ABB to Elizabeth Blackwell, December 26, 1902, Blackwell, LC.

36. ASB to ABB, November 24, 1901, Blackwell, SL.

37. Gilson ms., p. 320.

38. Cheney to ABB, May 16, 1898, Blackwell, SL.

39. Cheney to ASB, Blackwell, SL, repr. in Gilson ms., p. 322.

40. ABB, *Sea Drift, or Tribute to the Ocean* (New York: James T. White, 1902), p. 16.

41. Ibid., p. 139.

42. Ibid., p. 78.

43. Ibid., p. 204.

44. Unidentified newspaper clipping, Blackwell, SL.

45. ABB to Elizabeth Blackwell, December 26, 1902, Blackwell, LC.

46. ABB to family [Syria trip, 1903], Blackwell, SL.

47. Gilson ms., pp. 328-29.

48. Ibid., p. 331.

49. Agnes Blackwell Jones to Elizabeth Blackwell, December 16, 1903, Blackwell, LC.

50. Mary Grew, "Conference of the Pioneers," *Report of the International Council of Women, Assembled by the National Woman Suffrage Association, Washington, D. C., March 25 to April 1, 1888* (Washington, D. C.: Rufus H. Darby, 1888), p. 345.

ᔍ Chapter 15 ᔍ

1. ABB to ASB, April 18, 1905, Blackwell, SL.

2. Ibid.

3. ABB to ASB, received April 27, 1905, Blackwell, SL.

4. ASB, *Woman's Journal,* May 20, 1905.

5. ABB to ASB, received May 24, 1905, Blackwell, SL.

6. Sarah E. Burton to ABB, 156 East 27th St., March 14, 1902, Blackwell, SL.

7. ABB to ASB, received April 27, 1905, Blackwell, SL.

8. Quoted in Garry Wills, "Feminists and Other Useful Fanatics," *Harpers,* (Vol. 252) June 1976, p. 35.

9. Quoted in Rheta Childe Dorr, *Susan B. Anthony: The Woman Who Changed the Mind of a Nation* (New York: Frederick A. Stokes, 1928), pp. 92-93.

10. HWS, Vol. V, p. 139.

11. Ibid.

12. ABB to ASB, October 18, 1905, Blackwell, SL. I believe that at this time Blackwell sorted out and discarded a great portion of correspondence between herself and Sam during their marriage. Virtually no such letters are in any of the Blackwell papers, despite the fact that Sam and Antoinette were often in separate places and both were copious letter writers. In so doing, Blackwell would have been acting consistently with the then-prevailing view that a marriage was a private matter unrelated to a person's public self.

13. ABB to ASB, received December 15, 1905, Blackwell, SL.

14. Gilson ms., p. 8.

15. HWS, Vol. V, p. 185.

16. Dorr, *Susan B. Anthony,* p. 341.

17. Howland to ABB, March 15, 1906, Blackwell, SL.

18. "The Great Hope," September 19, 1912, Blackwell, SL.

19. ABB to ASB, December 30, 1907, 348 Bay Way, Blackwell, SL.

20. Gilson ms., p. 9.

21. *Oberlin Alumni Magazine,* Vol. IV, No. 10 (July 1908), p. 418.

22. *Oberlin Alumni Magazine,* Vol. V., No. 6 (March 1909), pp. 209-11.

23. Gilson ms., p. 4.

24. Ibid., p. 9.

25. ABB to ASB, received September 10, 1909, Blackwell, SL.

26. ABB to Howland, October 6, 1911, Blackwell, SL.

27. ABB to Howland, January 25, 1912, Blackwell, SL.

28. ABB to Howland, April 16, 1912, Blackwell, SL.

29. Ethel Jones Whidden, interview with author, October 1974.

30. ABB to ASB, March 1, 1911, Blackwell, SL.
31. Gilson ms., p. 13.
32. Ibid., p. 8.
33. ABB to ASB, April 11, 1911, Blackwell, SL.
34. ABB to ASB, received March 22, 1913, Blackwell, SL.
35. ABB to Howland, October 6, 1911, Blackwell, SL.
36. ABB to ASB, n.d., Blackwell, SL.
37. ABB, *The Making of the Universe* (Boston: Gorham Press, 1914), pp. 193-94.
38. Ibid., pp. 13-14.
39. Ibid., pp. 65-67.
40. Ibid., pp. 194-96.
41. Ibid., p. 189.
42. ABB, *The Social Side of Mind and Action* (New York: Neale Publishing, 1915), pp. 9, 11.
43. Ibid., pp. 128-29.
44. Ibid., pp. 114-15.
45. Ibid., p. 136.
46. Ibid., pp. 139-40.
47. ABB to ASB, March 27, 1915, Blackwell, SL.
48. *Boston Globe*, August 15, 1915.
49. Trustees of All Souls Church to ABB, April 15, 1920, Blackwell, SL.
50. ABB, *The Making of the Universe*, pp. 171-72.
51. ABB to ASB, n.d., Blackwell, SL.
52. Gertrude Brown, quoted in Mildred Adams, *The Right to be People* (Philadelphia: J. B. Lippincott, 1967), pp. 126-27.
53. The *Woman Citizen*, Vol. 2, No. 6 (January 5, 1918), p. 116.
54. ABB, *The Making of the Universe*, p. 172.
55. Emily Howland to ABB, August 27, 1919, Blackwell, SL.
56. *The Christian Register*, August 1, 1918, Blackwell, SL. Copy also in Woman's Rights Collection, LC.
57. ASB to ABB, September 6, 1918, Blackwell, SL.
58. Hanaford to ABB, March 2, 1918, Blackwell, SL.
59. Howland to ABB, August 27, 1919, Blackwell, SL.
60. Nettie R. Shuler to ABB, March 10, 1920, Blackwell, SL.
61. Handwritten account (apparently by Agnes Blackwell Jones), one page, Blackwell, SL.
62. For general information on the suffrage movement, see Adams, *The Right to Be People*, n. 52 above.
63. ABB to ASB, received September 10, 1909, Blackwell, SL.
64. Agnes Blackwell Jones to Kitty Barry, October 4, 1921, Blackwell, LC.

CHRONOLOGY

1819	Joseph and Abigail Brown move from Connecticut to New York.
1823	Samuel Charles Blackwell born, Bristol, England.
1825 May 20	Antoinette Louisa Brown born, Henrietta, New York.
Oct. 26	Erie Canal opened, Albany-Buffalo, New York.
1828	Antoinette Brown starts school, age 3.
1830	Brown family moves to new stone house.
1831	Congregational Church built, Henrietta.
1831-35	Charles Grandison Finney revivals, Rochester, New York.
1834	Antoinette Brown joins Congregational Church, Henrietta. Oberlin Collegiate Institute founded, Ohio.
1838	Antoinette Brown finishes elementary school, starts Monroe Academy.
1841 spring	Antoinette Brown holds first teaching job.
1843-45	Samuel, Ophelia, and Abby Frances Brown die of "lung fever."
1846 spring	Antoinette Brown begins studies at Oberlin College.
1846-47 winter	Antoinette Brown teaches in Rochester, Michigan, during long school vacation.
1847 Aug.	Antoinette Brown graduates from Ladies Literary Course; begins study in Theological Department.
1848	First Woman's Rights Convention, Seneca Falls, New York.

1850 Aug.	Antoinette Brown finishes theological course, Oberlin.
Oct.	First National Woman's Rights Convention, Worcester, Mass.; Antoinette Brown attends and speaks.
1852 May	Augusta Brown dies of "lung fever," Henrietta.
1853 spring	Antoinette Brown begins work as pastor, South Butler.
	Antoinette Brown meets Samuel Blackwell.
Sept.	"Half World's" Temperance Convention, New York City.
Sept. 15	Antoinette Brown ordained as minister, South Butler.
1854 July	Antoinette Brown leaves job in South Butler.
1855	Antoinette Brown lives in New York City, writes for *Tribune*.
May 1	Lucy Stone marries Henry Blackwell.
1856 Jan.	Antoinette Brown marries Samuel Blackwell, Henrietta.
summer	Blackwell clan moves from Cincinnati to New York-New Jersey.
Nov.	Florence Brown Blackwell born, New York City.
1858	Mabel Brown Blackwell born (April), dies (August).
1859 summer	Antoinette B. Blackwell and Susan B. Anthony lecture tour.
fall	Antoinette B. Blackwell preaches in New York City.
1860 Dec.	Edith Brown Blackwell born.
1861 April 12	Civil War breaks out (Fort Sumter).
1863 May	Woman's National Loyal League meets, New York City.
July 31	Grace Brown Blackwell born.
1865 April	Robert E. Lee surrenders, ending Civil War; President Lincoln assassinated.

?	Antoinette B. Blackwell has stillborn son.
1866	Blackwells spend summer in Chilmark, Martha's Vineyard. Agnes Brown Blackwell born.
1869	Publication of *Studies in General Science.* Split in woman suffrage movement.
Sept. 25	Ethel Brown Blackwell born.
1870	Hannah Lane Blackwell dies.
1871	Publication of *The Island Neighbors.* Samuel Blackwell gives up full-time job in New York City.
1873	Antoinette B. Blackwell attends founding meeting of AAW.
Aug. 30	Abigail Morse Brown dies, Henrietta.
1875	Publication of *The Sexes Throughout Nature.*
1876	Publication of *The Physical Basis of Immortality.*
1877 Mar.	Joseph Brown dies, Henrietta.
1878 Oct.	Antoinette B. Blackwell joins Unitarian Fellowship.
1880	Samuel Blackwell resumes full-time work in New York City.
1881	Antoinette B. Blackwell elected to AAAS.
1882	Florence Brown Blackwell marries Elliott Mayhew, Chilmark, Mass.
1883	Antoinette B. Blackwell and Lucy Stone attend Oberlin reunion.
1888	International Council of Women.
1890	Suffrage organizations merge into NAWSA.
1893	Publication of *The Philosophy of Individuality.* Columbian Exposition, Parliament of Religions, Chicago.
Oct.	Lucy Stone dies.

1895	Blackwells travel to England.
1897	Agnes Blackwell marries Samuel "Tom" Jones, New York City.
1901	Samuel Blackwell dies. Ethel Blackwell marries Alfred Robinson.
1902	Publication of *Sea Drift*.
1903	Antoinette B. Blackwell travels to Middle East. Founding of Unitarian Society, Elizabeth, New Jersey.
1905	Antoinette B. Blackwell travels to Portland, Oregon (NAWSA convention) and Alaska.
1906	Edith Brown Blackwell dies of typhoid fever.
1908	Antoinette B. Blackwell receives honorary D.Div., Oberlin.
1909	Henry Blackwell dies.
1910	Elizabeth and Emily Blackwell die, England.
1912	Antoinette B. Blackwell travels to Central and South America.
1914	Publication of *The Making of the Universe*.
1915	Publication of *The Social Side of Mind and Action*.
1920 Aug.	Woman Suffrage Amendment to U. S. Constitution ratified.
Nov.	Antoinette B. Blackwell votes in Presidential election.
1921 Nov.	Antoinette B. Blackwell dies, Elizabeth, New Jersey.

GENEALOGIES
Brown Family

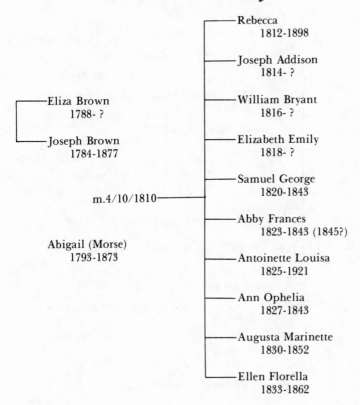

Eliza Brown
1788- ?

Joseph Brown
1784-1877

m.4/10/1810

Abigail (Morse)
1793-1873

Rebecca
1812-1898

Joseph Addison
1814- ?

William Bryant
1816- ?

Elizabeth Emily
1818- ?

Samuel George
1820-1843

Abby Frances
1823-1843 (1845?)

Antoinette Louisa
1825-1921

Ann Ophelia
1827-1843

Augusta Marinette
1830-1852

Ellen Florella
1833-1862

Blackwell family

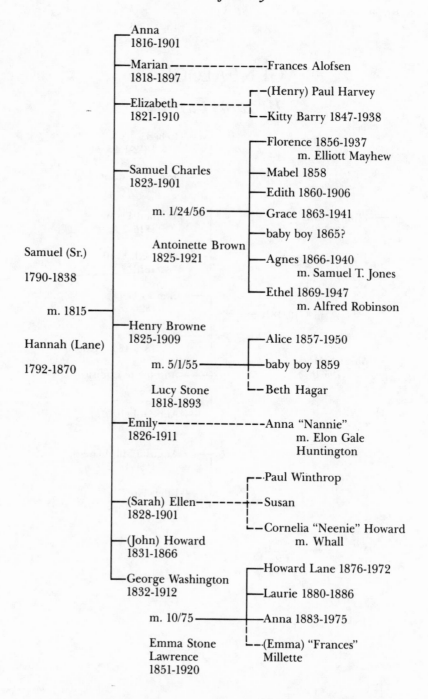

Anna
1816-1901

Marian ――――――――Frances Alofsen
1818-1897

Elizabeth ―――――― ┌─(Henry) Paul Harvey
1821-1910 └─Kitty Barry 1847-1938

Samuel Charles
1823-1901
m. 1/24/56
Antoinette Brown
1825-1921
┌─Florence 1856-1937
│   m. Elliott Mayhew
├─Mabel 1858
├─Edith 1860-1906
├─Grace 1863-1941
├─baby boy 1865?
├─Agnes 1866-1940
│   m. Samuel T. Jones
└─Ethel 1869-1947
    m. Alfred Robinson

Samuel (Sr.)

1790-1838

m. 1815

Hannah (Lane)

1792-1870

Henry Browne
1825-1909
m. 5/1/55
Lucy Stone
1818-1893
┌─Alice 1857-1950
├─baby boy 1859
└─Beth Hagar

Emily―――――――――Anna "Nannie"
1826-1911   m. Elon Gale
                     Huntington

(Sarah) Ellen――――┬─Paul Winthrop
1828-1901   ├─Susan
                   └─Cornelia "Neenie" Howard
                       m. Whall

(John) Howard
1831-1866

George Washington
1832-1912
m. 10/75
Emma Stone
Lawrence
1851-1920
┌─Howard Lane 1876-1972
├─Laurie 1880-1886
├─Anna 1883-1975
└─(Emma) "Frances"
    Millette

Broken lines indicate formal or informal adoptions. Sources: Elinor Rice Hays, *Those Extraordinary Blackwells* (New York: Harcourt, Brace and World, 1967), John Blackwell, and Gale Huntington.

INDEX

Numbers in italics refer to photographs and illustrations.

About the Author

Elizabeth Cazden was born in Ann Arbor, Michigan, in 1950. A history major, she graduated Phi Beta Kappa from Oberlin College in 1971; she began her work on Antoinette Brown Blackwell as a term paper for a course on "The History of Women in America." She graduated from Harvard Law School in 1978, and now practices law in Manchester, New Hampshire, where she lives with her husband and two children.

THE FEMINIST PRESS offers alternatives in education and in literature. Founded in 1970, this nonprofit, tax-exempt educational and publishing organization works to eliminate sexual stereotypes in books and schools and to provide literature with a broad vision of human potential. The publishing program includes reprints of important works by women, feminist biographies of women, and nonsexist children's books. Curricular materials, bibliographies, directories, and a quarterly journal provide information and support for students and teachers of women's studies. In-service projects help to transform teaching methods and curricula. Through publications and projects, The Feminist Press contributes to the rediscovery of the history of women and the emergence of a more humane society.